BASIC CRUISING SKILLS

by Gillian West

Illustrated by Chris Hui

Published by:

Canadian Yachting Association
Portsmouth Olympic Harbour
53 Yonge Street, Kingston, Ontario, K7M 6G4
Tel: (613) 545-3044   Fax: (613) 545-3045

www.sailing.ca

sailcanada@sailing.ca

ISBN 0-920232-27-2
Copyright Canadian Yachting Association

Cover photograph: Gary Gellert,
                      Humber College Sailing Centre

Layout and Design: Cameron Publishing & Typography

Canadian Yachting Association is a member
of the International Sailing Schools Association.

BASIC CRUISING SKILLS

by Gillian West
Illustrated by Chris Hui

This book is only part of the Canadian Yachting Association's Basic Cruising program. Please contact the Canadian Yachting Association for further information on sailing instruction in your area.
Phone (613) 748-5687.

No part of this book may be reproduced without prior written approval of the Canadian Yachting Association.

Acknowledgements

The publication has had the benefit of input of a great number of users of the Learn to Cruise system. Many students, instructors and schools have come forward with suggestions and ideas that have been incorporated. While I did not always agree with the decisions of the editorial committee, I sincerely hope that my contributions to this publication will benefit new sailors.

The nicest part of my involvement with this book was the helpfulness of my fellow sailors and others who became interested in the project. I would especially like to thank Peter Wood, Technical Director, CYA Training Division for his creative suggestions and guidance; members of the CYA Learn to Cruise Committee, who burned the midnight oil to help edit the book; Chris Hui, the illustrator, who was always ready to go the extra mile to get the artwork just right; Mary Scott, enthusiastic Girl Friday, who always met her deadlines; Mr. W. M. Leckie and Tim Brown for their advice; Pat Healey former CYA National Coach and meteorologist, who edited the chapter on weather; the Canadian Red Cross; the Canadian Coast Guard; the Jib Set Sailing School for permission to use its teaching materials; and my family, who allowed me to inundate their homes with a sea of paper. In addition, I am grateful to the many others who helped in smaller, but nonetheless vital roles.

This book will give you the foundation for the Ashore Knowledge of the Basic Cruising Standard and recommended procedures for the Afloat Skills components. A professional sailing instructor is essential to provide a complete program for learning good seamanship practices so you can enjoy many years of safe and fun-filled sailing.

TABLE OF CONTENTS

List of Illustrations vii
Preface xi

Introduction

The CYA Basic Cruising Standard 1
User's Guide to This Book 1
Equipping Yourself For Sailing 3

Section A: Getting Ready For Sailing

ASHORE KNOWLEDGE
Chapter 1 – Learning the Language 5
Chapter 2 – Some Basic Sailing Theory 16
    • Where Is the Wind? 16
    • The Sailing Circle 17
    • Points of Sail 18
    • Port and Starboard Tack 19
    • Changing Tack 19
Chapter 3 – People and Equipment 22
    • The Skipper and Crew 22
    • Minimum Required Equipment 23
    • CYA Recommended Gear and Equipment 26
    • Stowage 31
    • Self Test 32

AFLOAT SKILLS
Chapter 4 – Knots to Know 35
Chapter 5 – Lines 37
    • Taking Care of Loose Ends 37
    • Heaving a Line 39
Chapter 6 – Readying the Sails 40
    • Sail Care 40
    • The Mainsail 41
    • The Foresail 43
    • The Roller Furling Foresail 45
Chapter 7 – The Final Check 47
    • Checking Out the Boat 47
    • Putting on a PFD in the water 48

Section B: Safety and Maneuvering Under Power

ASHORE KNOWLEDGE
Chapter 8 – Avoiding Collision 49
   • Rules of the Road 49
   • Seeing and Being Seen 54
Chapter 9 – Safety 57
   • Sources of Fire and Explosion 57
   • Safe Refuelling Procedures 59
   • Overhead Power Lines 59
   • The Presence of Divers 60
Chapter 10 – Hypothermia 61
   • Preventing Hypothermia 61
   • Mild Hypothermia 62
   • Severe Hypothermia 63
   • Survival in Cold Water 63
   • Self Test 65

AFLOAT SKILLS
Chapter 11 – The Engine 68
   • The Outboard Engine 68
   • The Inboard Engine 71
Chapter 12 – Leaving the Dock 76
   • Steering 76
   • Casting Off 77
Chapter 13 – Getting to Know the Boat 80
   • Drifting 80
   • P-Effect 81
   • Figure Eight 81
   • Stopping 82
   • Reversing 83
Chapter 14 – Docking Under Power 84
   • Docking Under Power 84
Chapter 15 – Making Fast and Snugging Down 87
   • Making Fast 87
   • Snugging Down 88

Section C: Safety and Basic Sailing Skills

ASHORE KNOWLEDGE
Chapter 16 – Weather 91
   • Sources of Weather Information 91
   • Interpreting the Marine Forecast 92

- The Sun As Wind Generator 94
- Local Weather Hazards 95
- Fancy and Folklore 95

Chapter 17 – Coping with Wind and Weather 99
- Sail Selection: 99
- When the Wind Blows 101
- The Dreaded Lee Shore 102
- In Reduced Visibility 103

Chapter 18 – Coping with the Unexpected 105
- Springing a Leak 105
- Steering Failure 106
- Grounding at Anchor: 107
- Running Aground: 107
- Fouled Propeller 110
- Failure of Standing Rigging 110
- Broken Halyard 111
- Dragging Anchor 111
- Fire 111

Chapter 19 – Using the VHF Radio 112
- Making a Distress Call 112
- Self Test 115

AFLOAT SKILLS

Chapter 20 – Raising Sail 117
- Raising the Mainsail 117
- Raising the Foresail 121
- Unfurling the Roller Furling Foresail 122
- Safe Winch Techniques 123

Chapter 21 – How a Boat Sails 126
- How Sails Work 126
- The Keel's Job 126
- Sail Trim 127

Chapter 22 – Maneuvering Under Sail 131
- Heading Up and Bearing Away 131
- Slowing and Stopping 131
- Points of Sail 133

Chapter 23 – Tacking and Gybing 135
- Tacking 135
- In and Out of Irons 136
- The Gentle Gybe 137
- Sailing by the Lee 139

Chapter 24 – Coping with Stronger Winds 142
- Heaving To 142
- A Fisherman's Reef 144

- Reefing the Mainsail 144
- Shaking Out the Reef 146

Chapter 25 – Lowering Sail 148
- Lowering the Foresail 148
- Furling the Roller Furling Foresail 150
- Lowering the Mainsail 150

Section D: Navigation and Seamanship

ASHORE KNOWLEDGE

Chapter 26 – Reading a Chart 153
- Measuring Distance 154
- Depths and Heights 156
- Rocks, Wrecks, and Other Nasties 157

Chapter 27 – Aids to Navigation 160
- Lights 160
- Lateral Aids to Navigation 161
- Buoys 163

Chapter 28 – The Tide & Current Tables 167
- Reading a Tide Table 168
- Reading a Current Table 170
- Self Test 174

AFLOAT SKILLS

Chapter 29 – Crew Overboard Procedures 178
- Effective Techniques 178
- Triangle Method 180
- Using the Engine 182
- Recovery from the Water 182

Chapter 30 – Anchoring 185
- Ground Tackle 185
- Selecting an Anchorage 187
- Anchoring Procedure 188
- Weighing Anchor 190

Section E: You Are On Your Way

What Next? 192

Answers to Self Tests 194
Glossary 197
Index 203

TABLE OF ILLUSTRATIONS

Figure 1 – The CYA International Cruising Logbook and Seal 1
Figure 2 – Personal Equipment and Clothing for Sailing 1
Figure 1-1 – The Basic Cruising Keelboat 6
Figure 1-2 – Standing and Running Rigging 7
Figure 1-3 – Sails for a Sloop-rigged Boat 8
Figure 1-4 – Reefing Systems 9
Figure 1-5 – Pintle and Gudgeon 9
Figure 1-6 – Self-Bailing Cockpit 10
Figure 1-7 – Gooseneck 10
Figure 1-8 – Tang 10
Figure 1-9 – Turnbuckle 10
Figure 1-10 – Chainplates 11
Figure 1-11 – Shackles 11
Figure 1-12 – Fairleads 12
Figure 1-13 – Cleats 12
Figure 1-14 – Hanks 12
Figure 1-15 – Slides 13
Figure 1-16 – Winch 13
Figure 1-17 – Positions Relative to the Boat 14
Figure 1-18 – Windward, Leeward and Leeway 15
Figure 2-1 – Where Is the Wind Coming From? 16
Figure 2-2 – The Sailing Circle – No Sailing Zone 17
Figure 2-3 – The Sailing Circle 18
Figure 2-4 – Points of Sail 18
Figure 2-5 – Heading Up and Bearing Away 19
Figure 2-6 – Tacking 20
Figure 2-7 – Gybing 21
Figure 3-1 – Diagrams for Question #1 32
Figure 3-2 – Diagram for Question #4 33
Figure 3-3 – Diagram for Question #5 34
Figure 3-4 – Diagram for Question #6 34
Figure 4-1 – Figure Eight Knot 35
Figure 4-2 – Round Turn and Two Half Hitches 35
Figure 4-3 – Bowline 35
Figure 4-4 – Reef Knot (Square Knot) 36
Figure 4-5 – Double Sheet Bend 36
Figure 4-6 – Clove Hitch 36
Figure 5-1 – Types of Line 37
Figure 5-2 – Belaying a Cleat 37
Figure 5-3 – Coiling a Line 37
Figure 5-4 – Coiling a Line for Stowage 38

Figure 5-5 – Making Off a Halyard 38
Figure 5-6 – Heaving a Line 39
Figure 6-1 – Bending on the Mainsail 41
Figure 6-2 – Lowering and Stowing the Mainsail 42
Figure 6-3 – Bending on the Foresail With Hanks 43
Figure 6-4 – Flaking and Bagging the Foresail (HANKS) 44
Figure 6-5 – Bending on a Roller Furling Foresail 45
Figure 6-6 – Unfurling a Roller Furling Foresail 46
Figure 6-7 – A Furled Roller Furling Foresail 46
Figure 7-1 – Boat Preparation Checklist 47
Figure 7-2 – Putting on a PFD in the Water 48
Figure 8-1 – Opposite Tacks 50
Figure 8-2 – Same Tack 50
Figure 8-3 – Uncertainty 50
Figure 8-4 – Meeting Head-On (Rule 14) 51
Figure 8-5 – Crossing (Rule 15) 51
Figure 8-6 (a) & (b) – Overtaking: (Rule 13) 52
Figures 8-7 (a) & (b) – Risk of Collision: (Rule 7) 53
Figure 8-8 – Required Lights – Sailing Vessel Underway (Rule 25) 55
Figure 8-9 – Required Lights – Power Driven Vessel Underway
     (Rule 28) 55
Figure 8-10 – Required Lights – At Anchor (Rule 30) 55
Figure 9-1 – Safe Refuelling Procedures 58
Figure 9-2 – The Dangers of Overhead Power Lines 59
Figure 9-3 – The Presence of Divers 60
Figure 10-1 – The HELP Position 64
Figure 10-2 – Self Test Diagram for Question #1 65
Figure 11-1 – The Outboard Engine and Fuel Tank 69
Figure 11-2 – Typical Diesel Engine Controls 73
Figure 12-1 – How the Rudder Works 77
Figure 12-2 – Casting Off 78
Figure 13-1 – Drifting 80
Figure 13-2 – P-effect 81
Figure 13-3 – Figure Eight Maneuver 82
Figure 14-1 – Docking 84
Figure 15-1 – Made Fast and Snugged Down 88
Figure 16-1 – Halo Around the Sun 96
Figure 16-2 – Cirrus Clouds 96
Figure 16-3 – Cumulonimbus Cloud 96
Figure 17-1 (a) – Broad Reaching 100
Figure 17-1 (b) – Closehauled 100
Figure 17-2 – The Perils of Improper Stowage 102
Figure 17-3 – A Lee Shore 102
Figure 17-4 – Using the Bottom Contours 104

Figure 18-1 – Coping With a Serious Leak 105
Figure 18-2 – Using a Trailing Weight to Steer Downwind 106
Figure 18-3 – Kedging and Lightening Ship 108
Figure 18-4 – Heeling the Boat 108
Figure 18-5 – What to Do If You'll Be Aground for a While 109
Figure 18-6 – If the Standing Rigging Fails 110
Figure 19-1 – Familiarizing Yourself With the VHF Radio 112
Figure 19-2 – Coast Guard Assistance Is Available on Channel 16 114
Figure 20-1 – Raising the Mainsail 119
Figure 20-2 – Mainsail Luff Tension 120
Figure 20-3 – Raising the Foresail 122
Figure 20-4 – Placing Wraps on a Winch Safely 123
Figure 20-5 – Casting Off a Sheet Rapidly 125
Figure 20-6 – Easing a Sheet Gradually 125
Figure 20-7 – A Winch Over Ride 125
Figure 21-1 – Lift 126
Figure 21-2 – The Masthead Fly 127
Figure 21-3 – Principles of Sail Trim 128
Figure 21-4 (a),(b),(c) – Using the Foresail Telltales for Proper Trim .. 129
Figure 22-1 – Ease Sheets to Stop Your Boat While on a Close Reach .. 132
Figure 22-2 – Learning the Points of Sail 133
Figure 23-1 – Tacking 135
Figure 23-2 – Getting Out of Irons 137
Figure 23-3 – Performing the Gybe 138
Figure 23-4 – Sailing by the Lee 140
Figure 24-1 – Hove To 142
Figure 24-2 – Reefing the Mainsail 146
Figure 25-1 – Lowering the Foresail 149
Figure 25-2 – Lowering and Flaking the Mainsail 151
Figure 26-1 – The Title Block 154
Figure 26-2 (a) Mercator Projection   (b) Polyconic Projection 155
Figure 26-3 – Measuring Distance Using the Latitude Scale 156
Figure 26-4 – Symbols for Rocks 158
Figure 26-5 – Wrecks 158
Figures 26-6 – Submarine Cables and Pipelines 158
Figure 26-7 – Types of Seabed 159
Figure 27-1 – The Symbol for a Light 160
Figure 27-2 – Lateral System – Fixed Aids – Lighted 161
Figure 27-3 – Lateral System – Fixed Aids – Unlighted 162
Figure 27-4 – Lateral System – Port and Starboard Hand Buoys 163
Figure 27-5 – Lateral System – Port and Starboard Bifurcation Buoys ... 164
Figure 27-6 – Lateral System – Fairway Buoy 164
Figure 27-7 – Lateral System – Isolated Danger Buoy 164
Figure 27-8 – Cardinal Buoys 165

Figure 28-1 – Tide Table Coverage Areas 167
Figure 28-2 – Tidal Forces 168
Figure 28-3 – A Typical Tide Table 169
Figure 28-4 – A Typical Current Table 171
Figure 28-5 – Chart Illustrating Current Direction 173
Figure 28-6 – Diagram for Question #11 177
Figure 29-1 – The Triangle Method 181
Figure 29-2 – Methods of Recovering the COB 183
Figure 29-3 – A Collar With Buoyant Line 184
Figure 30-1 – Anchors 185
Figure 30-2 – Scope 186
Figure 30-3 – Selecting an Overnight Anchorage 187
Figure 30-4 – Anchoring Procedure 188

PREFACE

Basic Cruising Skills is the first in a series of student texts in the Canadian Yachting Association's Learn to Cruise Program.

In the past students of the Learn to Cruise Program have had to rely on commercially produced manuals by other authors or on manuals produced by commercial sailing schools specifically for their own requirements. In 1991 the Learn to Cruise Committee of the Canadian Yachting Association decided to produce a text which would closely follow the CYA Basic Cruising Standard.

Gillian West, a Vancouver based cruising Instructor-Evaluator, was commissioned to write Basic Cruising Skills. Gillian, a teacher by training, has been a CYA Cruising Instructor since the program was launched by CYA in 1976. She was the head instructor for many years at several sailing schools in Vancouver. Gillian has cruised extensively along the west coast of North America, has skippered a boat in the Victoria-Maui Yacht Race and is currently cruising her own boat on a circumnavigation of the world.

Chris Hui, a CYA Cruising Instructor from Vancouver drew the illustrations. The illustrations show a detail rarely shown in other basic instructional books. The illustrations complement the text to make it easier for the student to understand the terminology and techniques necessary to safely operate a cruising boat.

Finally, CYA would like to thank the members of the 1991 Learn to Cruise Committee who were supportive in their review of the various versions of the draft. The members at the time were Alan Redfern (Chairman), Jean Marc Abbott, Scott Hughes, David Layton, Paul Peachey, Simon Rosenman, Bruce Stott and Martin Wanless. CYA would also like to thank Agnes McLean, former Vice President, Training and Brian Lane, former Executive Director, for their encouragement of this project.

Canadian Yachting Association

To Maria from Graham, thank you.
A new adventure begins!

INTRODUCTION

THE CYA BASIC CRUISING STANDARD

Welcome to the world of sailing!

This is the introductory student book of the Canadian Yachting Association's **Learn to Cruise Program.** The Learn to Cruise Program, developed by the Canadian Yachting Association (CYA) in 1976, offers sequenced Standards, or levels of certification, through which you may progress to competency at the level to which you aspire, be it day sailing, coastal cruising or world cruising.

Whether you are a beginner taking lessons, or an experienced sailor challenging the Standard, everything you need to know to be successful in the examination for the **CYA Basic Cruising Standard** will be found in this book. The objective of this Standard is for you, upon completion, to be able to cruise safely by day in local waters, in moderate wind and sea conditions, as skipper or crew of a 20-30 foot sloop-rigged keelboat. Receiving your Basic Standard is somewhat akin to first receiving your driver's licence. You must follow up by practicing your skills to gain experience and confidence.

Testing for the CYA Basic Cruising Standard is in two parts: a written test on the **Ashore Knowledge** (theory) and an on-the-water test during which you demonstrate ability in the **Afloat Skills** (practical) portion of the Standard.

When you pass both parts of the examination you receive official recognition in the form of your **CYA International Cruising Logbook** which contains a CYA seal and the signature(s) of your evaluating CYA certified Cruising Instructor(s).

USER'S GUIDE TO THIS BOOK

Each section of the book is subdivided into Ashore Knowledge and Afloat Skills. Although tested separately, Ashore Knowledge and Afloat Skills are related in that knowledge is applied while you are afloat.

Figure 1 – The CYA International Cruising Logbook and seal.

To make the book flow, a few topics having both Ashore Knowledge and Afloat Skills components (for example, knots, anchoring) have been placed entirely in the Afloat Skills. Where this has been done, the Ashore Knowledge is indicated by the symbol for an open book and the Afloat Skills portion of the topic is indicated by this symbol for a sailboat.

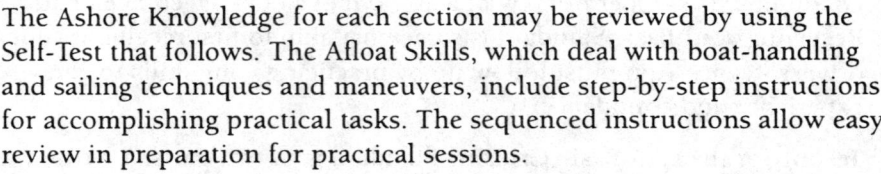

The Ashore Knowledge for each section may be reviewed by using the Self-Test that follows. The Afloat Skills, which deal with boat-handling and sailing techniques and maneuvers, include step-by-step instructions for accomplishing practical tasks. The sequenced instructions allow easy review in preparation for practical sessions.

Depending on the boat you are using, you may find that in a few instances you have to slightly modify the sequenced instructions. There is no such thing as a "generic" sailboat. Like cars, yachts come in a variety of sizes and models and each is "accessorised" differently – but, if you can handle one you can adapt to another.

The terms "boat", "yacht" and "vessel" are used more or less interchangeably. A yacht is a pleasure boat, either power or sail. "Vessel" is a general term meaning any type of a boat or ship. A boat or ship is traditionally referred to as a "she".

Bold print is used for emphasis. The first time a new term is introduced, except in diagrams, it will appear in ***Bold Italics***. These terms are defined in the glossary.

EQUIPPING YOURSELF FOR SAILING

Purchase only essential items and hold off on the others until you have been sailing. If you are involved in other sports, your wardrobe probably already includes items of suitable clothing. Some sailing schools provide their students with a lifejacket or **PFD** (Personal Flotation Device). If you are buying a PFD, see page 24 for information before you buy.

Dress in layers so you can adapt to abrupt changes in the weather. Carry an **extra layer of clothing** because, even on warm days, it can be much cooler on the water than on land. Carry also a **change of clothing** in case you get wet.

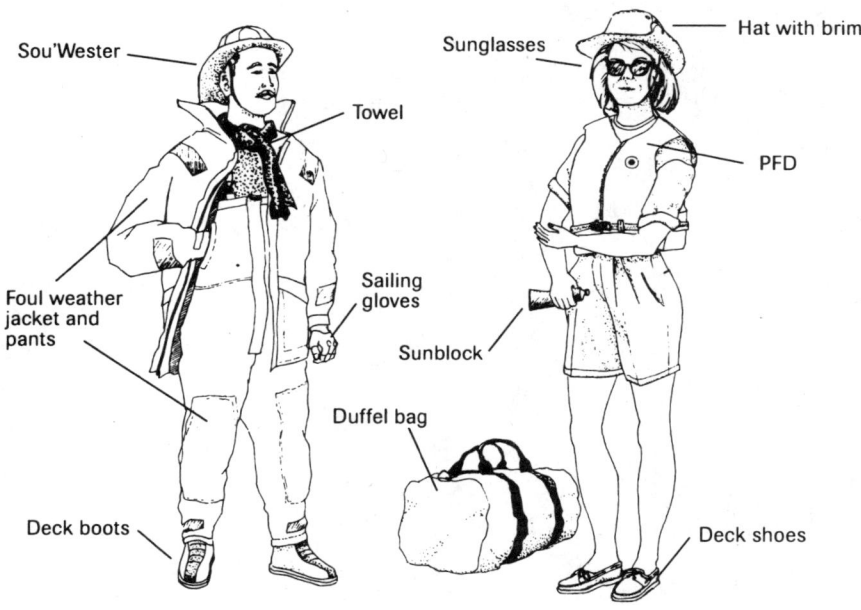

Figure 2 – Personal equipment and clothing for sailing.

Use **sunblock** year round. Wear good quality **sunglasses** with a cord or headstrap. In warm weather wear a **hat with a brim**. If you are sun sensitive, wear long sleeves and long pants.

For cool or rainy weather wear a **warm hat, a waterproof hood or hat** such as the traditional sou'wester, a **windproof shell** and **waterproof jacket** and **pants**. A **towel** worn as a scarf and tucked into your collar prevents rain and spray from seeping down into your clothing.

Deck shoes and **deck boots** have special non-skid soles. Avoid dark soled shoes as they leave tire-like marks on the deck. **Sailing gloves** with leather palms and cutaway fingertips increase your grip when handling lines and save your palms from rope burns.

Carry all your loose gear in a duffel bag. Include **medication** if you are prone to motion sickness. If you expect to be out on the water for more than an hour or two, take along water, juice, pop or a thermos of tea or coffee and an easily digestible snack.

SECTION A:
GETTING READY FOR SAILING

Section A introduces much of the terminology you are required to learn, discusses the responsibilities of skipper and crew, and teaches you how to prepare a boat to leave the dock.

ASHORE KNOWLEDGE

Main Topics:
- Learning the Language
- Some Basic Sailing Theory
- The Skipper and Crew
- Gear and Equipment
- Stowage

Chapter 1 – Learning the Language

Sailing, like other sports, has its own terminology. When faced with so many unfamiliar terms it may help to remember that salt water is in the blood of all of us. Our speech continues to be abundantly peppered with words and phrases originating from the days when men went down to the sea in tall ships.

For safety's sake communication aboard must be precise. You will soon recognize each term, associate it with its definition or function, and then incorporate it into your vocabulary. To assist you there is a glossary and an index at the back of the book.

Terminology varies very slightly with geographic location and among sailors, but the majority of terms used will be those presented in this book.

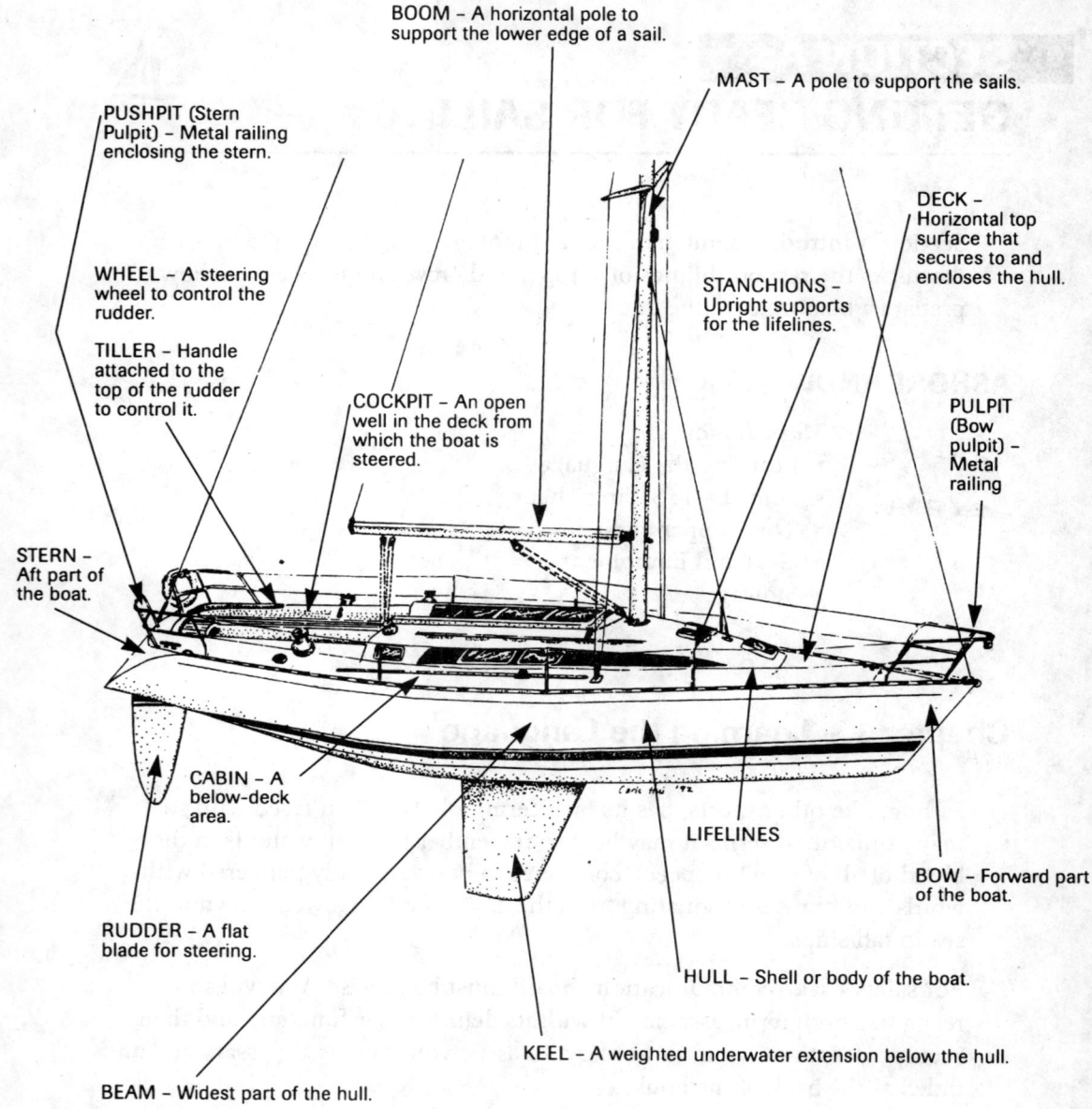

Figure 1-1 – The Basic Cruising Keelboat

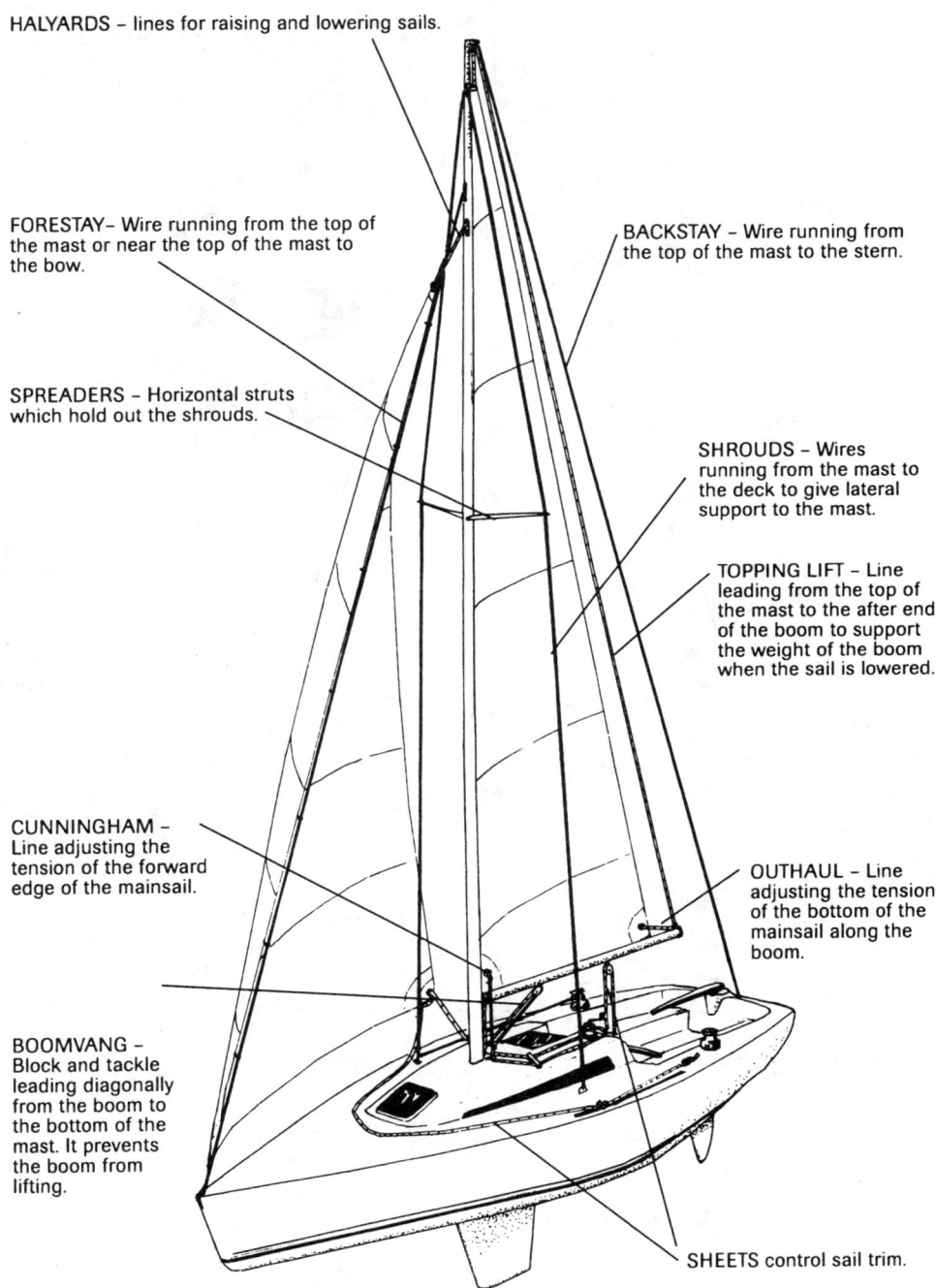

Figure 1-2 – Standing and Running Rigging.

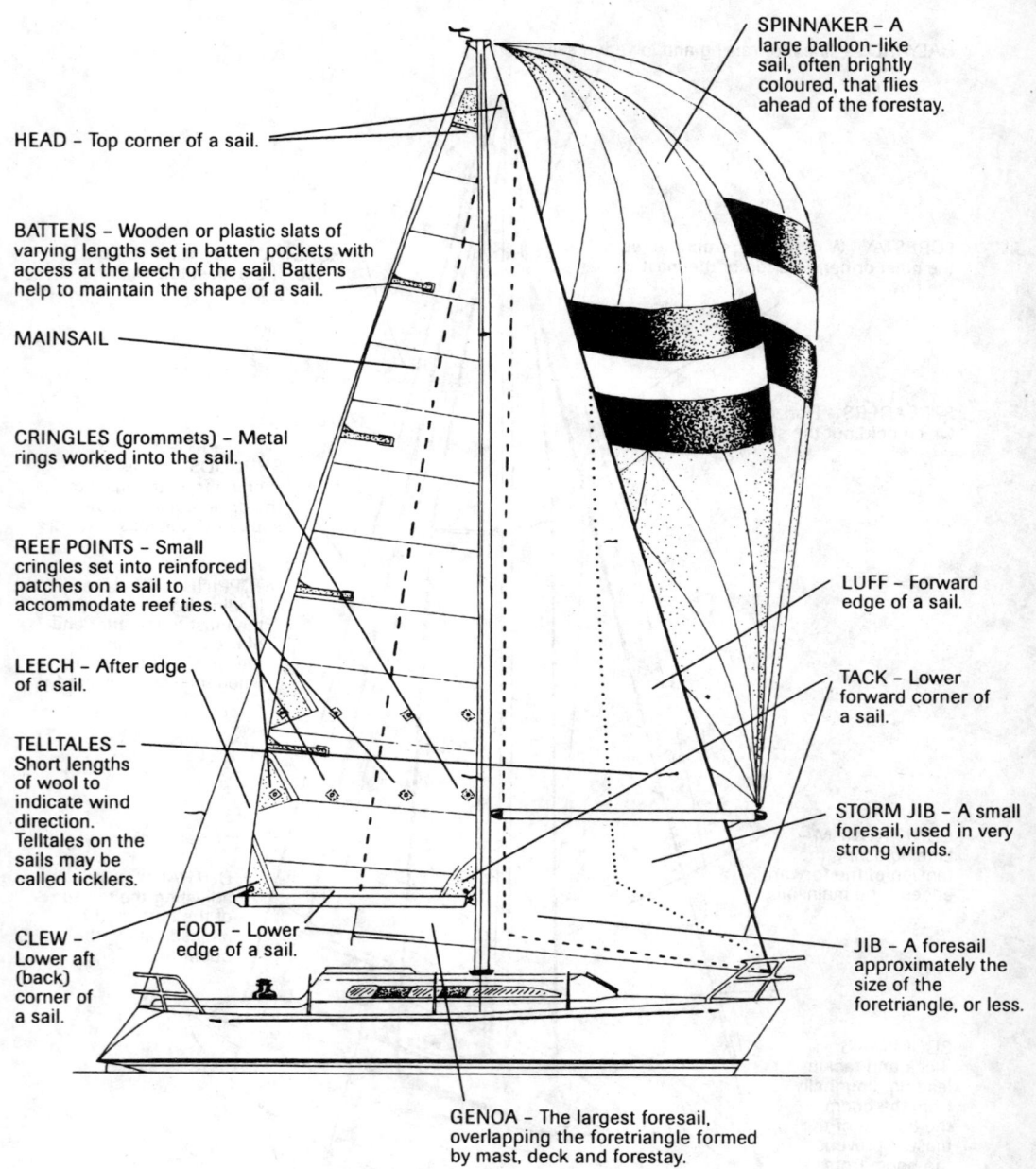

Figure 1-3 – Sails for a sloop-rigged boat.

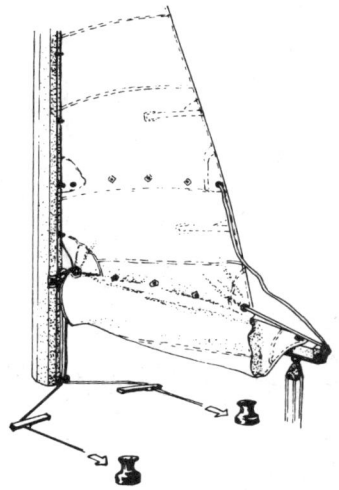 

Figure 1-4 – Reefing Systems

A sail may need to be reefed (reduced in size) so it can be adapted to an increase in wind strength.

Jiffy or Slab Reefing – is a means of reducing the size of a foresail or mainsail by partially lowering it and securing the lowered part with lines and ties. The illustration shows a mainsail reduced in size by this method.

Roller Reefing – is a means of reducing the size of a sail by using a control line to roll it around the forestay. Roller furling foresails are very common on cruising boats, though inmast mainsail reefing is not in general use at the time of publication.

Figures 1-5 and 1-7 through 1-16 illustrate fittings.

"Fittings" or "hardware" refer to a wide variety of devices, usually composed of metal or plastic, which may be attached to hull, rigging or sails to serve specific purposes.

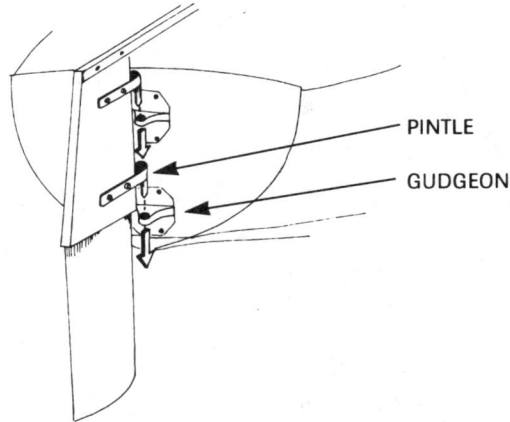

Figure 1-5 – Pintle and gudgeon – Two fittings working together to form a hinge. The pintle is the fitting with the pin. The pin is inserted into the socket of the gudgeon. Two sets of pintles and gudgeons mounted one above the other are used to attach a stern-hung rudder to the stern of a boat.

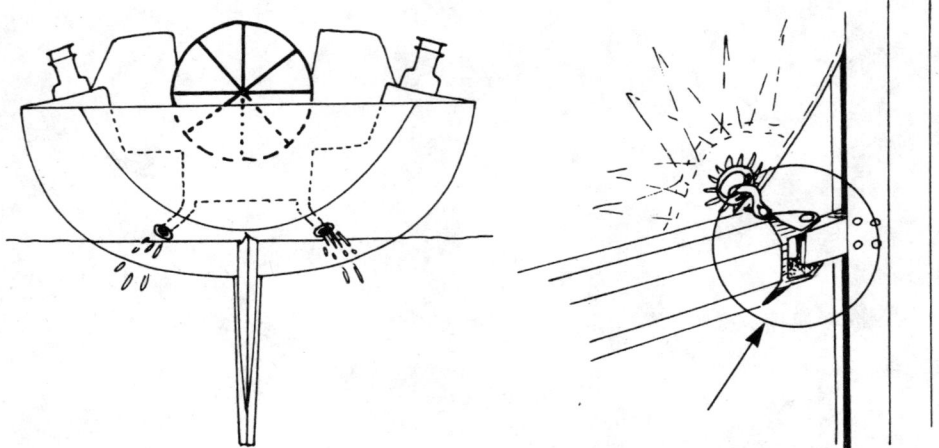

Figure 1-6 – Self-Bailing Cockpit – A cockpit with drainage to the outside of the hull.

Figure 1-7 – Gooseneck – A hinged fitting attaching the boom to the mast.

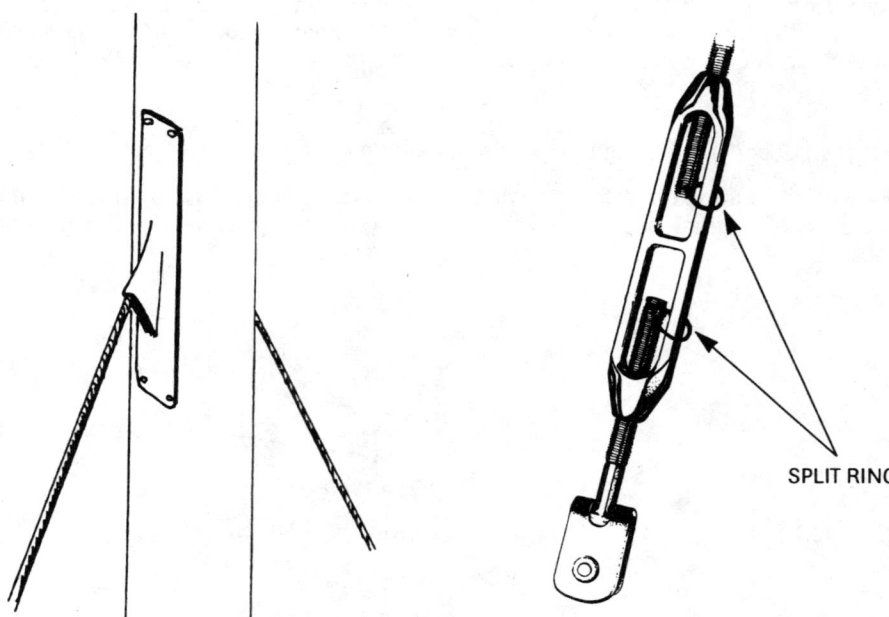

Figure 1-8 – Tang – A metal fitting used to attach the upper end of a shroud or stay to the mast.

Figure 1-9 – Turnbuckle – Long, threaded, adjustable fittings used to tension wires such as shrouds, stays and lifelines. A split ring is used to prevent the turnbuckle from unwinding.

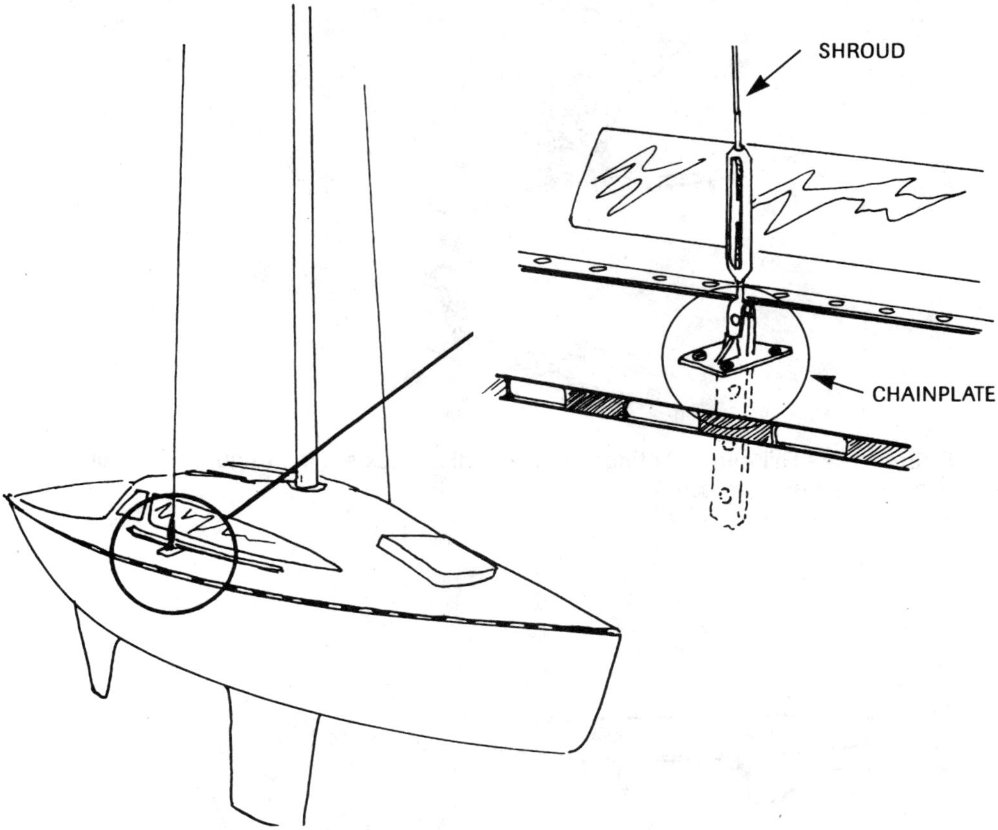

Figure 1-10 – Chainplates – Strong metal fittings attached to the hull externally or internally, to which the shroud turnbuckles are attached.

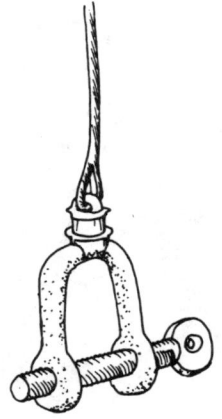

Figure 1-11 – Shackles – Metal fittings (usually U-shaped) that close with moveable pins. Shackles attach lines to fittings.

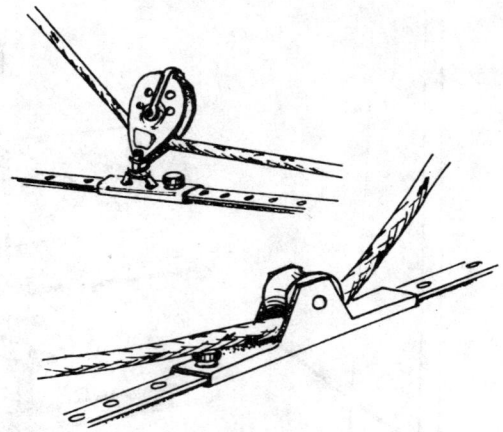

Figure 1-12 – Fairleads – Fittings through which lines are led to guide them or to change their directions.

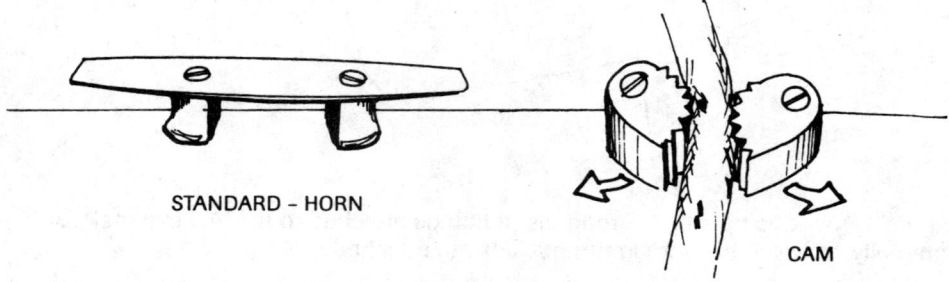

Figure 1-13 – Cleats – Fittings for gripping or securing lines. These take several forms.

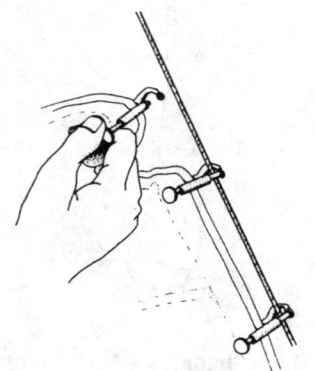

Figure 1-14 – Hanks – Clips on the luff of a foresail by which the foresail is attached to the forestay.

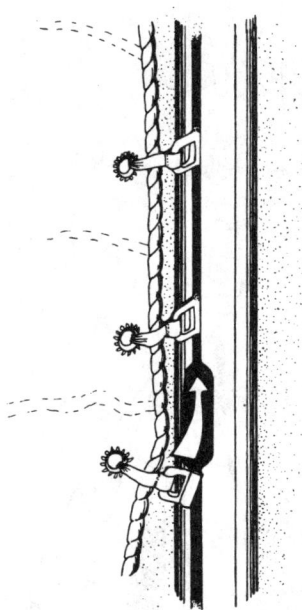

Figure 1-15 – Slides – Fittings attached to a sail by which the sail is attached to the mast or boom.

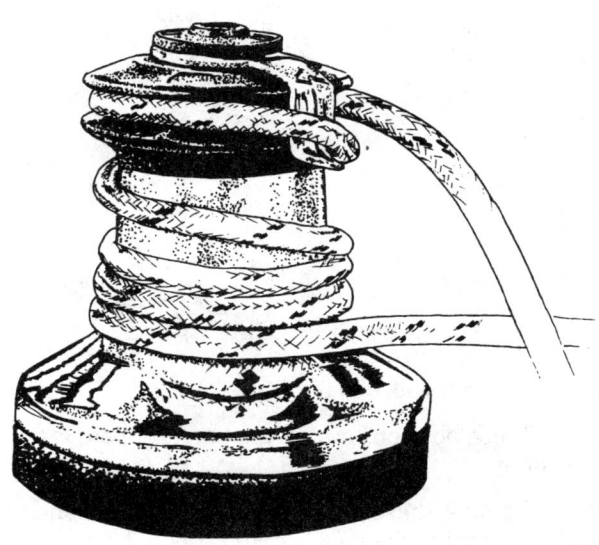

Figure 1-16 – Winch – A drum-like mechanical device which is rotated with a handle. A winch assists in hauling in sheets, halyards and other lines.

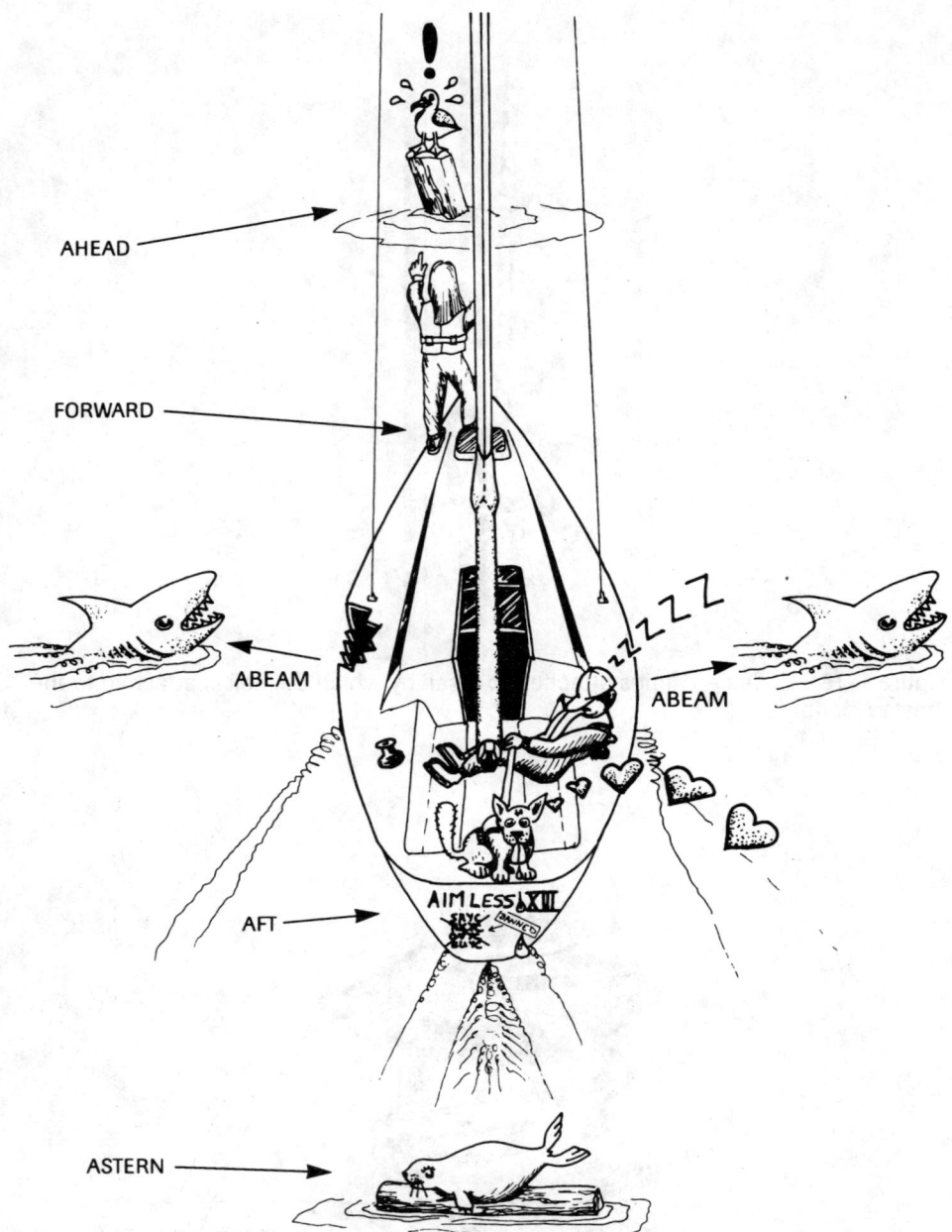

Figure 1-17 – Positions Relative to the Boat.

Forward & Aft – These positions are **on** the boat. Forward is towards the bow and aft is towards the stern.

Ahead, Astern, Abeam – These positions are **off** the boat and may be at any distance from it. Ahead is in front of the boat, astern is behind it, and abeam is at right angles to the boat's course on either side.

Port – When you face forward, the left side of the boat.

Starboard – When you face forward, the right side of the boat.

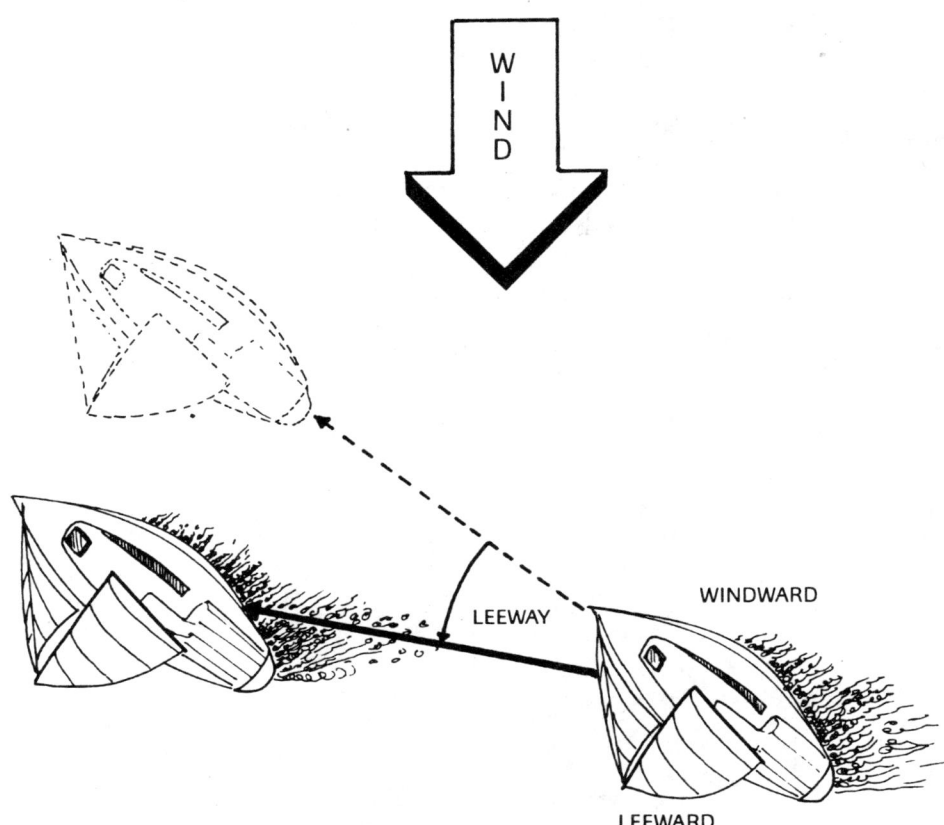

Figure 1-18 – Windward, Leeward and Leeway.

Windward – (also upwind or to weather) – towards the direction from which the wind is blowing.

Leeward – (also downwind or lee) away from the direction from which the wind is blowing.

Wind is named for the direction **from** which it is blowing. When the wind is blowing from the north, for instance, it is called a north wind. If you faced north at this time you would be looking to windward, whereas if you turned your back to the wind and faced south you would be looking downwind or to leeward.

Leeway – is the leeward motion of a boat, a side-slipping through the water caused by the wind against hull and rigging. The keel is not able to prevent leeway entirely.

Chapter 2 – Some Basic Sailing Theory

WHERE IS THE WIND?

This question, meaning "Where is the wind coming from?" is the question most asked of sailing students by their instructors, and with good reason. The wind is the power for a sailboat. Awareness of the wind's direction and strength allows you to make effective use of this power.

Wind is invisible of course, but you can see and feel its effects. Look about you. Which way is smoke blowing? Are flags limp or fluttering gently, or

Figure 2-1 – Where is the wind coming from?

are they flying out straight? In what direction are they blowing? Which way are the low clouds blowing? Are the branches of the trees waving or are the leaves barely moving? Sitting or standing birds like to face into the wind so their feathers don't ruffle. Which way are they facing? Is the water calm or rippled or wavy? Are there whitecaps? Which way are the ripples or waves travelling? (Be cautious with this. Wind and waves are not always going in the same direction.) What are other sailboats doing? If the wind is too light for you to feel it on your face, try wetting a finger in your mouth and holding it up. Can you tell which side feels coolest? Can you determine the wind direction with your eyes shut?

What are the telltales on your boat doing? The wind you sail by is the apparent wind which is shown on your boat by the telltales or wind instruments. This is further explained in Chapter 17.

THE SAILING CIRCLE

The sailing circle is an imaginary circle used as a device to explain the theory of sailing.

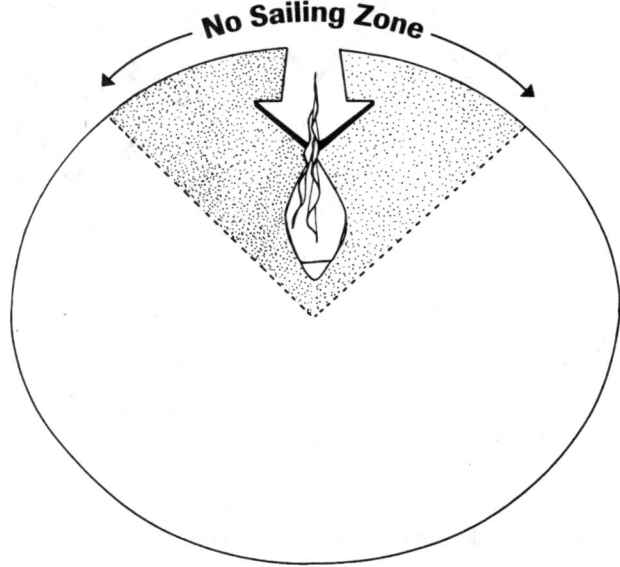

Figure 2-2 – The Sailing Circle – No Sailing Zone

The No Sailing Zone of the sailing circle extends from directly to windward of the center of the circle to an angle of approximately 45° on either side. A yacht cannot sail directly into the wind because her sails are not able to fill. Depending on the design of their hulls, sails and rigs, some boats can sail a little closer to the wind than 45°, while others are not able to sail quite as close.

As a yacht under sail begins turning into the No Sailing Zone, the luffs (forward edges) of her sails **luff** (flutter) because the sails are no longer completely filled with wind. The boat's speed soon decreases.

If the yacht continues to turn until she is **head to wind** (her bow is directly into the wind), her sails cannot fill at all. If she remains head to wind, she comes to a stop and loses steerage, meaning she will not steer, because a boat can be steered only when water is flowing over the rudder. The boat is **in irons**.

POINTS OF SAIL

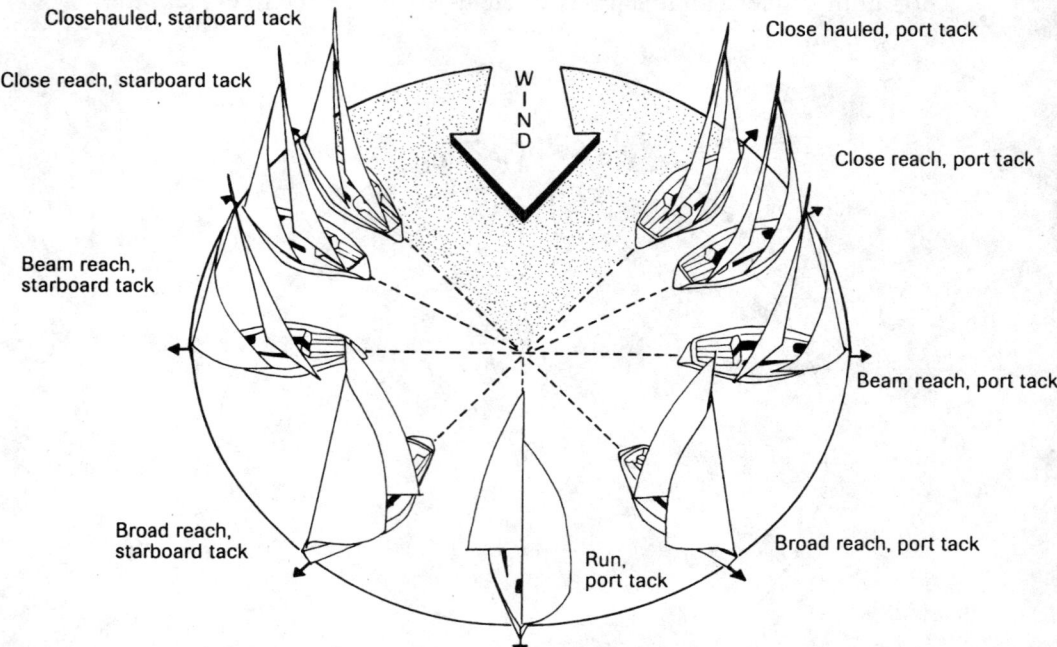

Figure 2-3 – The Sailing Circle – Points of Sail and Port and Starboard Tack.

A yacht sailing from the center of the sailing circle can sail in any direction except into the No Sailing Zone. There are five main directions with reference to the wind itself. Each of these is known as a ***point of sail***.

Sailing as close to the wind as possible, without the sails luffing, at an angle of about 45° to the wind direction, is ***closehauled***.

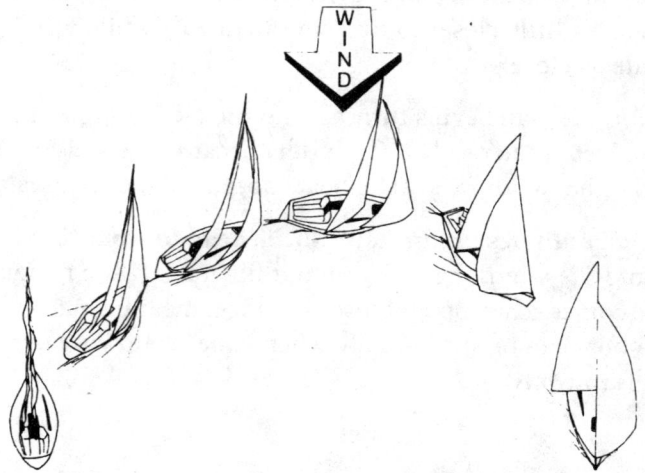

Figure 2-4 – Points of Sail – Another view. From left to right: head to wind, closehauled, close reach, beam reach, broad reach, run.

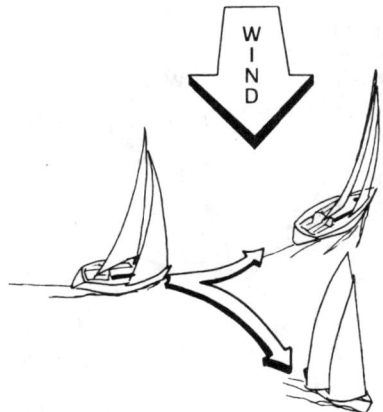

Figure 2-5 – Heading up and Bearing Away, Port Tack

Sailing directly downwind, away from the direction of the wind is **running** or on a run.

Sailing across the wind in any direction between closehauled and running is *reaching*. Sailing directly across the wind, with the wind on the beam, is a *beam reach*. Sailing in any direction between a closehauled and a beam reach is a *close reach*. Sailing in any direction between a beam reach and a run is a *broad reach*.

Heading up is altering course towards the wind. *Bearing away* is altering course away from the wind.

PORT AND STARBOARD TACK

While sailing, a yacht is on either a *port tack* or a *starboard tack* corresponding to her windward side. If her windward side is her port side she is on a port tack, and if her windward side is her starboard side, she is on a starboard tack (see Figure 2-3).

The windward side is the side closest to the direction the wind is coming from. Since confusion can result when the boat is on a run, with the wind coming from directly astern, "windward side" is also defined as the side opposite to that on which the mainsail is being carried.

A yacht, while sailing, is always **on a tack** except when she is in the process of **changing her tack**.

CHANGING TACK

A sailing vessel can change her tack in two ways: by *tacking* or by *gybing*.

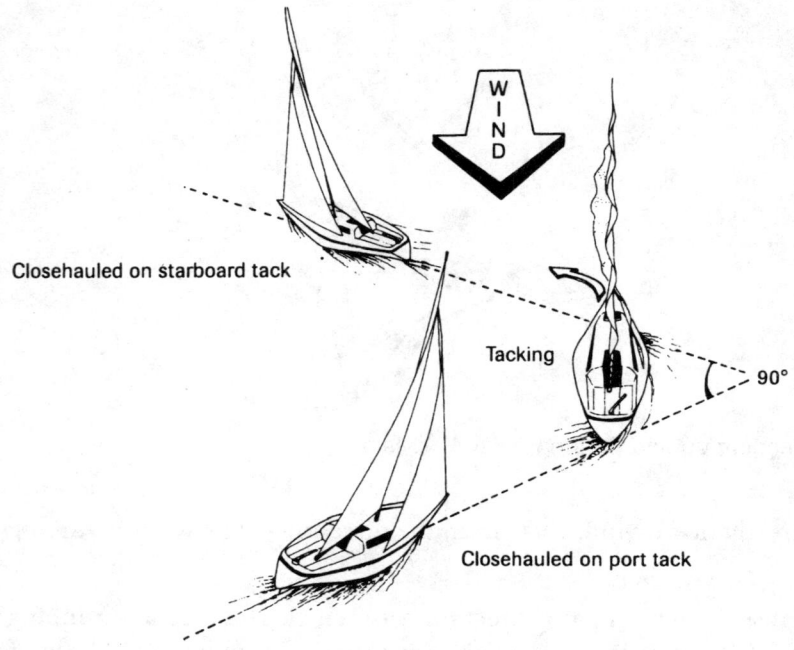

Figure 2-6 – Tacking

Tacking is turning the boat so her bow passes through head to wind. Starting from a close hauled course the boat alters course towards the wind, called heading up, until she is head to wind. She then alters course away from the wind, called bearing away, until she is closehauled on the new tack.

(Note: During a successful tack the boat does not pause while head to wind, thus she does not go into irons).

Because she is unable to sail directly into the wind, a sailing vessel has to travel to a destination to windward in a zig-zag fashion. She sails closehauled, tacks, sails closehauled on the opposite tack, tacks again, and so forth. This process is called beating.

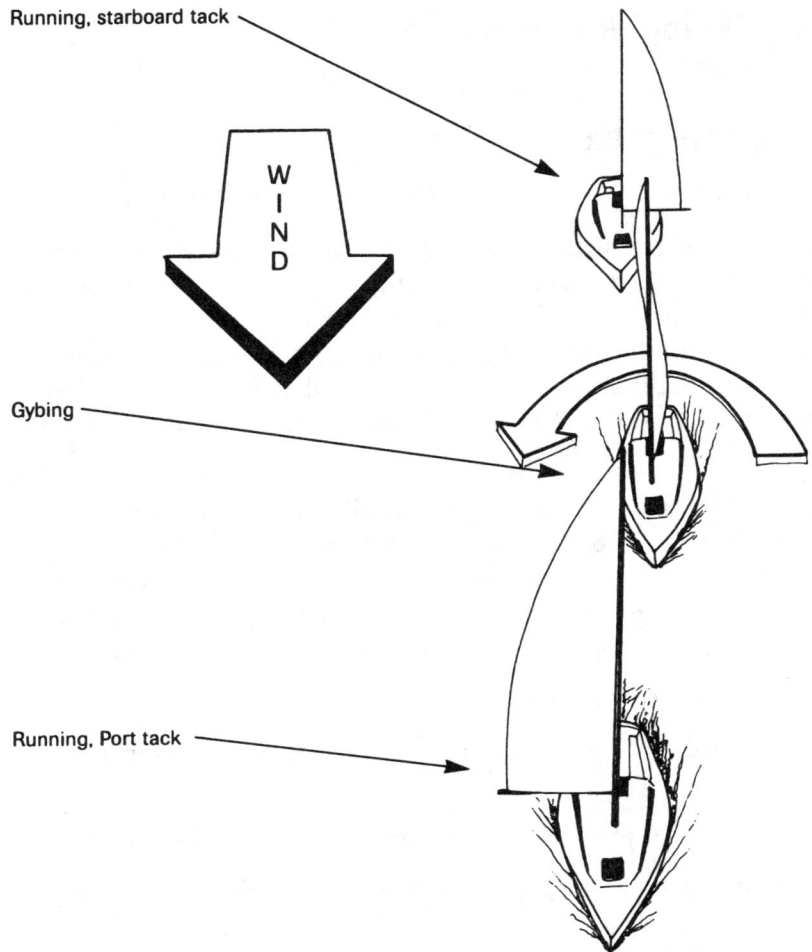

Figure 2-7 – Gybing

When changing tack by gybing, the boat bears away to a run and the sails are changed from one side of the boat to the other.

In summary, there are only two tacks, with five points of sail on each tack, and there are only two ways of changing tack. Once you have absorbed this ashore knowledge and can apply it afloat, you have become a sailor.

Chapter 3 – People and Equipment

THE SKIPPER AND CREW

The person in charge of the boat is the **skipper,** also **captain** or **master.**

The skipper's main responsibility is the **safety of the crew and the boat.** Prior to departure for a day sail or cruise, the skipper makes sure the boat is *seaworthy* (safe to go to sea). The skipper briefs the crew on the location and operation of lifesaving and other safety equipment. Before and during the trip, the skipper assigns duties and instructs the crew in the safe use of the vessel's domestic equipment, such as the **head** (marine toilet) and stove.

According to Maritime Law the skipper is at all times legally responsible and, although duties can be delegated the responsibility can not. The skipper is responsible for the actions of the crew. In the case of damage or injury severe enough for litigation, a court will usually apportion blame according to the percentage of fault of each party in that particular case.

Other functions of the skipper are:

- To make sure that the crew have the skills and are prepared for the proposed voyage.

- To navigate the boat properly in accordance with established practice.

- To coordinate the crew and to communicate with them clearly, firmly and pleasantly.

- To make all final decisions regarding the safety of the boat and the well-being of the crew. Except in emergencies, where quick action is essential, the good skipper welcomes input and ideas from the crew.

- To teach the crew to operate the boat and its equipment in the event of the skipper being unable to do so. Crew find the voyage much more enjoyable when they are allowed to handle the boat.

- To provide a good standard of care for those aboard. This includes keeping a watchful eye on crew to make sure they are moving about the boat safely. Crew must be made aware of any potential source of danger, such as a lifeline gate being open. Misuse of equipment can result in injury. For example, improper winch handling can cause crushed fingers. The skipper who fails to provide a good standard of care is risking a charge of negligence in case of an accident.

- To keep a running list in the ship's log of all losses or repairs needed, so that the boat can be restored to a seaworthy condition before leaving port again.

The **helmsman** is the person steering the boat. In this book we will refer to the helmsman as the helm. The **helm** may be a member of the crew designated by the skipper. To prevent confusion all commands come from the helm who, if not the skipper, operates under the skipper's direction. (The helm on a boat is also the steering mechanism.)

The responsibility of the crew is to **obey and assist the skipper**. "To obey" perhaps sounds rather feudal, but it is logical that the person who takes the responsibility makes the decisions. In case of emergency, action must be prompt and coordinated.

A good crew is a tremendous asset to a skipper. In fact, few boats leave their docks without crew. A good crew is sharp, supportive of and loyal to the skipper, and willing to work as part of a team. A crew member should not hesitate to ask questions to clarify duties or to determine the correct operation of equipment.

Depending on the length and type of cruise, requirements for crew knowledge and skill vary. However, most skippers are aware that today's new sailors, once trained, become tomorrow's experienced crew. If you have a cheerful disposition and show keenness to learn, you will almost certainly be welcomed aboard. Once you build up a reputation as a good crew, you are likely to find yourself in demand.

MINIMUM REQUIRED EQUIPMENT

The minimum required equipment for all pleasure boats, whether powered or not, is set out in the *Small Vessel Regulations* of the Canada Shipping Act. A summary of these regulations, in easy to understand language, is available in the Canadian Coast Guard publication *Safe Boating Guide*. The equipment required increases with the length of the vessel, and failure to have this equipment on board and in good condition and easily accessible is considered to render the vessel unseaworthy (unsafe to take to sea).

The word "approved" with regard to Department of Transport (DOT) required equipment means approved by the DOT. The *Collision*

> **SAFETY TIP:**
> When checking out your boat, make sure the minimum required equipment is on board.

Regulations referred to in the *Safe Boating Guide* are the *International Regulations for Preventing Collisions at Sea.*

LIFEJACKETS AND PFDS:

Both a **lifejacket** and a **Personal Flotation Device** (PFD) keep you afloat, but only the lifejacket turns you face up in the water. However, for constant wear when risk exists a PFD is recommended because it is less bulky and more comfortable. PFD's come in vest, keyhole, coat and coverall styles in a choice of orange, red or yellow. An approved PFD will have a DOT label inside. Make sure you have the proper size and that it is in good condition. Check the buoyancy of your PFD regularly and treat it with respect. Do not sit on it; do not leave it out in direct sunlight for days at a time; do not use it as a boat fender.

OARS, PADDLES AND ANCHORS:

An **anchor** keeps the boat stationary if there is no wind and the engine quits. It prevents the boat from drifting ashore or into a traffic lane. A small boat has a choice of oars with rowlocks or paddles **or** anchor because the smaller boat can be rowed **or** paddled home or to safety.

The chain, cable or rope attached to an anchor is the **rode.** When checking the anchor, make sure the rode is neatly **flaked** (piled back and forth so it can run freely), the shackle is secured with wire so the shackle pin cannot work loose, and the end of the rode is attached securely to the boat.

Anchoring is discussed in Chapter 30.

BAILERS AND BILGE PUMPS:

On cruising boats the bailer is usually a bucket. A small boat has the option of having either a bailer **or** a manual bilge pump, which is a hand-operated pump. On the larger boats both are required. A boat's **bilge** is the lowest inner part of its hull. A bucket is less effective on the larger boat because the person bailing is hampered by the higher steps leading from the cabin to the cockpit.

In addition, many boats have electric bilge pumps.

Empty the bilge before you leave the dock. If it refills you will know you have a leak and be able to tell how serious it is. Also, if the boat has shallow bilges and it heels (leans over) in a good breeze, water can escape from the bilge and slosh about in the cabin.

FIRE EXTINGUISHERS:

The letter or letters which appear on the label of a **fire extinguisher** denote the class or classes of fire that will be put out by the extinguisher. A *B* type fire extinguisher is suitable for combustible liquids such as gas and oil. A boat that is power driven or has a cooking or heating appliance that burns liquid or gaseous fuel requires a *B* type fire extinguisher.

A combination *BC* extinguisher is effective for *C* class (electrical fires) as well as *B* class fires. An extinguisher rated *ABC* is effective for *A* class fires (combustible solids, wood, paper) as well as *B* and *C* class fires.

The numerals *I* or *II* indicate the amount of foam, carbon dioxide, or dry chemical in the extinguisher. A *BII* extinguisher has more than twice the extinguishing capability of a *BI* extinguisher.

Fire extinguishers must be located in a convenient and accessible location. Check each fire extinguisher aboard to make sure the gauge needle is "in the green" and that an attached label shows it to have been serviced within the last year. Chemical and powder extinguishers should be inverted when checked to ensure the powder does not cake or solidify. Note the operating instructions and location of each extinguisher. If you have to use an extinguisher it will be most effective if you hold it upright and aim it at the base of the flames in a side to side sweeping motion.

LIGHTS:

The lights referred to are the boat's **navigation lights**. A small daysailer is not required to have permanently fitted lights. If she does, they must comply with the *Collision Regulations*. Navigation lights are discussed in Chapter 8.

SOUND SIGNAL DEVICES:

Sound devices signal alterations of course, the need for a bridge to be opened and in restricted visibility, whether the boat is powering or sailing. A compressed air horn or horn that you blow or operate manually is acceptable on small vessels.

CUSHIONS, HEAVING LINES AND LIFEBUOYS:

A buoyant object, for example, a **lifesaving cushion** or a **lifebuoy**, must be thrown immediately to a person who has fallen overboard. The buoyant **heaving line** is also thrown to the person so they can be pulled to the boat and assisted

aboard. The heaving line, being buoyant, may be grabbed anywhere along its length by the person in the water, and is less likely to foul the boat's propeller.

DISTRESS FLARES:

There are four types of approved **distress flares**: A,B,C and D. A,B and C flares are red and may be used day or night. A type *A* flare is a single parachute flare. A type *B* flare is a multi-star rocket consisting of at least two free-fall red stars. A type *C* flare is a hand-held flare. A type *D* flare is a buoyant or hand-held orange daytime smoke signal. All the boat's flares may be A,B or C type, but **only half the required number of flares may be the daytime D flares.**

Flares must be DOT approved and are valid for four years from the date of manufacture marked on each flare. Flares must be accessible and stored in a cool, dry location in a watertight container.

Make sure you know how to set off the flares on the boat you are using. Read the instructions on the flares when you are checking out the boat in preparation for departure. Aim the flares skyward, downwind and away from the boat and crew, and turn your face away before firing them.

C.Y.A. RECOMMENDED GEAR AND EQUIPMENT

FLASHLIGHT:

A **flashlight** is helpful by day for looking into darker nooks and crannies. At night a flashlight is invaluable for crew safety on deck, for checking the sails or for shining on the sails to make the boat more visible if you suspect you have not been seen by an approaching vessel. A flashlight can be used to signal SOS (· · · — — — · · ·) should you find yourself in distress at night.

Store extra batteries and bulbs in a watertight container.

A small personal flashlight is a useful item to keep in your pocket or duffel bag.

FIRST AID KIT:

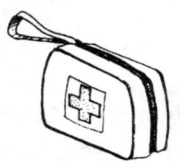

The extent of your first aid kit depends on the duration and destinations of your cruise. For day sailing the first aid kit can be quite simple, consisting of:
    A pain reliever (Aspirin, Tylenol, etc.)
    A variety of bandaids and bandages (including butterfly type)
    Gauze pads

Adhesive tape
One or two triangular bandages
Antiseptic
Tweezers
Scissors
Sunblock

Include a first aid manual and any motion sickness or prescription medication you may need. Check the first aid kit regularly.

A St. John or Red Cross first aid course and CPR course is a necessity for every cruising sailor. These organizations have a variety of excellent first aid kits for sale.

TOOLS AND SPARE PARTS:
Like the first aid kit, the number and type of tools and spare parts carried is dependent on the cruise. A minimum inventory for daysailing includes:

Knife
Screwdrivers (flat-head and Phillips)
Pliers
Vise grips
Adjustable wrench
Sail repair tape
Duct tape
Fuses
Shearpin for an outboard motor
Engine oil
Penetrating oil
Assorted spare nuts and bolts, screws and fittings
   (particularly shackles)
Spare line

SOFTWOOD PLUGS:

Through-hulls are entrances and exits for water in the hull. The entrance or exit of water is controlled by through-hull fittings with valves. A cruising boat normally may have five through-hulls: an entrance for sea water to cool the engine, an entrance and an exit for the head, and exits for galley sink and head sink drains. Other through-hull fittings may include a knotmeter (speedometer) paddle wheel and/or depth sounder transducer (sensor).

On board there should be a supply of tapered **softwood plugs** in various sizes. In case of a through-hull failing, there must be quickly available a plug of suitable size to push through the opening to stop the leak. An appropriately sized softwood plug should be linked to each through-hull fitting with a short length of line or soft wire.

Find and identify each through-hull fitting. Look for a softwood plug nearby. Open and close each valve to be sure it is not seized. On some boats, head and sink valves must be closed while the boat is sailing because of back-siphoning of water into the boat.

SAFETY HARNESSES:

The purpose of a safety harness is to prevent a crew member from falling overboard. It is essential to prevent a crew overboard situation. A safety harness for each crew member is a must. The tether should not be longer than the distance from the harness to the deck.

A safety harness is worn:

- if the weather is rough.
- if you are singlehanding (sailing alone).
- if you are on deck while travelling at night or in reduced visibility.

Secure your harness tether(s) to strong points on the boat and to fittings and lines especially set up for the purpose. Never attach a safety harness to a stanchion or lifeline. Improper attachment to the boat is dangerous because it gives a false sense of security.

RADAR REFLECTOR:

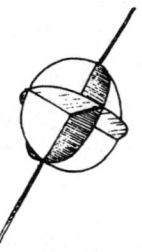

A fibreglass or wooden sailboat, even with a metal mast, does not show up well on a radar screen. To increase the probability of a boat being detected by the radar of other vessels, a **radar reflector** is displayed in the rigging. Many pleasure boats and most commercial craft are equipped with radar sets. At night, in fog or when visibility is reduced by heavy rainfall or snowfall, the radar screens of these vessels are likely to be closely monitored.

A radar reflector, consisting of a set of metal plates aligned at right angles to each other, reflects a radar signal back to the antenna of a radar set. The radar reflector is best permanently mounted, but on some cruisers is assembled and hoisted only when visibility is poor.

Do not rely on the radar reflector making your boat visible to other vessels. The effectiveness of a radar reflector may be limited by:

- the reflector being obscured by a wet sail, though a dry sail offers little hindrance to a radar beam.

- the reflector not being mounted properly. It should be mounted at least 4m (13 ft.) off the water and, unless it is the encapsulated type, in the "catch rain" position, with one pocket up and one pocket down.

- rough sea conditions, heavy rain or poor tuning by the operator rendering the radar set itself ineffective.

EMERGENCY STEERING:

In case of a steering failure, it is necessary to have a spare tiller. A boat with a wheel is usually equipped with an emergency tiller which can be mounted on the rudder post.

NAVIGATION CHARTS AND EQUIPMENT:

Use of charts, publications and equipment is covered in Section D. When checking out your boat in preparation for sailing, make sure that the following items are on board:

- Detailed chart or charts of the area in which you will be sailing, plus charts covering the entire area of your cruise.

- Publications for the area in which you are sailing.

These are:
Symbols and Abbreviations — Chart #1
Sailing Directions, Small Craft Guide or *Pilot*
Tide & Current Tables (if you are on tidal water)
The Canadian Aids to Navigation System
List of Lights, Buoys & Fog Signals
Radio Aids to Marine Navigation
The Collision Regulations.

The Canadian Coast Guard *Safe Boating Guide* is an excellent publication specifically developed for the boater and should be carried aboard all pleasure vessels.

Make sure all charts and publications are current editions. The date of printing and any corrections will be found in the lower margin of a chart.

- Basic navigation equipment consisting of:
  Parallel rules, protractor or plotter
  Dividers
  Pencil and eraser
  Paper or notebook
  Calculator (optional)

RADIO:

There should be at least one radio aboard capable of receiving up to date marine weather reports. Most cruisers are equipped with a marine **VHF radio** (VHF stands for "very high frequency"). The VHF radio is a short distance two-way radio with a range of up to about 30 miles depending on geographic features. It is used for getting marine weather reports and for communicating with other boats and shore stations.

COMPASS:

An accurate **compass** is without doubt the most important piece of navigation equipment aboard a boat. In poor visibility, at night, or when there are no buoys or landmarks ahead, a compass gives a constant reference by which the helmsman may steer a steady, desired course.

A magnetic compass is oriented to magnetic north. The compass card is graduated in increments totalling 360°, with 0° denoting magnetic north. A stationary reference to the fore and aft line of the boat is marked on the bowl surrounding the compass. This is the lubberline.

Each boat has its own magnetic properties which may be strong enough to cause the compass to give inaccurate readings. This error, called *deviation,* varies with the direction in which the boat is heading. A compass should be swung (adjusted) to minimize deviation. Any remaining deviation is then recorded on a deviation card so it can be compensated for on each heading steered.

The accuracy of a magnetic compass can also be affected by the composition or properties of nearby items:

- Iron, ferrous metals (metals containing iron) or magnets can seriously affect compass accuracy. Stainless steel may or may not affect the compass depending on its alloys. Do not leave tools, a radio, or metal kitchen gadgets near the compass.

- An electric current or magnetic field can disturb the compass. For this reason nearby wires are usually twisted to break up the electromagnetic field.

- Aluminum, bronze, brass and other non-ferrous metals do not affect the accuracy of a compass.

DEPTHSOUNDER OR LEADLINE:
A **depthsounder** is an indispensable safety and navigation aid on a keelboat. A depthsounder works by bouncing a sound pulse off the

bottom and then calculating depth based on the speed sound travels through water.

In conjunction with your chart, a continuous readout of depth while cruising helps you to avoid wandering into shallow water. The depthsounder is used also for anchoring, navigating in fog, and assisting in determining your position.

The traditional **leadline** is a reliable backup for the depthsounder. The leadline consists of a lead weight attached to a line that is marked at regular intervals. The lead is lowered to the bottom and the depth is noted. A leadline can be used to check the accuracy of the depthsounder.

BOARDING LADDER:

Whether a crewmember goes into the water inadvertently or to swim, a **boarding ladder** is by far the easiest method for getting back on board. The hull sides of a keelboat are high, making it almost impossible for a person in the water to climb aboard without assistance. Many boats have permanently fixed pull-down boarding ladders.

ONE CYA QUALIFIED PERSON:

It is desirable for at least one person on board to have CYA Learn to Cruise certification. While this does not guarantee that the person has good judgement, it does indicate that he or she has received training in safety, seamanship and navigation to the level of the Learn to Cruise certification.

Many experienced sailors have never taken a CYA course and are very competent, however it is common for self-taught or improperly taught sailors to have gaps in their knowledge, especially regarding safety procedures.

STOWAGE

Gear and equipment should be stowed in assigned and readily accessible places. Safety gear must be quickly accessible to all members of the crew. Tools, repair kits and spare parts may also need to be hunted out hastily. Loose items can cause injury when they appear unexpectedly underfoot or fly across the cabin in rough weather. No cans should be placed in lockers containing through hulls because they could shear off the through hull fittings. Delicate items such as cameras and binoculars can be broken when the boat tacks or heels to a fresh new breeze.

SELF TEST – ANSWERS ARE ON PAGE 194

1. Match the following terms to the numbers on the diagrams in Figure 3-1.

Pushpit _____   Clew _____

Stanchion _____   Jiffy/ Slab Reefing _____

Spreader _____   Pintle _____

Forestay _____   Gudgeon _____

Outhaul _____   Chainplate _____

Topping lift _____   Gooseneck _____

Boomvang _____   Turnbuckle _____

Genoa _____   Cleat _____

Reef points _____   Tang _____

Cringles _____   Shackle _____

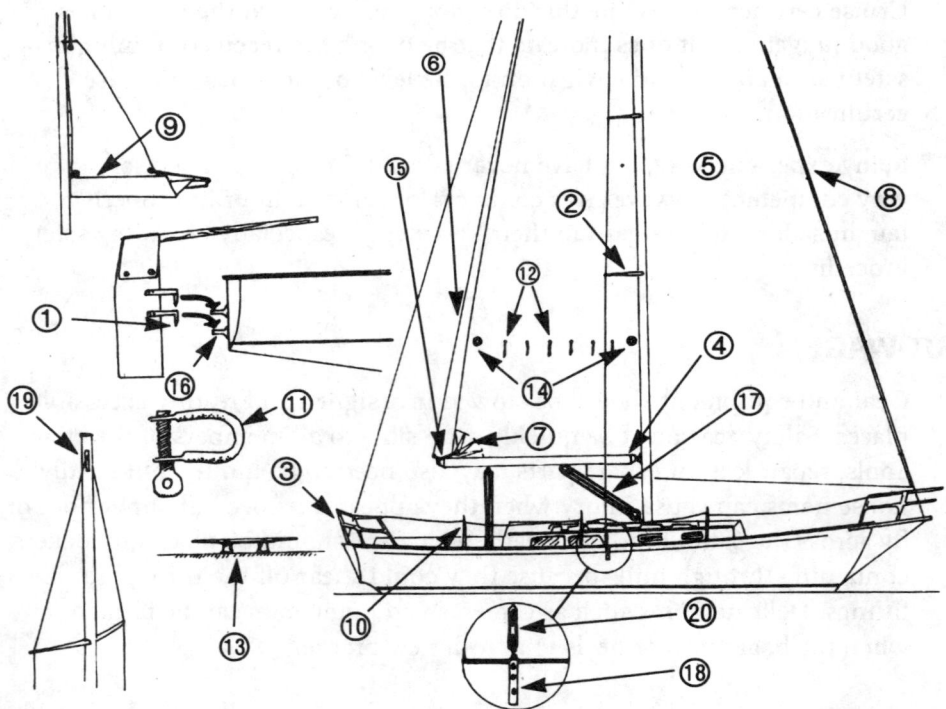

Figure 3-1 – Diagrams for Question #1

2. Name the terms defined:

(a) Away from the wind. _____

(b) The leeward motion of a boat caused by the wind.

_____

(c) Under sail, head to wind, with no steerage.

_____

(d) The bow passes through head to wind while underway.

_____

(e) Altering course toward the wind.

_____

3. What is the purpose of soft wooden plugs and where are they stowed?

_____

4. Match the following terms to the numbers in Figure 3-2.

Broad reach _____

Beam reach _____

Closehauled _____

Run _____

Close Reach _____

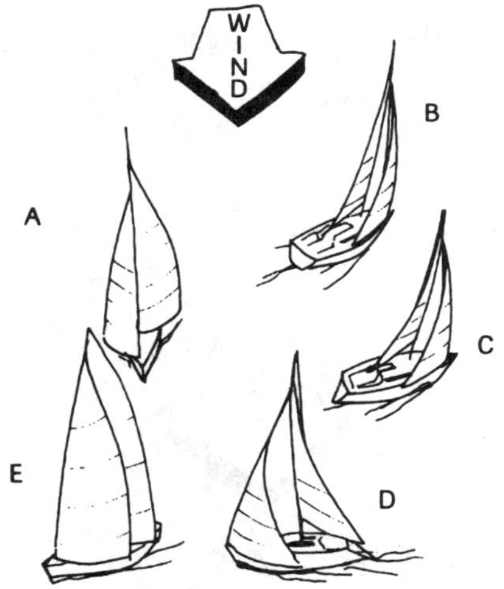

Figure 3-2 – Diagram for Question #4

5. In Figure 3-3 which boat is on a port tack? _____

6. In Figure 3-4 which boat is leeward boat? _____

7. What is the main responsibility of the skipper?
   _____

8. Approved distress flares are valid for how many years from the date of manufacture? _____

9. List three circumstances under which a safety harness is worn.
   _____
   _____
   _____

10. The accuracy of a magnetic compass can be affected by the presence nearby of: (answer Yes, No or Maybe)

    (a) Aluminum   _____   (d) A magnet   _____
    (b) Stainless steel _____   (e) Bronze   _____
    (c) Iron   _____   (f) Brass   _____

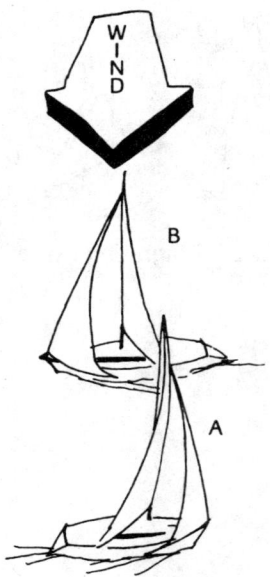

Figure 3-3 – Diagram for Question #5

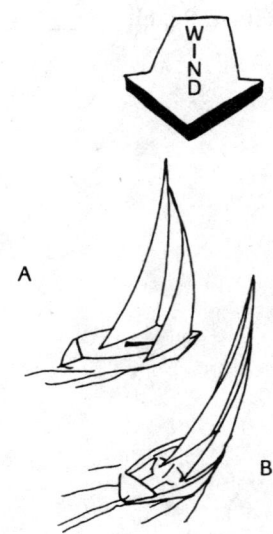

Figure 3-4 – Diagram for Question #6

GETTING READY FOR SAILING

AFLOAT SKILLS

Main topics:
- Knots and Lines
- Readying the Sails
- Sail Care
- Checking out the Boat
- Putting on a PFD in the Water

Chapter 4 – Knots to Know

There are literally hundreds of knots which sailors, truckers, mountain climbers and outdoor people use for specific purposes. Fortunately, the following six knots, when used appropriately, will carry you through almost any situation and they can be untied when required. Practice until you can tie them without hesitation. For security, leave several inches of **bitter end** (free end of the rope) when you tie a knot, and pull it tight.

Figure 4-1 – Figure Eight Knot

Used as a "stopper" knot. Tied in the end of a line, eg. a sheet. A figure eight prevents a line from pulling through a block or fairlead. It may also be used to temporarily prevent the end of a line from unlaying (unravelling). Leave sufficient bitter end to allow gripping with both hands.

Figure 4-2 – Round turn and Two Half Hitches

Used for tying a dockline to a ring or rail to secure the boat to a dock or float (a floating dock); also used for securing fenders to the boat. When tying the two half hitches, be sure to tie them in the same direction.

Figure 4-3 – Bowline

Used for making a temporary loop in a line. A bowline does not slip, jam or fail, yet is easily untied. It serves a variety of purposes, the most common of which is tying a sheet into the clew of the sail.

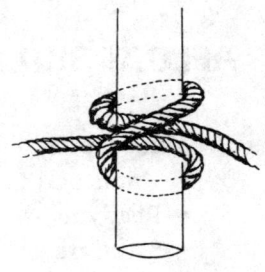

Figure 4-4 – Reef Knot (Square Knot)

Used for tying two ends of the same line, as when tying a reef in a sail. A reef knot is easily untied and may come undone if the line is subject to a lot of movement or flogging.

Figure 4-5 – Double Sheet Bend

Used for tying together two lines of unequal thickness. A double sheet bend will not jam or slip provided you make the initial bight (loop) with the thicker rope. This knot is useful for extending a line that is too short.

Figure 4-6 – Clove Hitch

Used for tying a line to a spar (piling, post or stick), for tying the tiller to center when the boat is docked, anchored, or at a mooring buoy. Beware of the clove hitch. Unless there is steady tension on the line, as in the case of tying the tiller, it can work loose. For this reason a clove hitch should not be used for permanently securing fenders to the boat. A clove hitch is suitable for hanging a coil of line from a rail or securing the end of a mainsail furling line to the boom.

A clove hitch may be tied around a spar or it may be made "on the bight" as two loops, one behind the other, which makes a clove hitch to put over the end of a spar. Be able to tie a clove hitch by both methods.

Chapter 5 – Lines

Braided Line

Laid Line

Figure 5-1 – Types of line

Except in a few instances, rope, once aboard a boat, is referred to as line. A line is a rope with a designated purpose. Most line used on pleasure boats is synthetic. Line may be braided or laid (made up of twisted strands)

Figure 5-2 – Belaying a Cleat

1. Make a full round turn.
2. Make a figure eight.
3. Finish with a half hitch. (Notice that the bitter end lies parallel to the figure eight turn.)

A line may slip or jam if it is incorrectly belayed, or made fast, to a horn cleat. If the cleat is vertically placed, as on a mast, make the half hitch on the top horn of the cleat so that, as the bitter end falls to the deck it doesn't weaken the hitch. If you are securing a line, for example a sheet, that might have to be released quickly, omit the half hitch and place two round turns on the cleat.

TAKING CARE OF LOOSE ENDS

What do you do with the leftover line after you have belayed the cleat? For that matter, what do you do with any other loose or leftover pieces of line, halyard or sheets? It depends on the circumstance. In most cases you will begin by coiling the line.

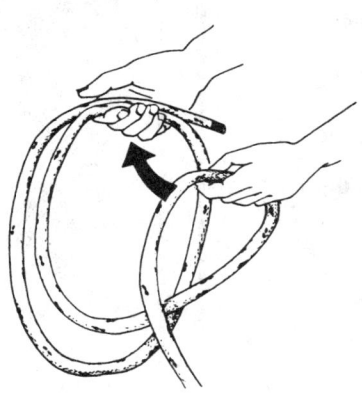

Figure 5-3 – Coiling a Line

To coil a loose piece of line (if right handed):
1. Starting with either free end, hold the line in your left hand.
2. Pass a uniform length of line from the right hand to the left. Make uniform sized loops in a clockwise direction.
3. If the line is laid line remove any twists by taking a slight turn clockwise with your right wrist as you coil. If the line is plaited or braided do not remove the twists. The line will fall into figure eight coils.

Note: If left handed, follow the diagram.

If you have belayed to a horn cleat on a dock or on deck, coil the line beginning at the **standing end** (the working end) and place the coil where it will be out of the way of traffic.

In some instances loose ends are not coiled. If the free end is very short, leave it uncoiled.

While the boat is under sail the free ends of the sheets are **flaked** so sheets can be released rapidly. The end of a sheet should be flaked by laying it back and forth loosely and piling it neatly near the cleat or winch.

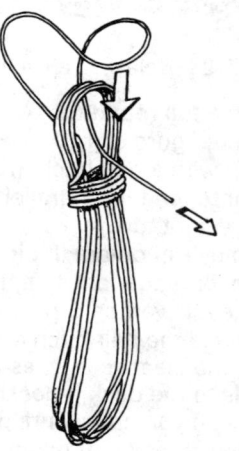

Figure 5-4 – Coiling a Line for Stowage

1. Coil the line as above until you reach last few feet of line.
2. Wrap the free end of the line around the top of the coil two or three times, starting from the bottom and working upwards.
3. Make a bight in the free end and pass it through the coil.
4. Pass the bight over the top of the coil.
5. Pull the end of the line taut to "lock" the coil.

Figure 5-5 – Making off a Halyard

The sails must be able to be lowered or reefed quickly in the event of a sudden increase in wind. To secure the free end of a halyard so it may be released without delay:

1. Starting at the standing end (the end by the cleat), coil the line.
2. Reach through the coil and grab the line midway between cleat and coil.
3. Make a bight in this section of line.
4. Twist the bight once or twice.
5. Hang the coil by slipping the bight over the top horn of the cleat or winch.
6. Pull down on the coil.

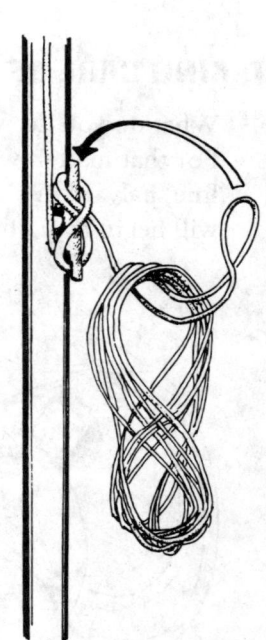

HEAVING A LINE

A correctly and accurately thrown heaving line can be a great help when docking is difficult; it can be literally a lifesaver when a crewmember has fallen overboard.

There are some excellent weighted throw-bags on the market which do not require the line to be coiled at the time it is thrown, saving time in deployment. The line has already been flaked into the bag (so it cannot kink) and the bag waits ready to be thrown in an instant.

Figure 5-6 – Heaving a Line

1. For your own safety, the end of the coil without the weight on it must be tied to a dockrail or shroud or, at the least, kept under one foot as you throw. Never throw a line with the end wrapped around your wrist.
2. Coil the line from the standing end in coils of approximately 1/2m (18") in diameter.
3. Divide the coil in half, keeping the coil with the weighted end in your throwing hand and the other part in your other hand. Do not throw underhand or overhand; either will shorten the distance you can throw. Hold your throwing arm stiffly about 45° away from your body.
4. Swing your throwing arm back, then forward to throw. As you throw, release the other half of the coil so it can follow the weighted coil.

When heaving a line to a person in the water, aim beyond your target in case the throw falls short. If the line does go beyond the person, the line, being buoyant, can be grasped anywhere along its length.

SAFETY TIP:
Never step on lines and sails. Lines roll underfoot and folds of sailcloth are as slippery as ice. Keep your feet on deck and well-braced against slipping.

Chapter 6 – Readying the Sails

Whether there is too little wind to sail or you plan only to motor, good **seamanship** (skill in handling and navigating a boat) requires the sails always to be prepared so they can be raised promptly. The sails are the boat's primary source of power and the engine is merely auxiliary power. In the event of engine failure, raise the sails. It is seldom that you are totally becalmed and if so, not usually for long.

BENDING ON, CHECKING AND STOWING SAILS

To **bend on** a sail is to attach it to a mast, boom or stay. To prepare for sailing you not only bend on the sails, if you personally have not used the sail, you raise each to check its condition and then lower and stow it.

When working with the sails the duties of crewmembers depend on the deck layout, location of controls and number of crew. The boomvang, for example, may be controlled from either cockpit or mast. The chief considerations are that operations are done in the correct sequence and that every crewmember is working from a safe position. As you learn the function of each part it is easier to remember the sequence. For instance, you will know that when lowering sail the topping lift must be **hardened** (tightened) before the sail is lowered, or the aft end of the boom will drop onto the heads of a surprised cockpit crew.

SAIL CARE

Most cruising sails are made of dacron, a cloth having the desirable quality of strength without stretch. Unfortunately its less desirable quality is its tendency to break down when exposed to ultra-violet rays. So, except when good seamanship requires them to be exposed to sunlight, sails should be covered by bags or sail covers. A roller-furling sail has an ultra-violet protective strip sewn onto its leech and foot which covers the sail when it is furled.

Sails are damaged when they are allowed to flog (flutter violently in the wind). Flogging breaks down the resins and fibers in the cloth. Be aware of this. For example, don't motor at high speed directly to windward with your mainsail up or delay in hardening the sheet after a sail has been raised.

Each foresail is designed for a certain range of windspeed. If you use a sail in stronger winds than those for which it is intended it will lose its shape and will no longer perform well.

The Mainsail

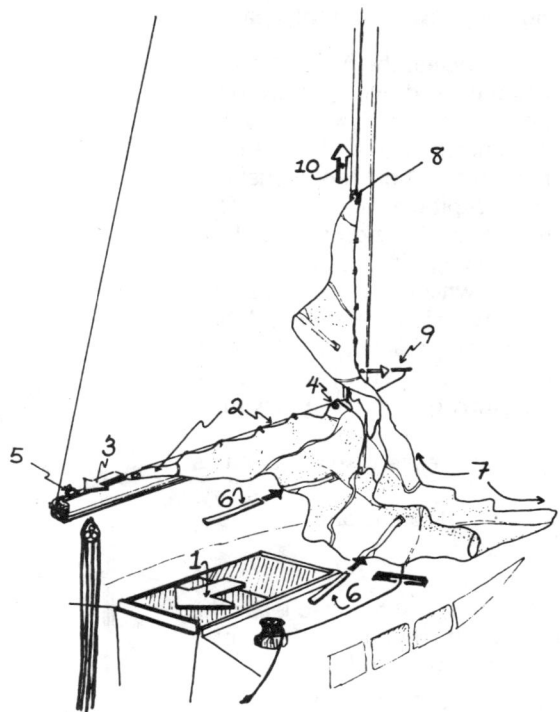

Figure 6-1 – Bending on the Mainsail (Numbers correspond to the first ten steps)

1. Slide the main hatch cover closed (to prevent crew falling down the hatch).
2. Take the sail out of its bag; find the clew and foot.
3. Starting near the gooseneck, slide the clew, then the foot, onto the boom.
4. Attach the tack to the gooseneck or to the fitting on the forward end of the boom.
5. Attach the outhaul shackle to the clew.
6. Place the battens in their pockets and secure them.
7. Run your hand along the luff of the sail from tack to head (to make sure the sail isn't twisted).
8. Attach the halyard shackle to the head of the sail and inspect the halyard for wear.
9. Remove the pin or open the fitting at the bottom of the mainsail groove or track.
10. Release the mainsheet, boomvang and cunningham. One crew slowly raises the sail part of the way up while another feeds the luff head first up the groove or track up the afterside of the mast. The sail is inspected as it is being raised. Look for wear, tears, missing or broken stitching, missing or broken battens, missing fittings, reefing lines and points.
11. When the luff is completely bent on, close the fitting or pin at the bottom of the mainsail groove or track.
12. Ease (let off) the halyard to lower the sail and cleat it off. Do not leave the sail raised at the dock.

SAFETY TIP:
When the mainsail is being raised or lowered, the boom must be free to swing. Keep clear of the danger area between the mast and the cockpit.

Figure 6-2 – Lowering and Stowing the Mainsail

1. Drop the halyard coil, uncleat the halyard, and ease it while reaching up and pulling down on the luff of the mainsail.
2. As soon as the sail is down cleat and make off the halyard and harden and cleat the mainsheet. One or more of the cockpit crew can now safely move to the boom to assist in flaking the sail. The secret to successful flaking of the sail is to pull aft on the leech of the sail while pleating the sail back and forth accordion-style along the boom. Make sure the battens are lying parallel to the boom.
3. Secure the sail along the boom with sail ties (use reef knots) or with a furling line (finished with a clove hitch).
4. Adjust boom height, if necessary, so the boom is horizontal.
5. Snug up the downhaul, if there is one, and the boomvang.
6. Flake the mainsheet.

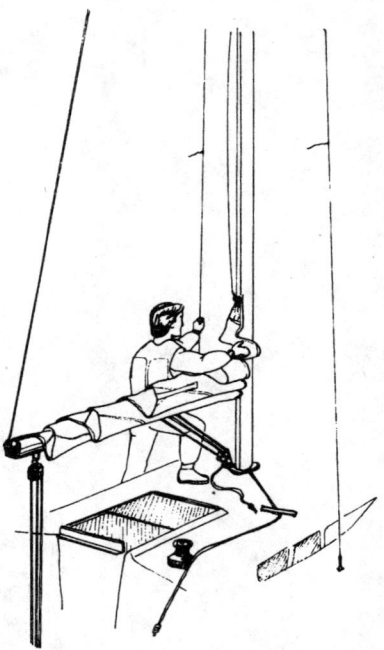

Because you are getting the boat ready to leave the dock the halyard remains attached to the head of the sail and the sail cover remains off.

The mainsail is seldom taken off the boom of a cruising boat. Normally you will find the mainsail secured to the boom, outhaul eased, the halyard removed from the head, and the mainsail cover on.

The Foresail

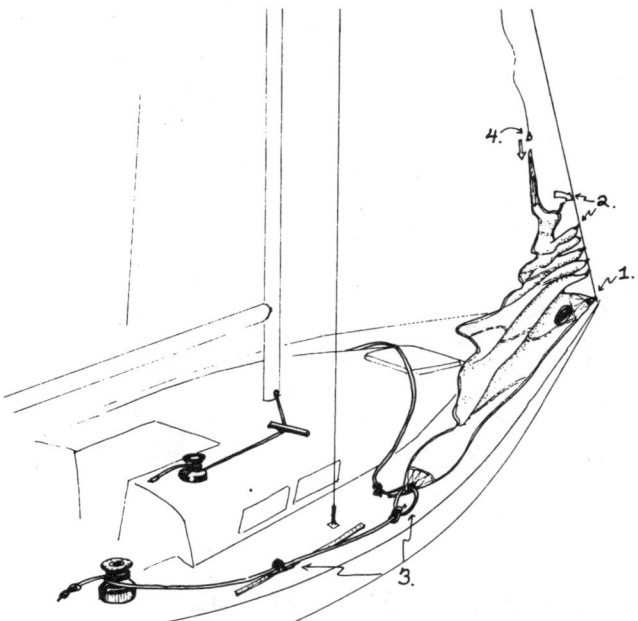

Figure 6-3 – Bending on the Foresail with Hanks. (Numbers correspond to steps 1–4.) Unless the boat has a roller-furling foresail, the foresails are usually stowed below in their bags.

When you remove the sail from its bag, secure the sailbag so it can't blow away.
1. Attach the tack to the shackle at the bottom of the forestay.
2. Attach the hanks to the forestay, working from the bottom up for convenience. Be careful not to twist the hanks or the sail will not run smoothly up and down.
3. Attach the sheets to the clew with bowlines and run one sheet down each side of the boat outside the shrouds and through the fairleads to the winches. Tie figure eight knots in the ends of the sheets.
4. Attach the foresail halyard shackle to the head of the sail. Make sure the halyard is not twisted around the forestay. Inspect the halyard for wear.
5. Raise the foresail inspecting the sail, for wear, tears, broken stitching, and missing or broken hanks.
6. While lowering the sail, one crew kneels on one knee on the foredeck, with forward arm around the forestay for personal safety. As the halyard is uncleated and eased the foredeck crew pulls down the luff of the sail. When the sail is most of the way down cockpit crew uncleat the sheet while the foredeck crew gathers in the foot of the sail to keep the sail out of the water.
7. When the sail is down, remove the halyard from the sail and shackle it to the pulpit. Harden, cleat and make off the halyard.
8. Pull the clew of the sail aft and flake the sail back and forth along the deck. Fold the sail in flat folds forward from the clew to the forestay, leaving the sheets to one side as you fold (see figure 6-4).
9. Work the sail bag over the folded sail, enclosing the sail right up to the hanks. Tighten the drawstring and secure the bag to the forestay by its cord. Harden and cleat the sheets (see figure 6-4).

Notice that, unlike the mainsail halyard, which remains attached to the mainsail whenever you are away from a dock, the foresail halyard is attached to the foresail only when the sail is raised. This is because, if left attached, it makes a nuisance of itself, flopping about and pulling the sail up the forestay. It may also jump off the **sheave** (roller) at the top of the mast, resulting in a jammed halyard.

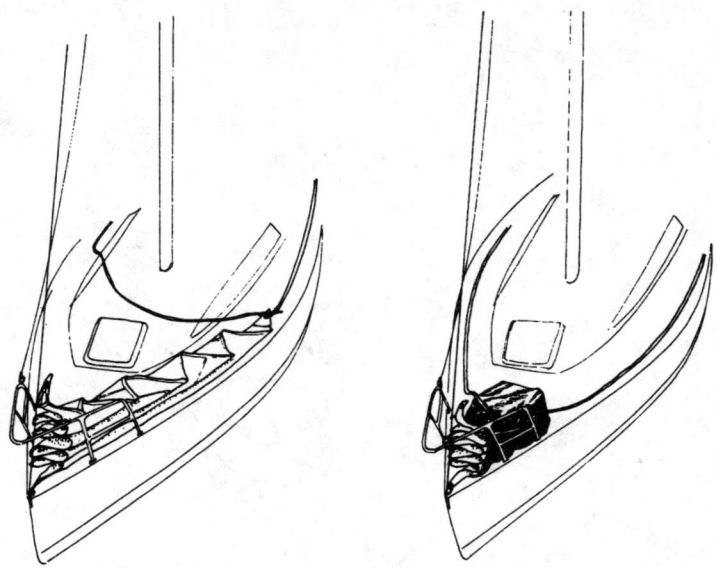

Figure 6-4 – Flaking and Bagging the Foresail (HANKS)

The Roller Furling Foresail

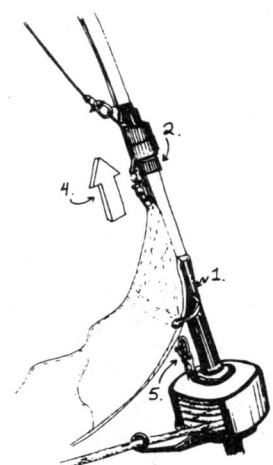

Figure 6-5 – Bending on a Roller Furling Foresail. (Numbers correspond to steps 1-5.)
If the sail is already furled, go directly to step 7.

1. Take the sail out of its bag and, starting near the head of the sail, feed the luff boltrope (a rope sewn onto or into the foot or luff of a sail) through the fitting at the base of the foil, appropriately called the feeder, and up into the groove on the foil.
2. After you have the luff started into the groove, attach the head to the swivel which is attached to the halyard. Check the halyard for wear.
3. Attach the sheets to the clew with bowlines and run one sheet down each side of the boat and through the fairleads to the winches. Tie figure eight knots in the ends of the sheets. If the foresail has been left on and furled since the boat was last out, the sheets are usually to be found coiled and hanging, one on each side of the pulpit. Uncoil the sheets and run one down each side of the boat and through the fairleads to the winches. Tie figure eight knots in the ends of the sheets.
4. Continue feeding the luff into the groove while raising the sail with the halyard. Raise the sail, checking for wear, tears and broken stitching.
5. Attach the tack of the sail to the fitting on the drum.
6. Tension, cleat and make off the halyard. Then go on to step #9.
7. Uncleat the furling line and make sure it will run freely. Maintain control of the furling line by taking a half turn around a cleat, so the sail doesn't wind out of control.
8. To unfurl the sail, haul on the leeward sheet (or either sheet, if the boat is head to wind) while keeping a light tension on the furling line. Maintain control; do not let the sail come out with a snap. Cleat & coil the furling line. While the sail is unfurled, look for wear, tears and broken stitching. Check the furling gear for smooth and easy operation and the furling line for wear.
9. To furl the sail, uncleat the furling line & make sure it will run freely. Haul on the furling line while keeping a light tension on the sheets. DO NOT PUT THE FURLING LINE ON A WINCH. Continue furling until the sheets are wrapped a couple of times about the sail so the sail will not tend to unfurl in a strong wind.
10. Cleat and coil the furling line. Tidy the sheets, cleating them loosely.

To prepare for sailing, the roller furling foresail remains raised and furled, the sheets bent on.

Figure 6-6 – Unfurling a Roller Furling Foresail

SAFETY TIP:
When hoisting or unfurling to check your sails at the dock, make sure your boat is head to wind. It is difficult and unsafe at all times to work with a sail that is full of wind.

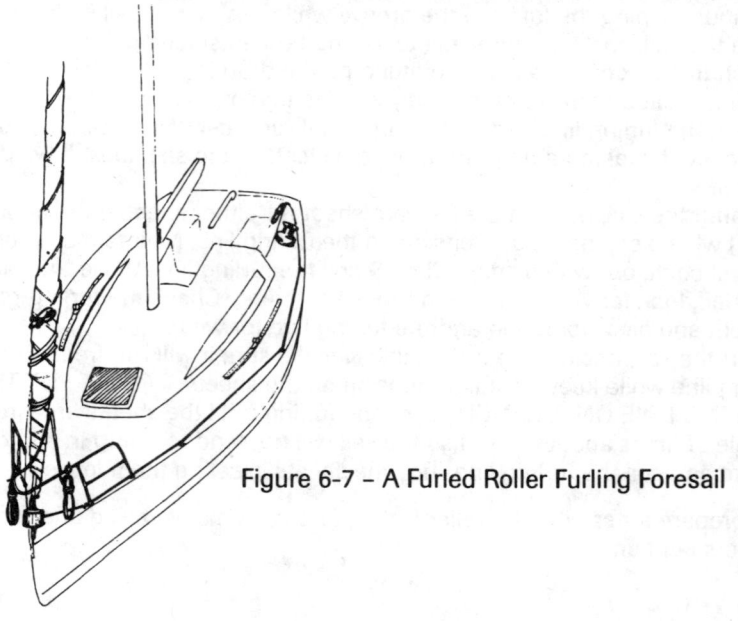

Figure 6-7 – A Furled Roller Furling Foresail

Chapter 7 – The Final Check

CHECKING OUT THE BOAT

As well as checking the sails and locating and inspecting the gear and equipment required by DOT and recommended by CYA, there are a number of other considerations before you take the boat away from the dock:

- Is there sufficient fuel, food and water?
- Have you inspected the rigging, lifelines, stanchions and steering? Perhaps the lifeline has a frayed section, or the tiller is cracked.
- Is there at least one winch handle on board? If not, the winch will be of little help when the wind pipes up.
- If in tidal water, have you checked the *Tide and Current Tables*? (see Chapter 28.)
- Do you know how to operate domestic or electronic equipment you will be using?
- Have you filed a Sailing Plan with your rental or charter company or with someone who loves you? There are ready-made Sailing Plan forms in the *Safe Boating Guide*.

You cannot afford to be casual about boat preparation. It is not only potentially dangerous but can mar an otherwise pleasant jaunt. You can speed up the process of preparation by making a checklist and dividing the work among the crew.

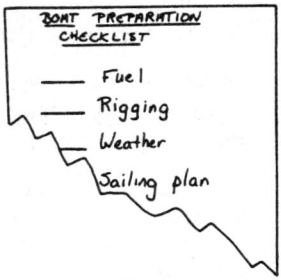

Figure 7-1 – Boat Preparation Checklist

PUTTING ON A PFD IN THE WATER

Before leaving the dock you should put on your PFD as a matter of habit. However, make sure you can also handle the scenario below.

Figure 7-2 – Putting on a PFD in the water

You fall into the water. You are not wearing your PFD! One is quickly thrown to you. You try to put it on in the usual way, like a jacket, but soon remember you can't because of the buoyancy of the water. Put it on this way:

1. Place PFD with inside facing up and neck away from you, slightly to one side and in front of you.
2. Insert your near arm into the PFD and roll onto your back, inserting your other arm.
3. Floating on your back, fasten the front.

Practice this on land, at the beach, or in a pool.

SECTION B:
SAFETY AND MANEUVERING UNDER POWER

The Ashore Knowledge part of this section begins with basic rules for preventing collisions and moves on to potential hazards to be aware of and to avoid. In the Afloat Skills you will start the engine, cast off, motor to open water to put the boat through her paces under power, practice docking, and bring the boat back to the dock.

ASHORE KNOWLEDGE

Main Topics:
- Avoiding Collision
- Safety
- Hypothermia

Chapter 8 – Avoiding Collision

RULES OF THE ROAD

Here lies the body of Michael O'Day,
Who died defending his right of way.
He was right, dead right, as he sailed along,
But he's just as dead as if he'd been wrong.

The *International Regulations for Preventing Collisions at Sea*, variously known as the *Collision Regulations*, Rules of the Road, or Colregs, apply to and are mandatory for all vessels. There are a number of Canadian modifications which apply in all Canadian waters. Local regulations, under the jurisdiction of Ports Canada, supersede the International Rules. The *Safe Boating Guide* contains illustrated and simplified excerpts from the *Collision Regulations*.

The word "way" appears frequently in boating. To **make way** simply means to pass or move, perhaps with reference to a direction or speed. If a boat is making **no way** or has "no way on," she is not moving. If she is making **headway** she is moving ahead; making **sternway**, moving astern. Earlier, *leeway* was defined as the leeward motion of a boat. If a boat is

taking way off she is reducing speed; **gathering way**, picking up speed. **Underway**, defined as "a vessel not at anchor, or made fast to the shore, or aground" can fool you. It merely means the boat is floating freely. It may or may not be making way.

When two vessels are approaching each other, one is the **stand-on** vessel and the other is the **give-way** vessel. "Right of way" is not properly used to apply to the stand-on vessel because the stand-on vessel is as obligated as the give-way vessel. She must "keep her course and speed" and "as soon as it becomes apparent to her that the vessel required to keep out of the way is not taking appropriate action, she must take action to avoid collision." The give-way vessel "shall, so far as possible, take early and substantial action to keep well clear." This means that if you have to keep out of the way of another boat you must make your intentions clear by an early and noticeable alteration of course.

RULES FOR SAILING VESSELS (RULE 12)

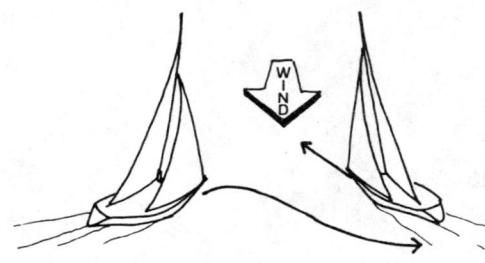

Figure 8-1 – OPPOSITE TACKS

When two sailing vessels are on opposite tacks, the vessel on port tack shall keep out of the way of the vessel on starboard tack.

Figure 8-2 – SAME TACK

When both sailing vessels are on the same tack, the vessel which is to windward shall keep out of the way of the vessel which is to leeward.

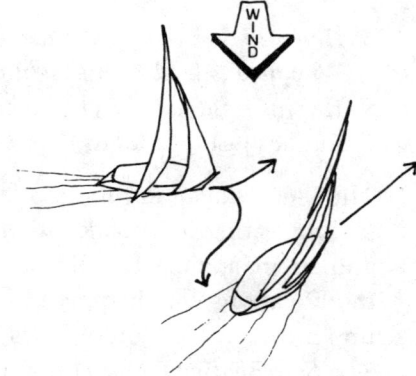

Figure 8-3 – UNCERTAINTY

When a sailing vessel on port tack sees a sailing vessel to windward and cannot determine with certainty what tack she is on, she shall keep out of the way of the windward vessel.

RULES FOR POWER-DRIVEN VESSELS:

The term power-driven vessel means any vessel propelled by machinery, so, whenever your engine is being used even if one or both sails are up, you are a power-driven vessel.

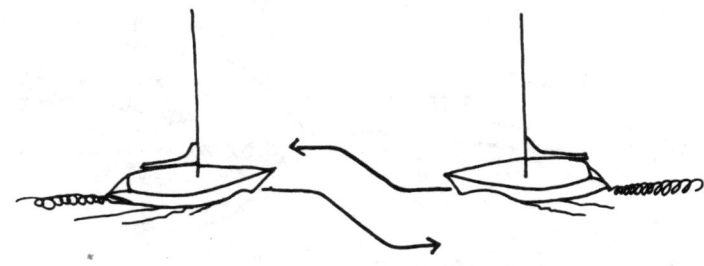

Figure 8-4 – MEETING HEAD-ON (Rule 14)

When two power-driven vessels are meeting on reciprocal or nearly reciprocal courses, each shall alter her course to starboard, so that each shall pass on the port side of the other.

In this situation, since each vessel must keep out of the way of the other, there is no stand-on vessel. Like two cars, coming from opposite directions, meeting on a narrow road, each moves over to the right to avoid collision.

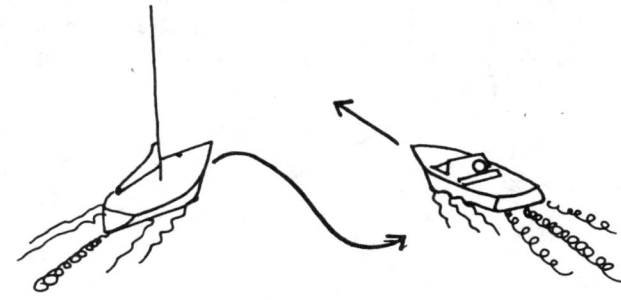

Figure 8-5 – CROSSING (Rule 15)

When two power-driven vessels are crossing, the vessel which has the other on her own starboard side shall keep out of the way and shall avoid crossing ahead of the other vessel.

We can liken this to two cars meeting at an unmarked intersection, in which case the car on the right has the right of way.

In Canadian waters a vessel crossing a river shall keep out of the way of a power-driven vessel ascending or descending the river, except on the St. Lawrence River northeast of Ile Rouge.

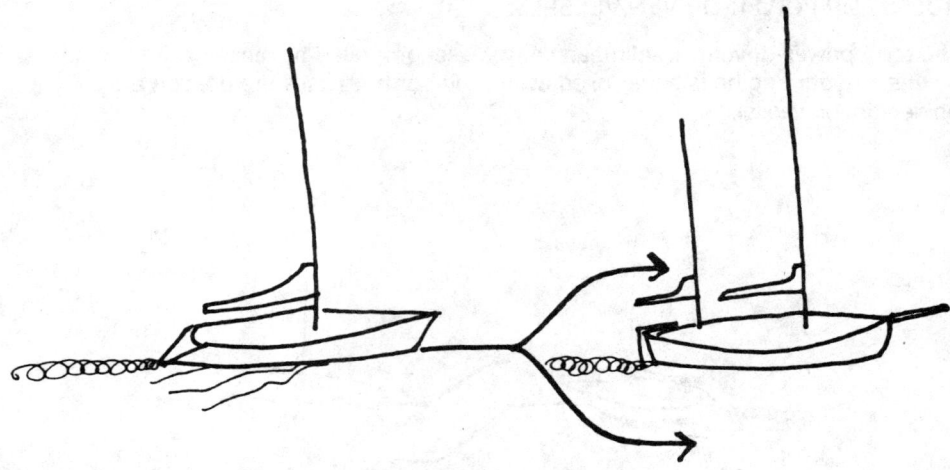

Figure 8-6 (a) – OVERTAKING: (Rule 13)

Any vessel (power or sail) overtaking any other vessel (power or sail) shall keep out of the way of the vessel being overtaken, until well clear ahead.

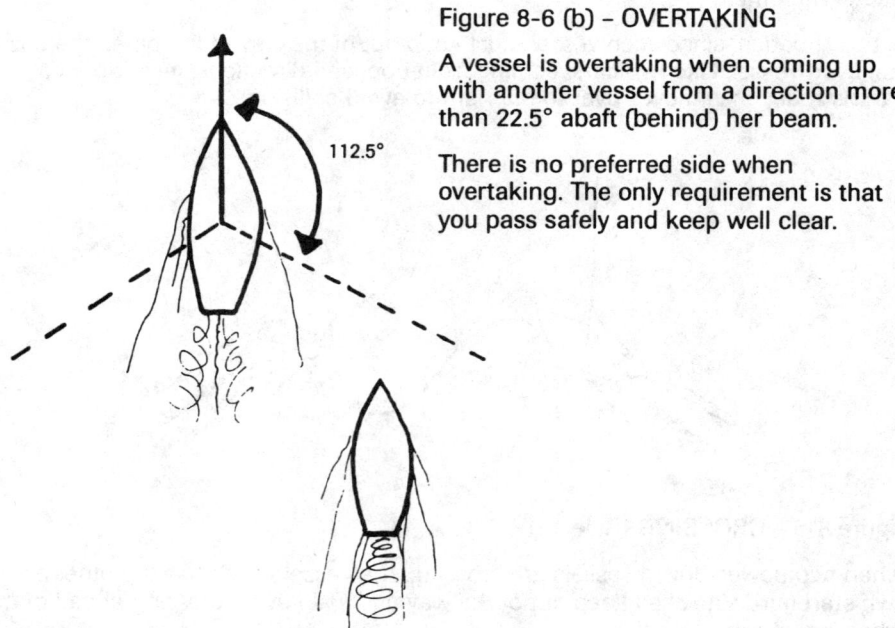

Figure 8-6 (b) – OVERTAKING

A vessel is overtaking when coming up with another vessel from a direction more than 22.5° abaft (behind) her beam.

There is no preferred side when overtaking. The only requirement is that you pass safely and keep well clear.

WHEN A SAILING VESSEL AND POWER-DRIVEN VESSEL MEET:

A power-driven vessel shall keep out of the way of a sailing vessel. (Rule 18)

The *Collision Regulations* are largely based on the concept that a more maneuverable vessel should keep out of the way of a less maneuverable vessel. In this case the power driven vessel is the more easily maneuvered of the two vessels.

This rule must be applied with caution and reservations. It does not apply in narrow channels, **traffic separation schemes** (shipping lanes), or when overtaking. Here are a few guidelines to assist you in applying this rule.

- **In a narrow channel stay well to the right hand side and do not impede the passage of a vessel which must stay within the channel** (eg. ferries, large commercial vessels). Cross the channel only when traffic permits.

- **Avoid a traffic separation scheme if possible.** If not, proceed in the appropriate lane and stay well to the side. If you must cross, cross as close to a right angle to the traffic flow as you can, and only when traffic permits.

- **Stay well clear of larger vessels that may be restricted in their ability to maneuver**, such as commercial fishing vessels while fishing, tugs with tows, dredges, and vessels engaged in underwater operations.

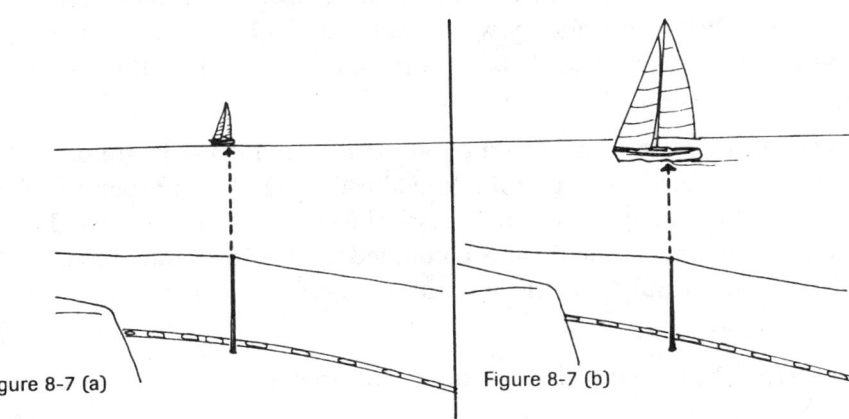

Figure 8-7 (a)   Figure 8-7 (b)

Figures 8-7 (a) & (b) – Risk of Collision: (Rule 7) – To tell if things are shaping up for a collision when you are on a converging course with another boat:

Figure 8-7 (a): Take a bearing on the approaching boat either with a compass or by aligning the boat with a fixed object on your boat such as a stanchion, winch or shroud. Maintain your heading and speed. Wait a short period.

Figure 8-7 (b): If the bearing on the approaching boat has remained the same you are on a collision course. When risk of collision exists, clarify the situation by asking yourself these questions:
- Am I under power or sail?
- Is the other boat under power or sail?
- What rule applies?
- What are my obligations?

- The operators of small power-driven vessels, such as runabouts and boats fishing for pleasure, may not realize they are required to keep out of the way of sailing vessels. Be cautious when approaching these boats.

The *Collision Regulations* require you to maintain a proper lookout not only by sight but by hearing as well. For instance, if you hear five or more short whistle blasts and see the vessel making these sounds heading your way, it is a danger signal meaning your intentions or actions are not being understood, or that the vessel is in doubt whether you are taking sufficient action to avoid collision.

You are also required to proceed at a safe speed taking into account the maneuverability of your boat, its stopping distance, the amount of traffic and the state of visibility.

SEEING AND BEING SEEN

The *Collision Regulations* require a vessel underway or at anchor to show the prescribed navigation lights from sunset to sunrise and whenever visibility is restricted by fog, mist, falling snow, heavy rainstorms and other causes.

In the daytime when visibility is good we can easily see whether an approaching vessel is under power or sail and in what direction it is moving. At night or when visibility is poor, a vessel's navigation lights give us this information.

Sidelights are a green light on the starboard side and a red light on the port side, each showing from dead ahead to 22.5° ***abaft*** (behind) the beam on its respective side. On a vessel of less than 20m the sidelights may be combined in one light. A combined light is frequently seen mounted on the pulpit, where it is not obscured by sails or other equipment.

The **sternlight** is a white light at the stern showing aft over an arc of 135°.

The sidelights and sternlight, if fitted together on the same plane, would show over an arc of 360°. One light, a tricolour, combining sidelights and sternlights and exhibited from the top of the mast is an option for a sailing vessel under 20m, but only when she is sailing.

The sidelights and sternlight may be thought of as the "basic" lights for most vessels over 7m (23 ft) underway. The number, colours and positions of additional lights on a vessel enable other vessels to determine the type of vessel, the direction in which the vessel is travelling and even its approximate size. The approaching vessel then knows what action to take.

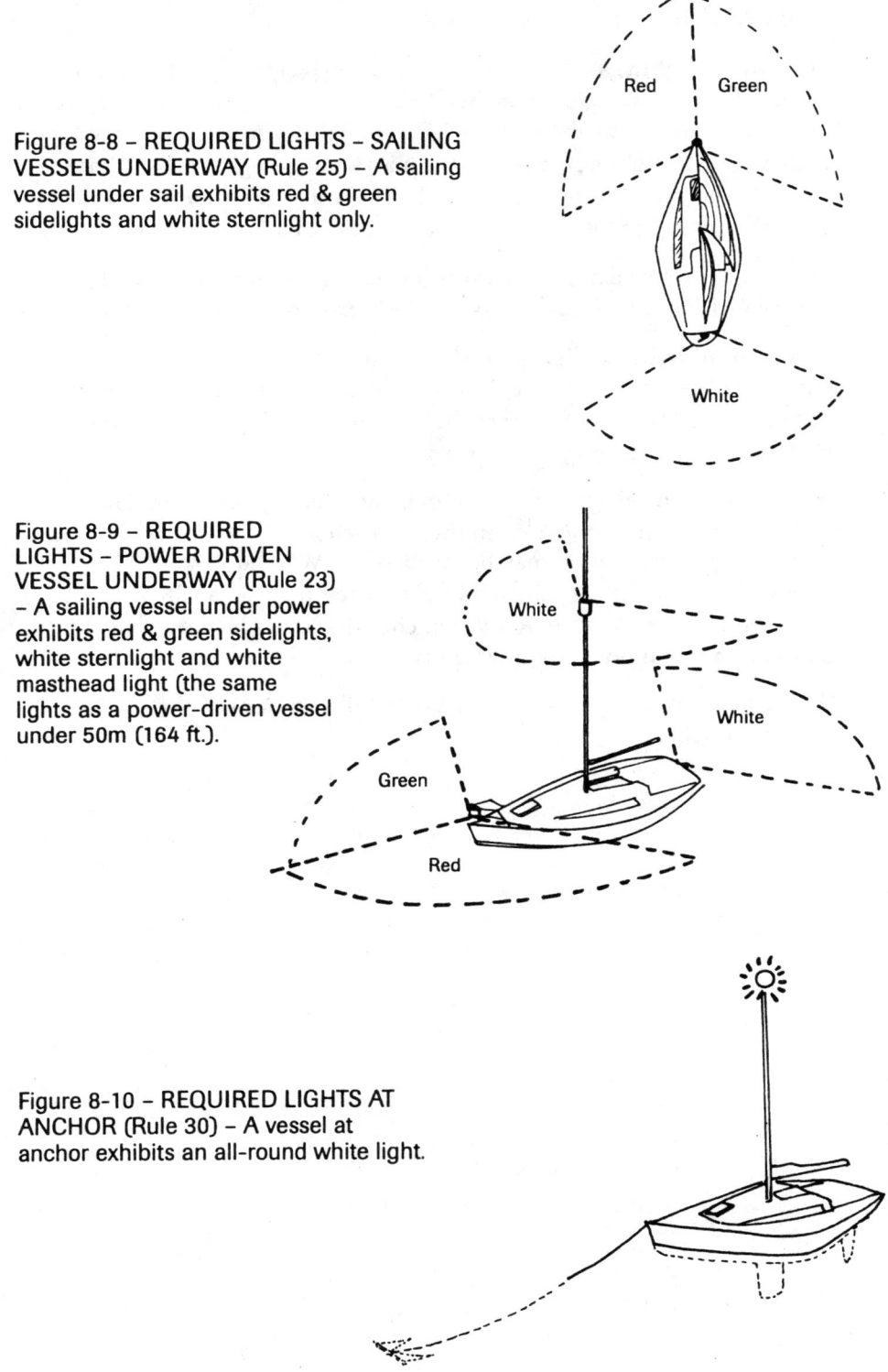

Figure 8-8 – REQUIRED LIGHTS – SAILING VESSELS UNDERWAY (Rule 25) – A sailing vessel under sail exhibits red & green sidelights and white sternlight only.

Figure 8-9 – REQUIRED LIGHTS – POWER DRIVEN VESSEL UNDERWAY (Rule 23) – A sailing vessel under power exhibits red & green sidelights, white sternlight and white masthead light (the same lights as a power-driven vessel under 50m (164 ft.).

Figure 8-10 – REQUIRED LIGHTS AT ANCHOR (Rule 30) – A vessel at anchor exhibits an all-round white light.

A sailing vessel under sail exhibits red & green sidelights and white sternlight only.

A **masthead light** is a white light placed over the fore and aft centerline of the vessel and showing over an arc of 112.5° on each side of the vessel. This is the same arc as the two sidelights together. On a sailboat the masthead light is not at the top of the mast as one might think. It is affixed to the front of the mast about half way up. (The **masthead** is not only the very top of the mast, it is the entire top half of the mast).

A sailing vessel under power exhibits sidelights, sternlight and masthead light, the same lights as a power-driven vessel under 50m.

An **all-round light** is a light that shows over an arc of 360°. A vessel less than 50m (164 ft) at anchor exhibits a white all-round light "where it may best be seen". This may be either the white electric light at the top of the mast or a lantern hanging in the rigging.

Unfortunately the electrical panels on many cruising boats are not labelled with current terminology used in the *Collision Regulations*. For example, the masthead light switch may be labelled "BOW," "BOW POWER," or "STEAMING," while the all-round light switch may be labelled "MASTHEAD" or "ANCHOR". When checking out a boat, try out the light switches and note down which is which.

The *Safe Boating Guide* contains additional illustrations of the navigation lights.

Chapter 9 – Safety

For the sailor who abides by the limits imposed by his or her level of skill and knowledge, cruising is a very safe recreation. The following are some potential hazards and how you can avoid or cope with them.

SOURCES OF FIRE AND EXPLOSION

Fumes from gasoline, propane, butane, alcohol and kerosene are the most common sources of fire and explosion aboard a boat.

Gasoline is extremely volatile. Gasoline for outboard motors must be stored above deck in vented containers. When refuelling, adhere strictly to the procedures listed below in Safe Refuelling Procedures.

Propane, a liquified petroleum gas (LPG), is a fast and very popular cooking fuel. Since propane is heavier than air, any leak will quickly allow gas to settle into the bilge where it is difficult to remove. To facilitate detection of this naturally odourless gas, a strong, unpleasant odour is added. Propane stoves and heaters that are properly installed and maintained are quite safe, with reliable alarm systems and tanks vented overboard. After using a propane stove, shut off the valve on the cylinder and bleed the propane out of the line by leaving one burner on until the flame is extinguished. Remember to then turn the burner control knob to "OFF."

Butane, also a liquified petroleum gas and heavier than air, should be treated with the same precautions as propane. Use all cooking, lighting and heating appliances in accordance with the manufacturer's instructions.

Two rarely considered gases that may be overlooked as sources of explosion aboard a boat are methane and hydrogen.

Methane, a by-product of the decomposition of human waste, can build up in the holding tank, head, and connecting or discharge hoses should they become plugged. Holding tanks are vented so methane can dissipate. Correct operation of the head and regular pumping out of the holding tank will ensure that methane gas does not build up.

A battery is an electro-chemical device which produces hydrogen when it is being recharged. The battery compartment must be well vented to allow the release of this highly explosive gas.

The human nose is a fairly sensitive gas detector. Sniff test, especially when first coming aboard and before lighting any appliance or starting the engine. Odours should always be investigated and no one permitted to smoke, light matches or change the position of electrical switches until the source of the odour has been identified and the boat ventilated thoroughly.

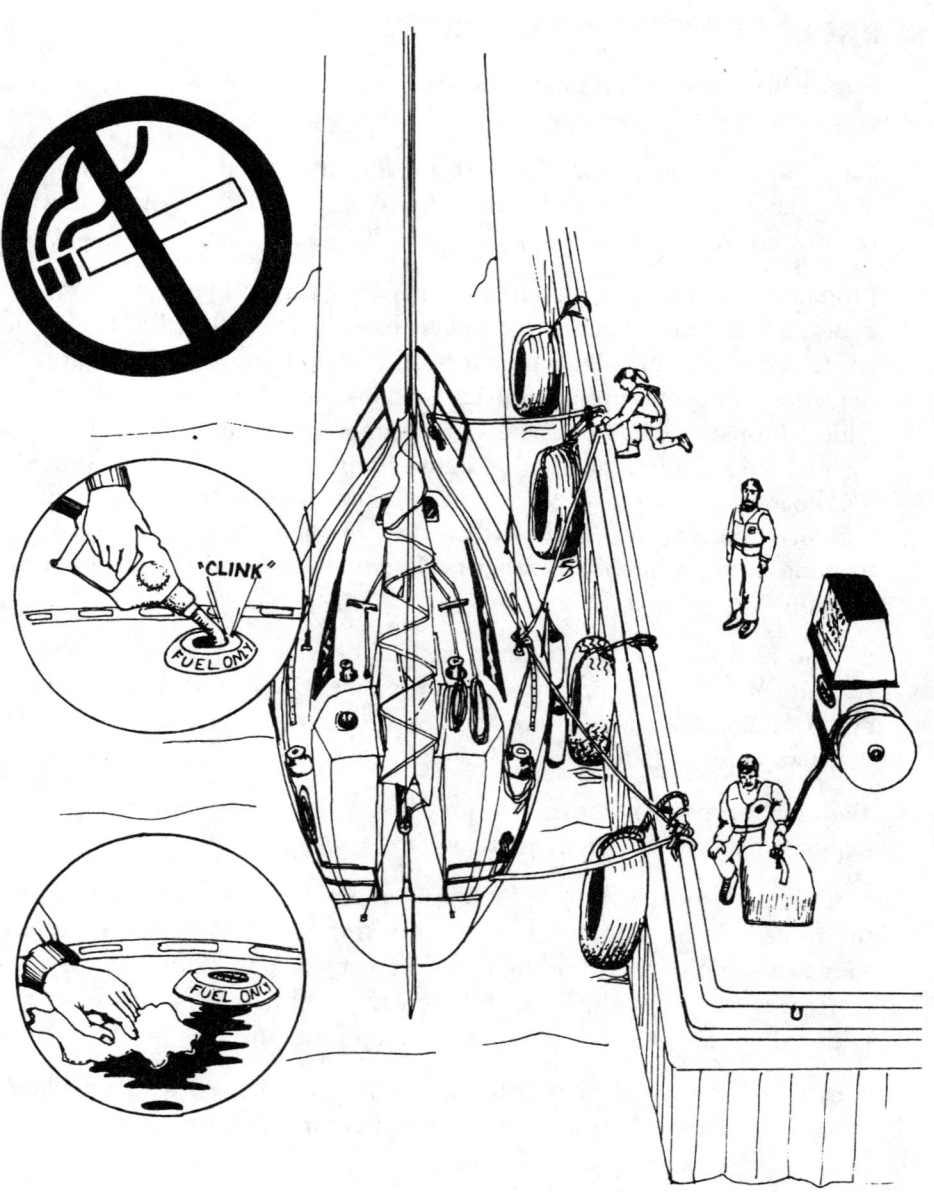

Figure 9-1 – Safe Refuelling Procedures

SAFE REFUELLING PROCEDURES

Memorize these:
1. Moor the boat securely.
2. Shut off engines; make sure all crew are off the boat.
3. Don't smoke and extinguish all open flames; close all windows and hatches (so fumes can't get into the cabin). It is safer to extinguish cigarettes and open flames before you approach the dock.
4. Take portable tanks ashore (to be filled).
5. Don't use electrical switches.
6. Ground the nozzle against the filler pipe (so no spark of static electricity can arc across); don't overfill.
7. Wipe up any spillage; turn on the blower (if there is one) for at least five minutes to clear the engine compartment of fumes.
8. Check for vapour odours.

It is good practice to start the engine before all crew get back aboard.

It is an offence punishable by a fine to pollute the water. Do not allow fuel to overflow while refuelling.

OVERHEAD POWER LINES

Very occasionally one hears of a helm either forgetting the tall mast or not keeping a proper lookout and taking a sailboat under a low power line, thereby electrocuting a crewmember. The mast is a very effective conductor of electricity and does not have to actually touch a power line for electric shock to happen. If the voltage is high the air will conduct

Figure 9-2 – The dangers of overhead power lines

electricity from the line to the nearby mast. Second to electrocution, dangers include burns, fire, and damage to the hull, rig or electronics.

PRESENCE OF DIVERS

While on the water, keep an eye out for flags signalling the presence of divers.

The blue and white International Code Flag "A" means "I have a diver down; keep well clear at slow speed." It is required by the *Collision Regulations* to be shown on vessels engaged in diving operations because their maneuverability is restricted. The red flag with the white diagonal stripe is required to be carried on a buoy marking an area where scuba* diving is in progress.

In actual practice in North America the red and white flag is in general use on both diving boats and floating markers.

Should you see either flag, give it a wide berth and reduce speed.

* Scuba stands for Self-Contained Underwater Breathing Apparatus.

Figure 9-3 – The presence of divers

Chapter 10 – Hypothermia

Hypothermia (exposure) is a very real hazard in our cool Canadian climate and cold waters. Hypothermia is the condition resulting from a lowering of the body's **core temperature** due to heat loss from the body. The core or deep body temperature is the temperature of the vital internal organs which include heart, lungs and brain. The main heat loss areas are the groin, where large blood vessels are close to the surface, the sides of the chest, where there is little muscle or fat, and the head including the neck. Over half the body's heat loss occurs through the head. Our mothers really did know best when they made us wear our wool hats in cold weather.

As the core temperature cools, the body goes into shock, which depresses normal bodily functions, such as breathing and heart rate. If untreated, hypothermia can be fatal. Death is usually due to cardiac arrest.

PREVENTING HYPOTHERMIA

The air temperature does not have to be extreme for hypothermia to become a threat. Sailors must also contend with the wind chill factor which can reduce the apparent temperature substantially.

To prevent hypothermia:

- Carry enough suitable clothing, with changes, for the worst conditions that could occur.

- Keep dry. Wet clothing loses its ability to insulate. The body loses heat much faster if your clothing is wet.

- Eat well and have non-alcoholic hot drinks in cool conditions. Alcohol impairs judgement.

- Watch yourself and fellow crewmembers for the first signs of impending hypothermia — shivering and numbness of hands and feet.

- Wear your safety harness, so you will stay on board when conditions make working on deck hazardous.

- Wear your PFD. Children and non-swimmers should wear their PFD's at all times while afloat. Students and new sailors should also wear them. Your PFD will help keep you warm, especially if you fall into the water. Wear it in the dinghy, when sailing at night, and whenever working on deck without one is unsafe.

MILD HYPOTHERMIA

SIGNS AND SYMPTOMS:

- **Uncontrollable shivering** as the muscles attempt to produce heat to counteract heat loss.

- Feeling of intense coldness. Numbness in hands and feet.

- Judgement may be impaired.

- Fatigue, weakness, loss of coordination. Even at this stage a person in the water will probably be unable to grab onto a line or climb a boarding ladder.

TREATMENT:

If the person is conscious, talking clearly and shivering vigorously (ie. mildly hypothermic):

- Get the person into the cabin and remove all wet clothing, **handling as gently as possible.** All hypothermic persons should be handled gently. Jolting can affect heart function.

- **Do not rub the surface of the body.** Massage sends cool blood to the core of the body, leading to **afterdrop** and possibly damaging surface tissues and nerve endings.

  Afterdrop is a further lowering of the core temperature caused when cool blood from the extremities moves to the core, further cooling it. Afterdrop can bring on cardiac arrest.

- Put on layers of dry clothing. Cover the head and neck with hat and scarf.

- Apply luke warm (40–45°C, 110–120°F) objects such as water bottles and chemical heat packs (hand warmers) when possible to head, neck and trunk. **Be careful not to burn the person.**

- Give a warm, nonalcoholic drink (soup, milk) if the person can hold a cup, and a sweet, high energy snack to provide quick energy.

- Do not give hot coffee, tea, or cocoa. They are cardiac irritants.

- **Do not give alcohol.** Alcohol does not warm the body. Dilation of blood vessels may cause heat loss and inhibit rewarming. Alas, the St. Bernard and its keg of brandy are an outdated, romantic legend.

SEVERE HYPOTHERMIA

SIGNS AND SYMPTOMS:

- **Shivering is reduced or absent.** This may be the result of the person becoming stiff and either becoming unconscious or showing signs of clouded consciousness, for example, slurred speech.

- Apathy, exhaustion, drowsiness.

- May appear dead, with little or no apparent breathing; dilated pupils; cold, waxy skin.

TREATMENT:

Once shivering has stopped, it is no use simply putting on dry clothing or wrapping the person in a blanket because the person cannot rewarm without an external source of heat. Heat must be donated to the person quickly.

- Wrap the torso, naked, in a sleeping bag or blanket with another naked person, or even two persons, so there is skin-to-skin contact providing a gentle transfer of body heat. **Handle the person very gently.** This is a good treatment also for mild hypothermia.

- Apply warm (40–45°C, 110–120°F) objects as for mild hypothermia.

- Direct steam from a kettle carefully under a makeshift hood over the person's head or exhale warm air close to the person's mouth in time with inhalations so he or she is breathing warm air.

- Call the Coast Guard on the VHF radio so medical aid can be available at the point of landing. Head for the nearest place medical aid can be made available.

- Perform rescue breathing if the person's breathing has stopped, and CPR if the heart has stopped.

SURVIVAL IN COLD WATER

When a person is immersed in cold water, heat is conducted away from the body much faster than heat loss in an equivalent air temperature. Survival time varies depending on clothing, activity, body mass, body fat, age, state of health, injury, and the will to live.

If you find yourself in cold water there are a number of actions you can take to buy survival time.

- **Keep calm and consciously control your breathing as much as you can.** Response to the initial shock of cold water is usually

hyperventilation (overbreathing). This can lead to uncontrolled aspiration of sea water as well as depleted carbon dioxide levels in the blood which could cause fainting and subsequent drowning. This phase will soon pass.

- **Keep your clothes, hat and shoes on.** They will provide some insulation and air trapped inside your clothing will offer some flotation. Make sure your PFD is secured snugly about your chest.

- **Stay as still as possible. Do not swim.** Swimming generates heat but more heat is lost than can be generated by the body.

- **Float in the HELP position** (Heat Escape Lessening Position), with elbows close to your sides and arms crossed in front, lower legs crossed, thighs together, knees bent, and head out of the water where its high rate of heat loss, especially in water, will be minimized.

Figure 10-1 – The HELP position

- **If you are not wearing a PFD, the best you can do is tread water.** This keeps your head out of the water, though cooling is still about 35% faster than keeping still in a PFD (which is an excellent reason for wearing your PFD!)

- **Do not use the drownproofing technique.** It is considered to be the express route to fatal hypothermia, though it does allow non-swimmers without flotation to escape drowning at least for some time.

Drownproofing, taught about 30 years ago, involves restful floating with lungs full of air which is interrupted every 10–15 seconds to raise the head out of the water to breathe. The problem is that the heat loss areas of the body, especially the head, are not protected from the cold.

- **Get out of the water if you can**. Even if you can climb only partly out of the water onto a floating object you will reduce the rate of heat loss. Do this as soon as possible before you lose the strength to help yourself.

SELF TEST – ANSWERS ARE ON PAGE 194

1. A scientific balloon has just floated down into the water. There is a small reward for turning it in. The crews of the boats in the picture have spotted it and are converging towards it at about the same speed. The skippers, seeing a traffic jam shaping up, must determine their obligations as set out in the *Collision Regulations*.

Assume that you are the skipper of each boat in Figure 10-2 and list all the other boats to which you must give way. (Hint: see figures 8-1 to 8-7.)

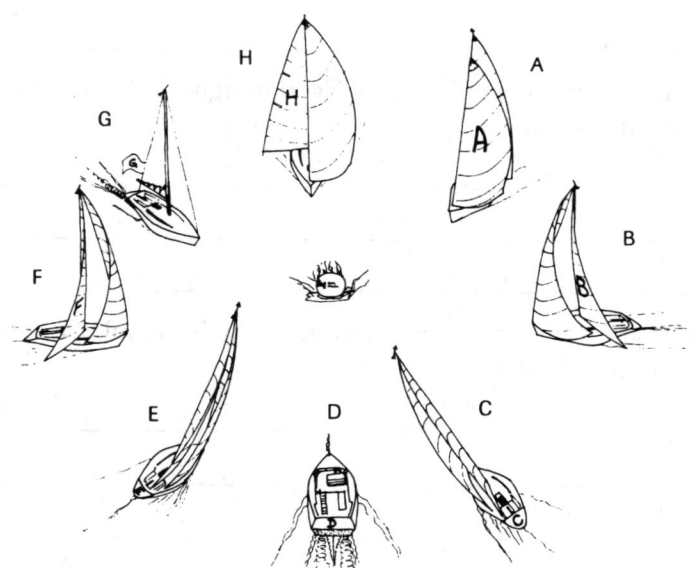

Figure 10-2 – Self Test Diagram for Question #1

Boat A gives way to boat(s) : _____

Boat B gives way to boat(s) : _____

Boat C gives way to boat(s) : _____

Boat D gives way to boat(s) : _____

Boat E gives way to boat(s) : _____

Boat F gives way to boat(s) : _____

Boat G gives way to boat(s) : _____

Boat H gives way to boat(s) : _____

Boat _____ is stand on vessel over all others and will arrive first to pick up the balloon.

2. Underway means _____
_____

3. Which is the preferred side when overtaking another vessel? _____
_____

4. There is no stand on vessel when two _____

    meet on _____

5. Navigation lights should be exhibited from _____ to _____

    and when _____

6. Name and give the colors of navigation lights exhibited by a sailing vessel under sail.
_____
_____
_____

7. Name and give the colors of navigation lights exhibited by a sailing vessel under power:
_____
_____
_____
_____

8. List two often overlooked gases that can cause explosion and fire aboard a boat and give a source for each:
_____
_____

9. What is the chief danger to the crew when a mast comes into contact with a power line? _____
_____

10. What action should you take when you see a flag denoting the presence of divers? _____

11. List three things <u>not</u> to do when treating a victim of mild hypothermia.

    _____

    _____

    _____

12. List three actions that will increase your survival time if you are immersed in cold water. You are wearing a PFD.

    _____

    _____

    _____

13. The three main heat loss areas of the body are _____,

    _____, and _____

14. What are the two first signs of impending hypothermia?

    _____

    _____

SAFETY AND MANEUVERING UNDER POWER

AFLOAT SKILLS

Main Topics:
- The Outboard Engine
- The Inboard Engine
- Steering
- Casting Off
- Getting to know the boat
- Docking Under Power
- Making Fast and Snugging Down

By the completion of the Afloat Skills in Section A, the boat was ready for departure. In the Afloat Skills of this section you learn to handle the boat under power. In the narrow channels of marinas and harbours it can be virtually impossible to maneuver or dock a boat under sail.

> **SAFETY TIP:**
> Get on or off the boat holding a shroud for support. Secure handholds aboard are the shrouds, forestay, backstay, mast, handrails, pulpit and pushpit. Treat lifelines with caution. They have been known to give way. When working about the boat keep in mind the saying "One hand for you, and one hand for the ship".

Chapter 11 – The Engine

THE OUTBOARD ENGINE

Small cruisers are frequently powered by outboard engines of less than 10 HP mounted by a bracket on the **transom** (a flat section of the hull at the stern) or by clamps to an engine well near the stern.

PRE-START CHECK:

- **Pull the starter cord handle out slowly to check for wear on the cord and smooth operation of the starter mechanism.** You may wish to remove the engine cover to see if there are spare cotter pins and shearpins by the motor.

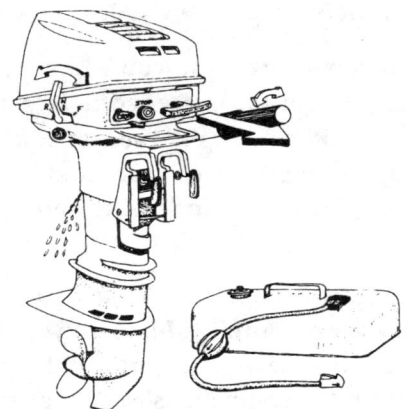

Figure 11-1 – The outboard engine and fuel tank

- **Lower the engine into the water** so both cooling water intake and propeller are immersed. Check that mounting is secure and that the engine is facing center.

- **Shake the fuel tank(s)** to be sure there is sufficient fuel (the gauge may not read correctly) and to mix the oil and gas. The majority of outboards use 50:1 gas to oil outboard mix available at many fuel docks, though occasionally you may have to mix your own. Fuel consumption is about 4.5 litres (1 gal.) per hour for engines less than 10 HP.

- **Open the vent on the gas tank,** and the gasoline shut-off lever if there is one on the engine. Opening the vent prevents a vacuum building up in the tank and causing an airlock. Close the vent while sailing, as the fuel could spill.

- **Connect the fuel line between tank and engine,** making sure the arrow on the priming bulb points towards the engine. **Squeeze the primer bulb** two or three times until it firms up. This primes the engine by pumping fuel into the carburetor.

- **Check that the gear shift lever is in neutral position.** Electric starts usually will not work unless the engine is in neutral — a safety feature.

- **Turn the throttle to the start position**. If the throttle is misaligned with the label or the label is unreadable, open the throttle about 2/3 full.

- **Engage the choke.** This may not be necessary if the engine is warm from recent use.

STARTING AND WARMUP:

- **Look behind you before starting** so you will not give a crewmember a black eye when you pull out the starter cord. Depending on the position of the engine, either grasp the starter cord handle with one hand or stand facing the engine, legs apart, and grasp it with both hands so you can pull between your legs. Ensure you are in a stable stance.

- Pull the starter cord handle out a few centimeters to engage the starter gear, then **pull with short, rapid pulls** to prevent flooding, keeping the cord as horizontal as possible and keeping hold of the handle while allowing it to return. If the engine fails to start after two or three times, disengage the choke and try again.

– or –

Press the electric start button if the engine has an electric start.

- **Disengage the choke** once the engine has started. With some engines if this isn't done immediately the engine will stall; with others the choke must be disengaged slowly.

- **Turn the throttle down to just above idle.**

- **Check for the flow of cooling water.** If there is none, turn off the engine at once to prevent damage, and investigate.

- After making sure that the spring lines are secure, reduce the throttle gently to the shift position (to prevent stalling) and engage forward gear. **Warm up the engine in forward gear for about 2 or 3 minutes with throttle at half speed**. An engine warms up best under load. **Note: Never change gears unless the throttle is in shift position.** (slow RPM's).

- **Throttle down and shift into reverse gear** to make sure the gear is functioning, then return to neutral.

- **To stop the engine**, turn throttle to idle, then press the stop button or with some models, turn the throttle down all the way.

STARTING PROBLEMS:

- **Broken starter cord:** Tie a figure eight knot in the end of a piece of light line. Insert the knot into one of the notches in the flywheel (you may have to unscrew a cover to get at it). Wind the line clockwise around the flywheel once or twice and pull normally to start the engine.

- **Flooding**: Repeatedly trying unsuccessfully to start the engine fills the carburetor with gas. You may even smell gas. To clear a flooded carburetor:
  - disconnect the fuel line from the engine.
  - disengage the choke and open the throttle fully.
  - pull the starter cord handle repeatedly until the engine shows signs of starting.
  - reconnect the fuel line and start as usual.
- **Airlock**: If the engine starts well, then dies after a few minutes, check that the vent on the gas tank is open.

THE INBOARD ENGINE

Diesel inboard engines are the engines most often seen aboard larger cruising sailboats. They are sturdy, economical, safe and reliable. A diesel engine, unlike a gasoline engine, has no spark plugs or carburetor. Fuel ignites from being compressed in the cylinders. A diesel engine has no choke and is unlikely to have an engine compartment blower fan to clear the engine compartment of fumes.

BEFORE STARTING:

- **Sniff for fumes as you come aboard.** If there are fumes, ventilate, including turning on the engine compartment blower fan, if there is one, and investigate. Proceed no further until the boat is clear of fumes.

- **Locate the engine manual.** Use it while familiarizing yourself with the engine.

- **Remove the engine access panel(s).** To do this you may have to remove the companionway stairs.
  - **Visually inspect the engine** for fuel, water and oil leaks, loose wires or hoses, loose or broken engine mounts, and an excess of water in the engine sump. Bail the water out.
  - Locate the engine oil dipstick and the engine oil filler cap. Pull out the dipstick and wipe it off. Replace the dipstick and pull it out again. The oil level should be between the two lines on the lower end of the dipstick. **Add oil, if necessary**, but don't overfill. Reseat the dipstick fully, otherwise oil may spray and make a mess.
  - If the engine is fresh water cooled, **open the heat exchanger cap** (radiator cap) and, **if fresh water needs to be added, top up.**
  - **Check the belt(s)** for wear and proper tension.
  - **Open the cooling water intake seacock and the fuel shutoff valve**, if closed.

- **Replace and secure the engine access panel(s)** and stairs.

- **Check the battery (or batteries).** If there are gauges the voltage should be greater than 12 volts.

- **Turn the battery selector switch to battery "1" or battery "2".** There may also be a main switch to turn on.

- **Turn on the blower** if there is one. If a gasoline engine, the blower must be on for 5 minutes before starting. You may have to turn the battery selector switch and possibly a main switch before the blower will work.

While the engine is running it is recharging the battery or batteries. **It is good practice to recharge the batteries daily.** One system is to alternate from one battery to the other each day the boat is in use.

The battery selector switch is turned to "OFF" at the end of the day if the crew is leaving the vessel.

The battery switch can be put on "BOTH" or "ALL" (the label depends on the make of switch) **if each individual battery does not have enough charge to start the engine.** If it is necessary to charge both batteries, switch to "BOTH" or "ALL" before starting the engine. It is not recommended that you switch from one battery to the other or to "BOTH" or "ALL" while the engine is running. Never turn the battery selector switch to "OFF" while the engine is running because it could damage the alternator.

- **Check the fuel supply.** There may be a fuel gauge on or by the engine panel in the cockpit, or on the fuel tank(s). The ignition or key switch has to be turned on for the gauge in the cockpit to work. Fuel consumption for 2 and 3 cylinder diesel engines is approximately 2.5 litres (.5 gals.) per hour. You can cut down the rate of consumption considerably by reducing speed.

STARTING AND WARMUP:

- **Check the engine manual for specific procedures for starting and stopping.**

- **Check that the cooling water intake seacock is open.**

- **Make sure the gear control lever is in neutral.** Controls for the transmission and throttle may be single lever or two lever type.

- **Advance the throttle to about 2/3 full.**

- **Make sure the stop button or handle is pushed all the way in** (diesel)

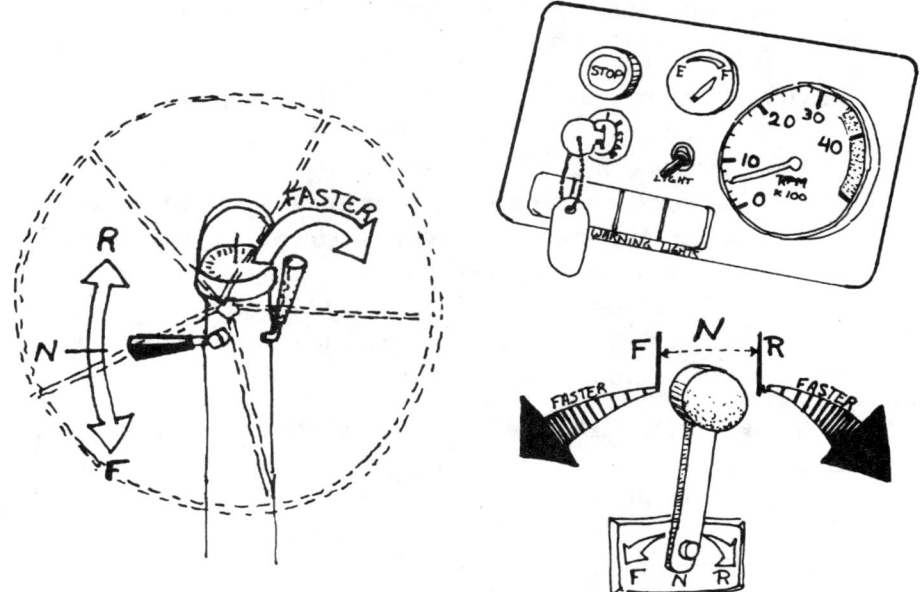

Figure 11-2 – Typical diesel engine controls. Forward and reverse transmission controls on some boats may be opposite.

- **Engage the choke** if the engine is cold (gasoline). A diesel engine may have a **preheating mechanism** for use in cold weather (see engine manual).

- **Turn on the key.** An oil pressure audio-alarm may sound but will stop when the engine starts and pressure reaches the normal operating range.

- **Press the starter button or turn the key fully** and crank until the engine starts. If the engine does not start, do not crank for more than 10 seconds. Wait 10 seconds before trying again. If a gasoline engine does not start after a couple of tries, restart in about 10 minutes when fumes have had time to disperse and flooding has cleared.

- **When the engine has started, reduce the throttle to about 1200 RPM's** (or as recommended in engine manual).

- **Check for cooling water coming out with the exhaust.** If none, stop the engine at once to prevent damage.

- **Reduce or disengage choke** (gasoline). Disengage choke completely as soon as possible.

- **Check the temperature, oil pressure and ammeter gauges** or look to see that oil pressure and ammeter (alternator non-charging) lights are out.

- The blower on gasoline powered boats should remain on the entire time the engine is in use.

- **Check the transmission.** First, make sure the spring lines are secure and there are no lines in the water. Throttle down to idle and shift into reverse. After a few moments, shift into forward, with a slight pause in neutral. **The throttle must always be at idle before shifting gears and, if going from forward to reverse or vice versa, always pause momentarily in neutral.** Advance the throttle slightly and warm up in gear for a few minutes. All engines warm up best under load. A diesel engine does not stall, so you can shift back to neutral and get underway only a couple of minutes after starting.

- **TO STOP THE ENGINE** (gasoline):
  – Throttle gradually all the way down.
  – Gearshift lever to neutral.
  – Press stop button/turn off key.
  – Turn off blower.

- **TO STOP THE ENGINE** (diesel):
  – Throttle gradually all the way down.
  – Gearshift lever to neutral.
  – Wait approximately 30 seconds.
  – Pull stop button or handle which shuts off the fuel and wait until engine stops.
  – When engine stops, push in stop button or handle all the way.

NOTE: Some diesel engines are stopped by simply turning off the key. They are fitted with an electric solenoid which controls the fuel to the engine. In this case omit this and the last step.
  – Turn off the key (you should listen for the oil pressure audio-alarm again before the key is turned off). **The key must be turned off after all the other steps, otherwise you may drain the battery.**

OPERATING GUIDELINES WHILE UNDERWAY:

- Cruising RPM's vary from engine to engine, and are usually about three quarters of maximum. Consult the engine manual for the boat you are using.

- Keep an eye on all warning lights and gauges and heed any audio-alarm. Check flow of cooling water periodically.

SAFETY TIP:
If you need to look inside the engine compartment while the engine is running, be very careful that hair, clothing or hands do not get caught in the alternator or water pump belts or other moving parts.

If there is any problem with oil pressure, engine temperature, alternator charging or if cooling water ceases to flow, stop the engine at once.

- **Put the gear shift lever in reverse while sailing.** You will get rid of an annoying noise and there will be less propeller drag to slow the boat.

- **When motor sailing (both motoring and sailing):**
  – do motor-sail with the sail(s) filled to prevent flogging of the sails.
  – **do not allow the boat to heel (lean over) more than 15°** as the oil supply to the engine may not circulate properly, resulting in serious damage to the engine.
  – **do not** motor into the wind with the foresail raised.

Chapter 12 – Leaving the Dock

STEERING

- Sit or stand where you can both see ahead and control the engine.
- **With wheel steering the boat is steered like a car.** Usually the wheel is marked so you can tell when the rudder is centered.
- **With tiller steering the tiller is pushed away from the direction you wish to turn.** When a keelboat turns it pivots around a point on its keel which is roughly halfway between bow and stern. When you push the tiller to port you are actually turning the stern to port, which results in the bow turning to starboard. Pushing the tiller to port turns the rudder in the same direction as turning a wheel to starboard.

Steering with a tiller while moving astern is especially easy. Just point the aft end of the tiller where you want to go.

- Remember, **a boat loses steerage and will not steer if there is no water flowing over the rudder.** The slower a boat is moving, the slower water is flowing over the rudder, and the slower her response to the helm (steering mechanism). Another very important point is that it doesn't matter what gear you are in, it's the direction the boat is moving (water is flowing over the rudder) that dictates how the boat will steer (see figure 12-1).

PREPARATION FOR CASTING OFF

- **The secret of successful arrivals and departures is planning and communication.** When planning your departure:
  - Consider how the wind or current will affect you.
  - Note any hazards such as shallow areas or a dinghy hanging from the stern of a nearby boat.
  - Communicate your plan to the crew. Explain what is going to happen, what duties each crewmember will perform and what commands you will give.
- Put on PFD's.
- Note how and where the boat is tied up so you can duplicate the arrangement on your return.
- Turn on the depthsounder and instruments.
- Make sure the rudder is fully operational. Unlock the wheel or untie the tiller.
- Start and warm up the engine (gasoline).

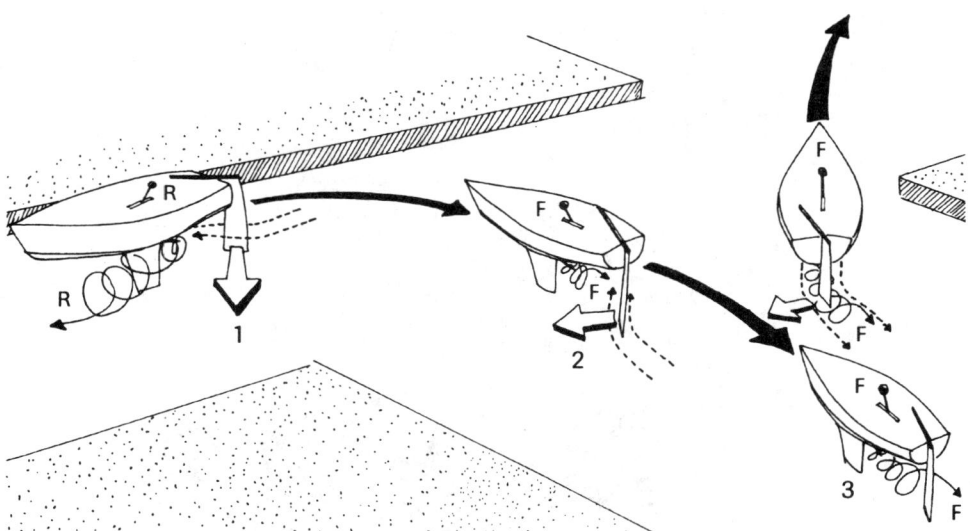

Figure 12-1 – How the rudder works.

1. The boat is leaving the marina in reverse gear with water flowing over the rudder, and is turning to port.
2. Even though the boat has been put into forward gear the helm realizes the boat is still moving astern and steers accordingly.
3. The boat has come to a stop and has no steerage.
4. The boat has begun to move forward in the water, with water flowing over the rudder. The helm steers accordingly.

There is no mystery to giving commands. They must be loud enough to be heard by all crew and they must indicate clearly what you want done. If you should say "Let go" in referring to a line instead of "Cast off", for example, so long as the intent is unmistakable it is no problem. Persevere and soon the proper commands will come automatically.

If you want something done that requires no preparation, simply give the command. If preparation is required, say "Ready to ...", wait for crew to respond "Ready" and then give the command. Watch for this distinction as you go through *Basic Cruising Skills*. Let's first cast off assuming there is no wind or current. The other possibilities are all variations of this.

CASTING OFF

- The helm assigns crew to their duties, one person on the dock for the **forward spring** and **bow breastline** (bow line) and one on the dock for the **aft spring** and **stern breastline** (stern line)(see figure 15-1). If there are other crewmembers, at least one should be assigned to staying aboard and fending off, if necessary, with a **roving fender**, a loose fender which is used wherever needed for fending off.

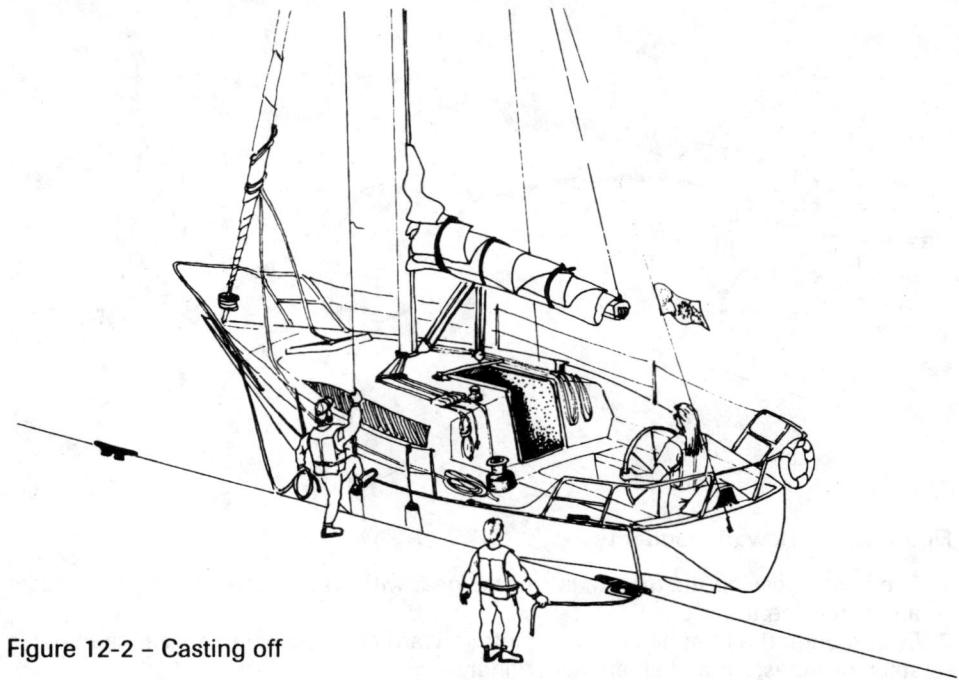

Figure 12-2 – Casting off

- Command "CAST OFF THE SPRING LINES." The two crew on the dock uncleat or untie and remove the two spring lines, placing them aboard.

- Command "READY TO CAST OFF THE BOW LINE." "READY TO CAST OFF THE STERN LINE."

- Each crew on the dock uncleats or unties his or her respective breastline, keeping one turn of the line around the ring, cleat, or rail to which the line was secured and the free end of the line coiled in hand. (A cruising boat can be impossible to hold stationary or pull in to the dock just by hanging onto the docklines. Even this one turn will allow you to hold a good-sized keelboat against a strong wind). At this point, each crew will respond "READY."

- The helm checks for traffic, then commands "CAST OFF THE BOW LINE," followed by "CAST OFF THE STERN LINE," and "STEP ABOARD."

- Each line handler removes the turn from ring, cleat or rail, fends off if necessary, pushes off only if asked to do so, and steps aboard with the line, holding onto a shroud for support. Under some circumstances the crew at the stern may have to board there, preferably at the gate.

SAFETY TIP:
Never fend off with your hands or feet. Use a fender.

- Once aboard, the bow line crew moves to the bow, holds onto the forestay for support, and maintains a lookout until asked to return to the cockpit. The stern line crew makes sure no lines that can foul the propeller are trailing in the water.

- As the dockline crew steps aboard, the helm engages gear so the boat is not dead in the water beside the dock with all crew aboard. The boat is eased away from the dock, the helm making sure the stern does not hit the dock and throttling down as soon as there is steerage way. If the boat has to be turned sharply around the corner of the dock it must not be turned until past the pivot point.

- Keep speed very low in the marina area.

When well clear of the marina the helm orders the mooring lines and fenders to be removed and stowed and the lifeline gate closed. It is considered very bad form to travel with your fenders dangling alongside, yet it is so easy to forget they are there. The lines are coiled for stowage and together with the fenders are hung or placed in a locker, usually the cockpit locker, where they are easily accessible.

Variations on casting off as outlined above depend on the state of the wind and current and the configuration of the dock. At this level you are not expected to be able to deal with all circumstances without assistance.

Some common situations are:

- **Wind blowing off the dock:** This is an easy one. Springlines are removed first then bow line and stern line crew each take a turn with their lines around a ring, cleat or rail on the dock and step aboard with the lines doubled back to the boat. On command they cast off their lines. (The sternline must not get into the propeller!)

- **Wind blowing onto the dock:** You will have to back out because the bow will be blown onto the dock. The spring lines and then the stern line are cast off, with the bow line being cast off last. The bow must be protected either by the crew with the roving fender or with a secured fender and the bow line crew fending off as necessary.

- **Wind or current from ahead:** The bow line is removed first to allow the bow to swing away from the dock. The forward spring line is cast off last to stop the boat going astern. Care must be taken to protect and fend off the stern.

- **Wind or current from astern:** The aft spring line is last to be cast off to stop the boat from moving forward before all is ready. Care must be taken to fend off to avoid hitting a boat docked immediately ahead of your vessel.

Chapter 13 – Getting to Know the Boat

The following drills performed in open water where there is little traffic will give you an opportunity to familiarize yourself with the boat, to practice steering and to determine the boat's handling characteristics under power. Experiment with power handling every time you use an unfamiliar boat so when you arrive at your destination you are not embarrassed by hitting the dock or, even worse, another boat.

DRIFTING

With your boat head to wind, throttle down to idle and put the gearshift in neutral. Let the boat drift for a few minutes with the helm unattended. How does the boat lie in relation to the wind?

A keelboat will usually lie in an attitude anywhere from beam to the wind to stern to the wind. In the case of casting off with the wind blowing onto the dock it was stated that you would have to back away because the bow would be blown onto the dock. **The bow of a keelboat will blow downwind, away from the wind, faster than the stern because it is lighter and its underwater shape provides less resistance.** This knowledge is essential to correct power handling in windy conditions.

Try drifting with helm held *amidships* (in the centre of the boat), then while *lying ahull* (drifting without sails, the wheel locked to windward or tiller lashed to leeward). Does the position of the rudder make any difference?

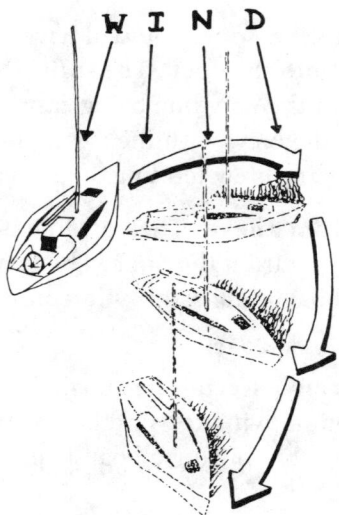

Figure 13-1 – Drifting

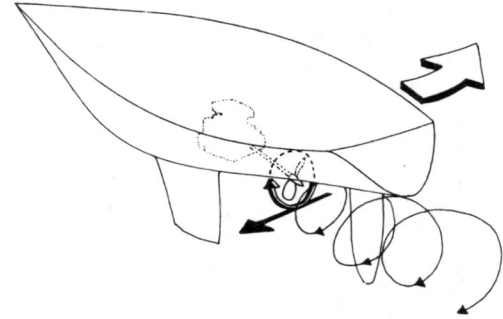

Figure 13-2 – P-effect

P-EFFECT

Motoring in forward gear at very slow speed, take your hands off the helm. Does the boat turn in a large circle to port or starboard? The majority of boats will turn to port because they have right hand propellers, that is propellers which, when viewed from astern, rotate to the right (clockwise) when the engine is in forward gear. A right hand propeller, when the boat is in forward gear, "walks" the stern to starboard and consequently the bow turns to port. This phenomenon is called **P-effect**. A left hand prop will have the opposite effect.

While the P-effect doesn't change the way you steer (ie. move the helm to turn to port or starboard), it does affect your steering, especially when power is applied suddenly. Instead of fighting the P-effect you can use it to assist in docking and in maneuvering in tight spaces. At a more advanced level you will learn to use the P-effect and drifting behaviour together to handle a boat under power in a strong wind.

FIGURE EIGHT

At very slow speed, put the helm **hard over** (all the way over) and turn the boat in a circle.

As the circle is completed and you cross your **wake** (the waves created by the boat's passage), put the helm hard over the other way and again turn the boat in a circle so that you have made a figure eight in the water. If you have an inboard engine you may be able to detect a difference in size of the two circles because of the P-effect (a small outboard engine produces negligible P-effect). With a right hand propeller the circle to port should be slightly smaller. A left hand propeller will result in a smaller circle to starboard. An average cruising boat turns in about one and a half times her length.

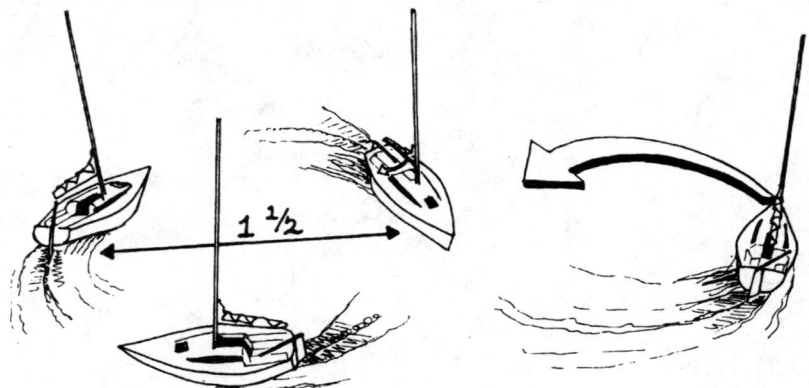

Figure 13-3 – Figure eight maneuver.

Advance the throttle to cruising speed and repeat the figure eight. Notice the larger turning radius and the heeling effect.

If you turn an outboard engine to one side, you increase the boat's turning ability.

STOPPING

Boats differ in the distance they take to stop. A heavy boat carries its way longer than a light boat. A supertanker is an extreme example of a heavy vessel needing a long stopping distance — several miles!

While moving at a slow to moderate speed bring the boat to a stop. A high speed emergency stop is of little use in a sailboat. At cruising speed you can turn away faster than you can stop. In a marina you travel very slowly.

Stopping distance will be affected by wind and current direction.
If going with either you need more distance than when going against wind and current.

STOPPING UNDER POWER:

Proceeding without altering course:
- Throttle to idle.
- Shift into neutral. Pause slightly.
- Shift into reverse.
- Throttle up to two-thirds full.

When stopped:
- Throttle to idle.
- Shift into neutral.

If using an inboard engine you probably noticed the stern pulling to one side as you throttled up in reverse gear. The P-effect again! Only this time you were in reverse gear so a right hand prop would be rotating to the left, causing the stern to walk to port, and a left hand prop would be doing the opposite.

After you have mastered stopping in open water, practice keeping a straight course and coming to a full stop with your bow half a boat length away from a buoy or other object in the water.

REVERSING

When reversing there is greater water pressure on the rudder so, to avoid damaging the rudder, do not let go of the helm.

Bring the boat to a stop. Shift into reverse and apply throttle to get the boat moving. Once the boat is moving at slow speed, throttle down to maintain this speed. Notice that the P-effect diminishes once the boat is moving at a steady rate. Turn the stern to port, then to starboard. Apply more throttle and try to steer backwards in a straight line, keeping your bow pointed towards a chosen landmark.

As you apply more throttle you may notice an increase in pressure on the rudder and another brief bout of P-effect as you gather more way. **When motoring in reverse with an inboard engine, every time you apply throttle you experience the P-effect**. You can keep this to a minimum by keeping your speed low and constant.

Chapter 14 – Docking Under Power

DOCKING UNDER POWER

When coming into harbour:
- Keep a close watch for traffic, especially in the area of ferry routes, fuel docks, launching ramps and marina entrances.
- Obey the speed limit.
- Use the *aids to navigation* (these are discussed in Chapter 27).

CONSIDERATIONS BEFORE DOCKING:

- **Docking speed is just enough speed to maintain steerage.** When docking bow first a good way to control your speed is to keep the throttle at idle, working only the gear lever. Shift into neutral to slow the boat; into gear again to increase speed. If there is a strong wind or current you will have to use more throttle.

- **Try to dock into the wind and/or current if possible,** either forward into them or backing into them, so they will act as brakes.

- **If the only docking possible is downwind or down current, go in bow first,** stopping the boat with reverse gear and the aft springline (tie it on amidships before docking).

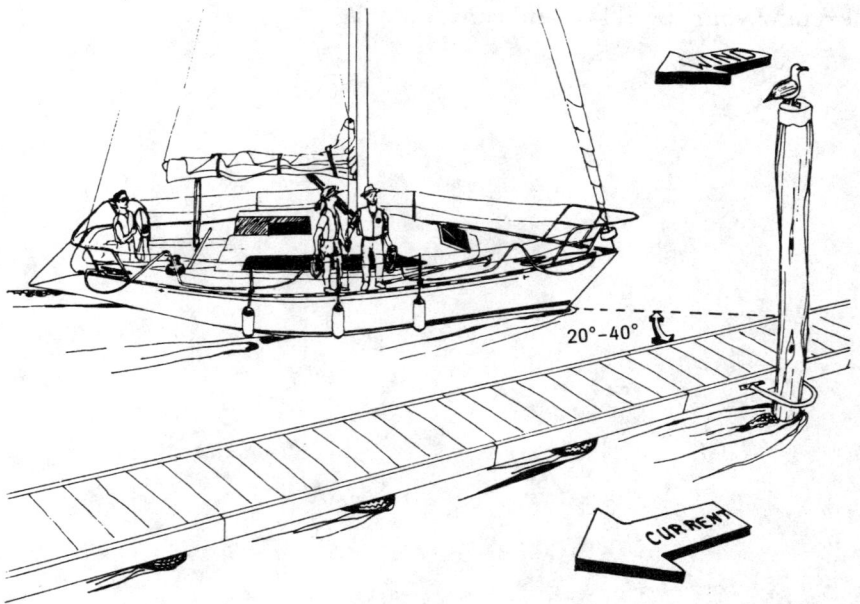

Figure 14-1 – Docking

- **If the wind is blowing onto the dock, stop a little further off the dock than if there is no wind,** and let the wind blow you in.
- **If the wind is blowing off the dock get in as close as possible, making sure the crew have been advised to step ashore smartly when commanded to do so.** Do not let the crew step ashore if it is unsafe. Go around again.
- **If you have an inboard engine, consider how P-effect will affect the stern when you apply throttle in reverse to stop the boat.** For example, barring other considerations, it will be easier when docking bow first to dock port side to the dock because, as you reverse, P-effect will walk in the stern.

DOCKING UNDER POWER:

- Make a reconnaissance pass, coming in fairly close to the dock. Consider the effect of wind and current direction and strength. Note any obstructions, for example, docked boats.
- Retreat and decide upon your approach. Have a contingency plan.
- Assign one crewmember to the bow line, one to the stern line, and any other crew to be ready to fend off with the roving fender, if necessary. When approaching the dock only bow line and stern line crew should be on the docking side so the helmsman has the best possible visibility.
- Command "MOORING LINES AND FENDERS STARBOARD SIDE TO" (the dock). You can of course, dock port side to.
- The bowline is led from the starboard bow cleat, through the bow **chock** (guide) and aft outside the lifelines, then back over the lifelines onto the deck. The sternline is led from the starboard stern cleat, through the stern chock and forward outside the lifelines, then over the lifelines into the cockpit. Crew should make sure neither line can fall into the water. Except under specific circumstances, the springlines are rigged after the boat is docked.
- Fenders are secured at the beam to the lower lifeline or to the base of a suitably placed stanchion. If unable to determine correct fender height, secure them so their bottoms are almost, but not quite, touching the water.
- Command "READY TO STEP ASHORE."
- Bow line and stern line crew move to the shrouds with their lines, each holding a shroud for security. They respond "READY". Under some circumstances the stern line crew may open the starboard gate and step ashore from there when commanded to do so, for example, when docking stern first.

- Docking, like parallel parking, is done "by formula". Approach the dock slowly, at an angle of about 20° to 40°, compensating for wind or current, bow pointing to where you want the stern to be when the boat is docked. If you have misjudged and you are uneasy with the approach, don't hesitate to go around again.

- Control speed on the approach by selecting neutral gear and applying forward gear without throttle as necessary. Avoid shifting into reverse to slow down because of the P effect.

- When the bow is as close to the dock as it will be when secured alongside, turn the boat so the centerline will be parallel to the dock. This swings or pivots the stern in toward the dock.

- Move the helm to center, apply reverse gear to stop. When stopped alongside command "STEP ASHORE" as you return gear to neutral.

- Bow and sternline crew step ashore (**they never jump!**) with their lines. They do not pull on the docklines unless asked to or unless there is an obvious difficulty. They each take a turn around the ring, cleat or rail on the dock. The skipper may ask crew to harden or ease one or both lines to adjust the boat's position, then will command "MAKE FAST THE LINES."

- Height and placement of fenders is adjusted, as necessary.

- The boat is ***made fast*** (secured) to the dock with the breast and spring lines.

- The engine is shut off.

BACKING IN:

Advantages of docking stern first are better visibility for the helm and ease of exit if conditions are difficult when you wish to leave, because the boat responds more positively when moving forward.

Some tips for backing in:
- Do not try to back in with the wind on your bow or across the dock. You will be moving very slowly and the wind will blow your bow off either into the dock or away from it.
- Tie a fender near the stern to protect the hull.
- Start backing in well away to give you time to overcome any P-effect and to get into a steady, low docking speed which you can maintain. You do not want to apply throttle when you are approaching the dock.
- Approach the dock at an angle of 30° or so, aiming the center of your stern at the centre of the space in which you are docking.

- Do not throttle down until you can coast in. When the stern is the distance from the dock as it will be when docked, turn the helm sharply to clear the dock and swing in the bow. When the boat is parallel to the dock, put helm to center, shift into forward and apply throttle to stop the boat.

It is quite acceptable when casting off or docking to move a boat along a dock or turn it by handling the dock lines and using the engine as necessary to bring the vessel into a desired position.

Chapter 15 – Making Fast and Snugging Down

MAKING FAST

Making fast means securing the boat to the dock. Usually the boat is made fast to the dock with a bow breastline, a stern breastline, a forward springline and an aft springline. However, depending on the number and spacing of rings, cleats and dock rails and the configuration of the dock itself, there may have to be a special arrangement. The object, when making fast, is to have the boat secured so that it can move only slightly in any direction.

The breastlines run from bow and stern to nearby rings, cleats or rails on the dock. Do not pull in the bow breastline too snugly, because the fore and aft centerline of the boat should be parallel to the dock. Allow a little slack in both lines so the boat is not held tightly against the fenders and dock.

The forward spring line runs from the dock adjacent to the bow to a strongpoint on the hull amidships (midway between bow and stern), for example, the base of the shrouds. **The aft springline runs from the dock adjacent to the stern to a strong point on the hull amidships.** Springlines should also have a little slack, to allow a small amount of fore and aft movement.

Fenders must be placed at proper locations and heights so they are effective in protecting the hull. Push and pull the boat about to make sure that if the boat rotates slightly the fenders still afford protection.

Lines and fenders should be secured with round turns and two half hitches or belayed to a cleat. After making fast, coil the bitter ends of the lines and place them at the edge of the dock so they will not trip passersby.

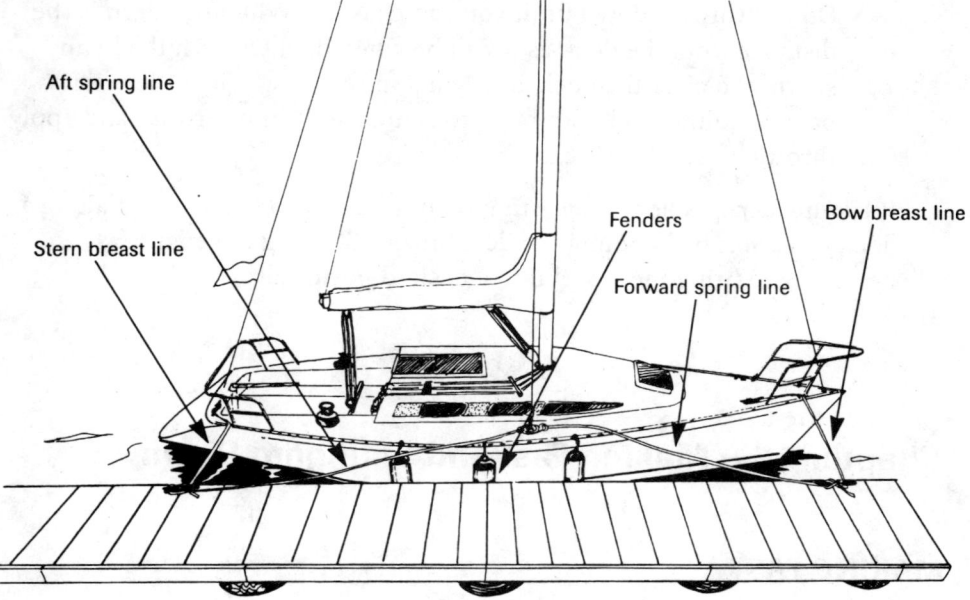

Figure 15-1 – Made fast and snugged down

Fenders – Bumpers made of soft material which hang over the sides of the hull to protect it when tying alongside a dock or another vessel.

Breast lines – Mooring lines (docklines) running from the bow and stern to the dock at approximately right angles to the dock. Breast lines prevent a boat from moving out from the dock.

Spring lines – Mooring lines running diagonally from the dock opposite bow and stern to a strong point (eg. midship cleat, chainplates, or toe rail) at the beam of the boat. Spring lines prevent a boat from moving ahead and astern.

SNUGGING DOWN

Snugging down is simply "putting your boat to bed" and leaving her shipshape. The term is rather descriptive, reminiscent of warmth and peace and shelter from the raging storm! Following is the procedure for snugging down when a boat is to be left unattended overnight or longer. If you have been cruising or taking a liveaboard course you will need to spend more time cleaning and tidying below deck and in lockers.

THE ENGINE:

- Refuel. It prevents condensation in the tanks.

Outboard Engine:

- Drain the carburetor so that varnish in the gasoline does not gum up its moving parts. To drain the carburetor: Disconnect the fuel line

and leave the engine running in neutral gear, throttle advanced, until the engine stops.
- Coil the fuel line on top of the gas tank, close the vent on the tank and make sure the end fitting is not resting in water or dirt.
- Tilt up or raise the engine to stop seawater corrosion of the lower unit.

Inboard Engine:

- Turn off the engine. Remove key.
- Close fuel tank valve (gasoline engine only).
- Close engine intake seacock (but post a warning in a place where it is sure to be seen!).

THE SAILS:

Foresail:

- **Roller furling:** Make sure the sail is tightly furled with a couple of wraps of the sheets around it. Coil and hang the sheets on the pulpit.
- **Genoa** or **Jib:** Unhank the sail from the forestay. Coil the sheets separately for stowing and, if the sheets are wet, leave them outside the bag so they will dry more easily. Stow the bagged sail below.

Mainsail:

- Unshackle the main halyard from the sail and shackle it away from the mast to the toerail or handrail. **Snug up** (tighten) the halyard, cleat it, and make it off.
- Make sure the boom is horizontal.
- The boomvang and mainsheet should be just taut, then cleated. Coil and hang the bitter end of the mainsheet.
- Put on the mainsail cover.

Halyards:

All halyards on the boat should be silenced, that is, secured so they are held well away from the mast so the halyards will not set up a clanking sound on the mast if the wind gets up.

OTHER PROCEDURES:

- Center and lock the wheel or tie the tiller with a clove hitch. This prevents the rudder banging back and forth in the waves or in the wakes of passing vessels.

SAFETY TIP:
Do not leave cockpit lockers open. Someone may fall in.

- Stow loose items and valuable items below, for example boathook and winch handles.
- Clean and tidy galley and navigation station. Shut off propane at tank after burning out the line.
- Check bilge. Pump out if necessary. If there is an automatic bilge pump, leave it on "AUTO" (automatic) position.
- Shut off electronics and electrics.
- Turn battery selector switch to "OFF."
- Connect shore power, if required.
- Close seacocks in head and galley.
- Remove personal gear, food and garbage.
- Note in the ship's log:
  – deficiencies, damage, losses
  – boat refuelled
  – water tanks filled
  – battery last used
  – engine seacock closed
- Wash the deck, cockpit and **topsides** (hull above the waterline).
- Fill the water tanks.
- Close and lock the boat. Return the keys.

SECTION C:
SAFETY AND BASIC SAILING SKILLS

For this section The Ashore Knowledge addresses general weather information, sail selection, coping in less than ideal conditions, and what to do when things go wrong. Learning and practicing the basic skills you will need to safely sail your boat is covered in the Afloat Skills.

ASHORE KNOWLEDGE

Main Topics:
- Weather
- Sail Selection
- Sailing in Less than Ideal Conditions
- Coping with the Unexpected
- Using the VHF Radio

Chapter 16 – Weather

Being weather-wise increases both your cruising enjoyment and your safety. The weather must always be taken into account when you are planning to sail. While on the water, listen to a marine forecast every few hours and keep a weather-eye out for signs of deteriorating conditions. You can over time, by careful observation of nature's signs, become a good amateur forecaster.

SOURCES OF WEATHER INFORMATION

- **VHF Radio:** Marine forecasts and warnings may be obtained on the weather channels 21B, 83B, WX1, WX2 and WX3. Continuous Marine Broadcasts by the Canadian Coast Guard and Weatheradio Canada broadcasts on VHF are made as soon as possible after the forecasts and warnings have been issued by Environment Canada. They also include the latest local weather observations.

MAFOR code is used on the Great Lakes and St. Lawrence River for weather broadcasts. After the MAFOR code there is a translation of the code in plain language.

- **Telephone:** In larger centers marine forecasts may be obtained by telephone. Look in the Government of Canada listings for Canadian Coast Guard, Marine Weather or Environment Canada, Atmospheric Environment Service, Marine Forecast.

- **Commercial Radio Stations:** Except for Weatheradio Canada (Environment Canada) forecasts, the information does not include wind speed and direction and sea state, which are of vital interest to sailors.

- **Newspapers:** Clip and save weather maps for several days to see emerging weather trends. There may or may not be a marine forecast and the forecast given may not be as up to date as one given by radio.

- **Television:** Good general information may be obtained but there is often insufficient detail regarding local or marine conditions. The dedicated weather channel on cablevision is more detailed than the general forecasts on TV news.

- **Airport Weather Offices:** If you are unable to obtain a marine forecast a local airport may prove to be a good source of weather information.

- **Weatherfacsimile:** Weatherfax machines are becoming common aboard boats cruising in exposed waters or making extended passages. Weatherfax receives and reproduces radio-transmitted weather maps

- **Polling the Weather Office Facsimiles:** Some Environment Canada Offices offer marine maps and forecasts which can be obtained by calling the weather office from a facsimile machine.

INTERPRETING THE MARINE FORECAST

The Continuous Marine Broadcast on the VHF radio is broadcast continuously 24 hours a day. The forecast is valid for 24 hours and a new forecast is issued every 6 hours. **Monitor each new forecast. Rapid changes can occur in the weather and you should always have a contingency plan for this possibility.** If you are planning a cruise, track the weather for a few days beforehand.

The format of a marine forecast is:

- **Synopsis:** Describes the location and intensity of weather systems affecting the area and indicates their movements during the forecast period. A general description of the present and forecast winds is included.

- **Forecast:**
  - Wind Speeds: Average wind speeds expected are given in **knots** (nautical miles per hour). **Gusts** or **squalls** (sudden temporary increases in windspeed) are mentioned if they are expected to be much higher than the average winds. A **wind warning** may be given (see below).
  - **Wind direction:**
  - **Weather and Visibility:** A brief description is given of the sky condition (sunny, cloudy) and weather (rain, showers). Visibility is only mentioned if it is reduced. A **weather warning** may be given, for example, severe thunderstorms.
  - **Sea State:** This is the combined wave and swell height in feet or metres. A **swell** is a rounded wave that remains after the wind that caused it to form is no longer acting upon it.

There is no swell in enclosed waters. The average height of the higher waves is the figure given for sea state. Sea state may be described as calm, rippled or waves and/or low, moderate or heavy swell.

- **Outlook:** The outlook describes the winds expected during the 24 hour period following the forecast.

In addition, the Continuous Marine Broadcast includes local weather reports and may include Notices to Shipping.

- **Local Reports:** These are weather observations made by lighthouse keepers and ships' personnel. They are useful for determining whether predicted weather is arriving on time and for finding out what the weather is doing at your destination.

- **Notices to Shipping:** Notices to Shipping deal with navigation hazards, lights extinguished and buoys out of position, etc.

There may be considerable local variation from forecast winds and weather because:
  - of geographical characteristics.
  - forecast weather systems may slow down or speed up or may reach only one part of a large forecast region on time.
  - forecasts cannot be overly long or detailed.

Because of local variations you must develop the ability to supplement the official forecast with your own forecast.

The terms "bad" or "rough" in regard to weather depends on your skill and experience. **As a novice it is safe for you to sail in light winds**

(0–11 knots) working up to moderate winds (12–19 knots). You may find sailing in Small Craft Warning conditions far too much of a handful, whereas an experienced keelboat sailor with a good crew would enjoy it thoroughly. Wind strength increases as the square of its velocity, thus a 20 knot wind is not twice as strong as a 10 knot wind, but 4 times as strong.

It would be foolhardy for any pleasure sailor to even consider setting out in gale force or greater conditions.

Wind warnings	Winds are Expected to Exceed
Small Craft Warning (Strong Winds)	20 knots
Gale Warning (Gale Force Winds)	34 knots
Storm Warning (Storm Force Winds)	47 knots
Hurricane Force (Hurricane Force Winds)	63 knots

The size of waves that form depends on:

- the speed of the wind.
- the duration of time the wind has been blowing.
- the *fetch,* which is the distance over water the wind has blown.

The longer the wind blows and the longer the fetch, the larger the waves will become until they reach a maximum size for the windspeed and fetch. If the wind starts to blow strongly, head to shelter before the waves build up.

THE SUN AS WIND GENERATOR

Weather is caused by the uneven heating of the earth by the sun. Nature is perpetually trying to achieve a state of equilibrium (and is always ultimately thwarted!) Wind is air set in motion horizontally to equalize air temperature and barometric pressure between one location and another. Clouds, rain and snow form when air saturated with water vapour, which has evaporated from the earth and its oceans, condenses.

Differences in temperature and pressure occur on a planetary scale, creating the broad major wind belts of Earth. They occur also on a large scale that causes weather systems, and on a local scale. Weather on a local scale is the trickiest to predict. It is affected by landforms, vegetation, bodies of water, and even by man's cities and large buildings.

LOCAL WEATHER HAZARDS

Canada has the widest range of weather of any country in the world. Canadians must deal with icebergs off Newfoundland, waterspouts on the Great Lakes, sixty knot thunderstorms on the Prairies and **tide-rips** in British Columbia. A major hazard in one region may be rarely a hazard or even non-existent in another. For example, thunderstorms are a frequent threat in summer to the lake sailor, whereas they are only occasionally experienced by the coastal sailor.

When attempting to predict the weather, make it a practice to look for more than one indicator as a single indicator can be misleading.

- Look for clues on the horizons and note any changes, especially in the westerly quadrant.

- Read the sky. Observe the type and direction of clouds. Clouds are visible evidence of instability and turbulence in the atmosphere.

- Note changes in wind direction and speed.

- Watch for dark patches or lines on the water which indicate rough water and approaching wind.

- Develop awareness of changes in air temperature.

Your instructor will be able to advise you which of the weather hazards listed below apply to your sailing area, though you should be able to recognize all indicators of poor weather in case you charter a boat elsewhere. When sailing in unfamiliar waters you can find out about local weather hazards by reading the *Small Craft Guide* or *Sailing Directions* and by chatting up knowledgeable locals, such as sailors, fishermen, Coast Guard personnel and the Harbourmaster. The following information applies to the mid-latitudes of the northern hemisphere.

FANCY AND FOLKLORE

Some of the sayings and rhymes of folklore in regard to weather are simply nonsense, for example "If March comes in like a lion, it will go out like a lamb". However the following well known verse is fairly reliable:

Red sky at night,
A sailor's delight.
Red sky at morning,
Sailors take warning.

Figure 16-1(a) Halo around the sun   Figure 16-1(b) – Cirrus clouds

Figure 16-2 – Cumulonimbus cloud

Versions of this saying date back to the Bible (Matthew XVI: 2-3). In the North Temperate Zone weather patterns move roughly from west to east. When looking to the west at the setting sun we are previewing tomorrow's weather. If the air to the west is full of moisture the sun appears yellow or grey or you can see only clouds. But if the air to the west is dry, the sun reflects dry dust particles and appears red and tomorrow should be fair.

Red in the morning is a less reliable predictor. Perhaps it can be argued that because good and bad weather comes in cycles, the passing of a good cycle (clear in the east) means bad weather is on its way. No one has ever erred in predicting rain — eventually!

Use the following information in conjunction with regular marine weather forecasts.

LOCAL HAZARD	IDENTIFIED BY	WARNING TIME
Figure 16-1(a) or Figure 16-1(b) **Deteriorating Weather**	• A thin, transparent wispy veil of high cloud (cirrus cloud) • Halo around the sun or moon followed by lower, thicker clouds • Wind backs* from west to south or east	6-24 hours

* In the northern hemisphere when the wind backs it shifts in a counter-clockwise direction, for example, from west through south to east. A backing wind often heralds the approach of poor weather, whereas a veering wind, which shifts in a clockwise direction, is considered to indicate improving weather.

The above signs of deterioration after a spell of fair weather are common to all areas of the country. Keep an eye on the rate of deterioration and consider heading for harbour. The weather may deteriorate only to an unsettled, cloudy condition or it may deteriorate into heavy rainfall with strong winds from the south or east.

LOCAL HAZARD	IDENTIFIED BY	WARNING TIME
Figure 16-2 **Thunderstorms and associated hazards:** • **violent gusty winds** • **line squalls*** • **lightning** • **decreased visibility** • **waterspouts****	• Huge, towering cauliflower-shaped clouds with flat, dark bottoms and flat fuzzy tops spreading out to form an anvil shape (cumulonimbus clouds) • These develop to the west and may be isolated clouds or a wall of clouds • A massive windshift usually precedes a thunderstorm • There is often a "calm before the storm" followed by a fast-approaching line of dark water • Heavy static on the radio may indicate nearby thunderstorm activity	15-30 min.

* GUSTS & SQUALLS are temporary increases in wind speed. The difference between them is that a gust only lasts a few seconds while a squall lasts a few minutes.

** A WATERSPOUT is a funnel-shaped vertical column of water similar to a tornado but is generally less violent. Waterspouts are to be avoided.

Thunderstorms usually occur in the afternoon in the lake areas of central Canada. They occur less frequently on the Atlantic and Pacific coasts. At the approach of a thunderstorm, get all sails down quickly. Thunderstorms are mercifully brief, though nasty while they last. Fatalities from lightning are rare on the water.

LOCAL HAZARD	IDENTIFIED BY	WARNING TIME
Fog*	• Presence of fog banks • Fair calm weather with a sharp temperature drop overnight	Minutes

* Fog is cloud at ground level.

Fog can thicken suddenly and can envelop your boat rapidly. Do not set out in fog. Keep a good lookout and anchor or enter harbour if fog is threatening. If caught in fog, follow the guidelines in the next chapter. Know your position at all times. The combination of fog and icebergs can be a problem in Newfoundland waters.

LOCAL HAZARD	IDENTIFIED BY	WARNING TIME
Strong Outflow Winds	Rough water at the entrances to coastal inlets in mountainous areas.	None

Strong outflow winds blowing out from inlets can cause a boat to find itself with too much sail up. Keep a lookout ahead if transiting the entrances to the inlets. Outflow winds can be a hazard in British Columbia particularly.

LOCAL HAZARD	IDENTIFIED BY	WARNING TIME
Tide Rips*	Short, steep waves in or at the entrances of coastal passes, rivers and channels, and near capes.	None

*These are areas of rough water caused when the wind blows in opposition to a strong tidal current. Plan transits of passes to coincide with the times of minimal current predicted by the Current Tables. Keep an eye on the state of the water surface when approaching a pass.

LOCAL HAZARD	IDENTIFIED BY	WARNING TIME
Sudden Strong Winds	Often not forecast, and no prior indication	None

Strong winds with little warning are hazards in Newfoundland and the Bras d'Or Lakes of Cape Breton Island, though they can occur anywhere. Reduce sail promptly and seek shelter.

Because sailors were so dependent upon the wind and because most of their education was oral, it is not surprising the number of rhymes that predict the weather.

A veering wind will clear the sky;
A backing wind says storms are nigh.

This is true and describes a storm whose center is passing to the north of you. But just the opposite works for a storm passing to the south!

Sea gull, sea gull, sit on the sand,
It's a sign of rain when you are at hand.

Birds seem to spend more time on the ground during dropping or low pressure.

Some true observations about clouds are:
The higher the clouds,
the better the weather.
Halo around the sun or moon,
It is going to rain very soon.

Halo's form in the ice crystals of the high clouds before a warm front brings rain.

People in the Atlantic Provinces say of their hurricane season:
June too soon,
July stand by,
August look out,
September, you'll remember.

Chapter 17 – Coping with Wind and Weather

SAIL SELECTION

As windspeed increases, the amount of sail area a boat can carry decreases. Wind speed figures given in the table below correlate only approximately to sail selection because boats vary considerably in the sail they can carry for any given windspeed. Learn the sequence of sail reduction so that you can apply the sequence to any boat you may sail.

TRUE WIND SPEED	SAIL SELECTION
0–12 Knots	Genoa and full main
13–18 Knots	Jib and full main <u>or</u> genoa and reefed main
19–26 Knots	Jib and reefed main
26–32 Knots	Jib or reefed main

A boat carrying too much sail for the wind condition **heels** (leans over) excessively. **Excessive heel is undesirable because the boat does not sail efficiently.** The boat makes a lot of leeway. Also, the shape of the hull underwater is no longer symmetrical and the curved part of the hull on the leeward side digs deeply into the water. Immerse the bowl of a spoon into a sinkful of water and try to pull it horizontally in a straight line. You will find that it wants to turn in the direction of its curve. Similarly a boat that is heeled wants to turn to windward rather than moving forward in a straight line. In addition, the sails of the heeled boat are no longer vertically over the hull. The force of the wind on them will cause your boat to turn to windward. You have to apply excess rudder to keep the boat from turning to windward, creating drag which slows the boat.

The tendency of a boat to turn to windward is called **weather helm**. A boat sailing a straight course with little application of rudder is said to have **neutral or balanced helm**. The tendency of a boat to turn to leeward is called *lee helm*. If you sail a boat in light to moderate winds with mainsail only, the force of the wind on the sail will be behind the boat's pivot point and the boat will have weather helm. If you sail in the same conditions with only a jib the boat will probably have lee helm because the force of the wind on the sail will be ahead of the boat's pivot point. By using the correct sail combination you can balance the helm. In lighter winds it is desirable to have a neutral helm. The boat is said to be **in balance**. In stronger winds a slight weather helm is preferred because it assists the boat to move well to windward. Lee helm is not desirable.

True, Apparent & Boat Wind

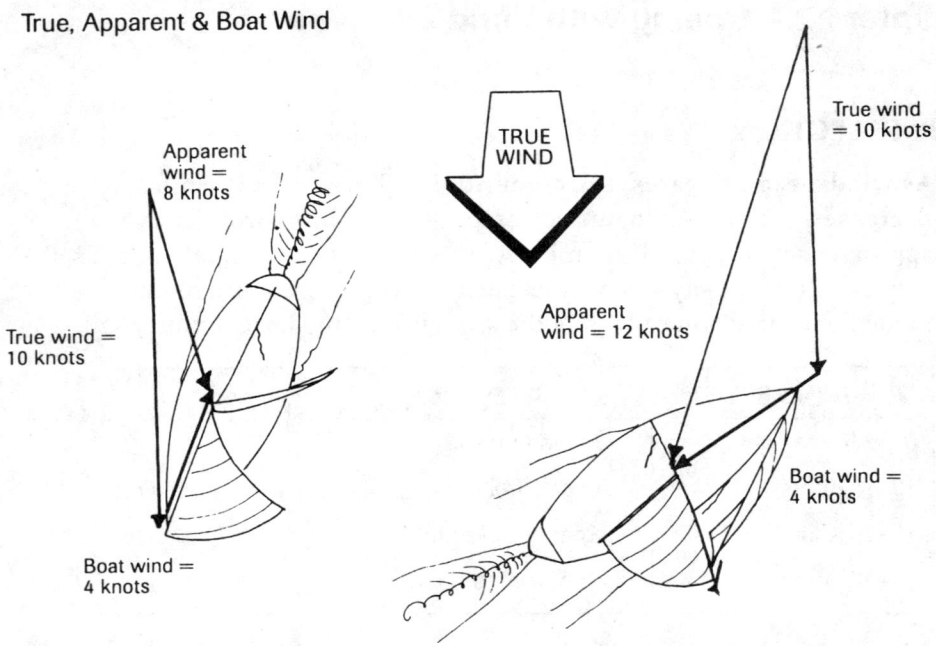

Figure 17-1 (a) Broad reaching   Figure 17-1 (b) Closehauled

The apparent wind speed is less when you sail downwind on a broad reach than it is when you are sailing closehauled [figure17-1 (b)]. This means that you can carry more sail when sailing on a broad reach [figure17-1 (a)] than you can when sailing closehauled. The farther off closehauled you are sailing, the less wind pressure there is on your sails.

Although you get an exciting impression of speed when your boat is heeled and foaming water rushes past below you, your boat is labouring. You will sail faster and more comfortably by reducing sail area to keep the boat more in balance and upright.

When there is too much wind for the genoa and full main you have the choice of changing to a jib and keeping the full main or keeping the genoa and reefing the main. Again, heel and helm balance will be the basis for your decision. If the wind is increasing rapidly you can move directly to a jib and reefed main. However, if you have too little sail up the boat will not move well and will be tossed about more in the waves.

A roller furling genoa loses its shape if more than about one-third of it is reefed. At this point you should drop the genoa and change to a jib.

The wind speed referred to in the table on page 99 is true wind speed. The **true wind** is the wind you feel when the boat is not moving (at anchor, tied to a dock or mooring buoy). When the boat is moving forward it creates a wind from ahead equal to the boat's speed. This is called **boat wind**.

(Think of the wind you feel when motoring along on a windless day). When the boat is sailing the wind you feel and steer by and set your sails by is the **apparent wind,** which is a combination of the true wind and boat wind.

WHEN THE WIND BLOWS

Sooner or later you will find yourself in strong winds. If you have practised your boat handling skills in gentler winds you will welcome the challenge. In heavier winds deficiencies in sailing technique become evident and can be dangerous. It is easy to become careless in light winds because you can usually "get away" with unsafe practices. Make a habit of working the boat safely and correctly at all times, then coping in heavier winds will be a breeze.

When the wind begins to blow hard:

- Make sure all aboard wear foul weather gear, PFD's and safety harnesses.
- Close hatches and **portlights** (windows).
- Reduce sail.
- Secure all loose items on deck such as paddles or boathook and check below to make sure everything is stowed in lockers.
- Discuss each maneuver beforehand, making sure the crew understands what is required and what commands will be given. You may opt to use a rough weather maneuver, for example, **heaving to,** covered in the Afloat Skills of this section.
- Seek shelter only if the harbour or anchorage is familiar and has an easy entrance that is safe to negotiate in the current conditions. Otherwise you are safer to ride out the rough weather at sea.
- Do not try to motor in heavy seas. You can damage the engine and you will be more comfortable and will have a smoother, steadier ride under sail. The boat is designed to be sailed.

> **SAFETY TIP:**
> Be conservative with sail selection. It is much easier to increase sail area if you have been too conservative than it is to struggle to reduce sail in a strong wind. A good trick on a windy day is to put a reef in the mainsail before leaving the dock, then when you hoist the sail outside the harbor it will already be reefed.

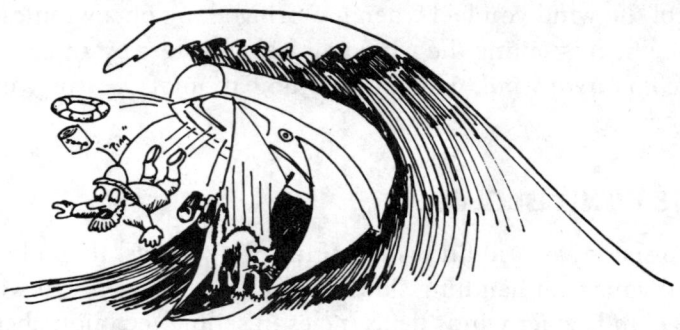

Figure 17-2 – The perils of improper stowage

- Keep well away from your lee shore.
- Do not lock your sheets onto cleats with half hitches. Simply add an extra round turn so you can release sheets quickly if necessary.

THE DREADED LEE SHORE

A lee shore is the shore to leeward of your boat. In strong winds the danger of your lee shore is your shipwreck. The shore to a boat's leeward only becomes a dangerous lee shore when the wind is blowing strongly onto it. Any boat unfortunate enough to be blown onto its lee shore can be pounded to pieces in the surf. The two most common causes of shipwreck are lee shores and navigational errors.

To avoid becoming a lee shore statistic:

- Be sure you know how to recognize your lee shore.

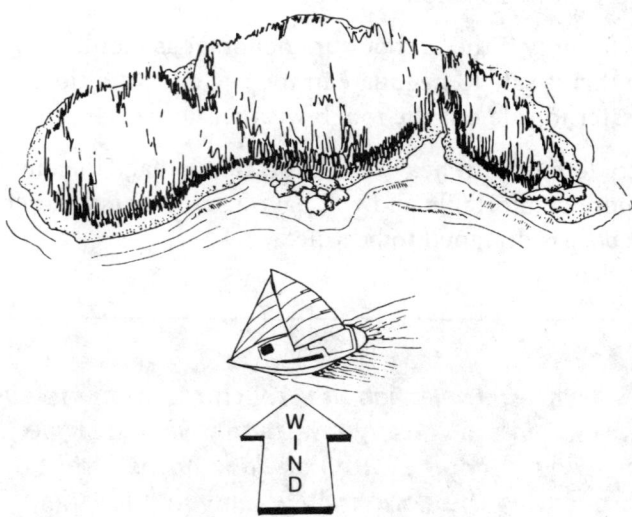

Figure 17-3 – A lee shore

- Improve your skill in sailing to windward.

- In strong winds keep a close watch on your position to determine if you are being driven onto your lee shore. If you are, sail and motor as well, if necessary, to get well to windward.

- If, in spite of your efforts, you are getting close to a lee shore, lower your anchor with most of its rode and hope that it will dig into the bottom and keep you off the shore.

- Under another scenario, when you are at anchor and the wind begins to blow briskly into the anchorage, raise anchor without delay and move to an anchorage which is not a lee shore.

IN REDUCED VISIBILITY

Good or bad weather can bring a reduction in visibility. Fog, mist, heavy rain, snowfall, smoke or smog can restrict visibility, in some instances quite suddenly.

As soon as you notice the visibility is deteriorating or if you see a fog bank rolling towards you:

- Determine your position and plot it as accurately as you can on your chart. Update your plot as often as possible. For example, you may find yourself close to a buoy or light. If you keep track of your speed, time travelled and direction of travel from your first plot you should be able to work out an approximate position.

- Assign a crewmember to keep a lookout at the bow.

- Slow down so you are travelling at a safe speed for the conditions.

- Display the appropriate navigation lights so your boat is as visible as possible.

- Turn on the depth sounder and assign a crew member to monitor it. (see Figure 17-4)

- Make sound signals as required by the *Collision Regulations*.
  If sailing: long, short, short. — • •
  If powering: one prolonged blast. —

A prolonged blast is 4–6 seconds in duration and a short blast is approximately 1 second in duration. The intervals between signals must be not more than two minutes, although they can be less.

- If you hear a sound signal, respond with yours immediately.

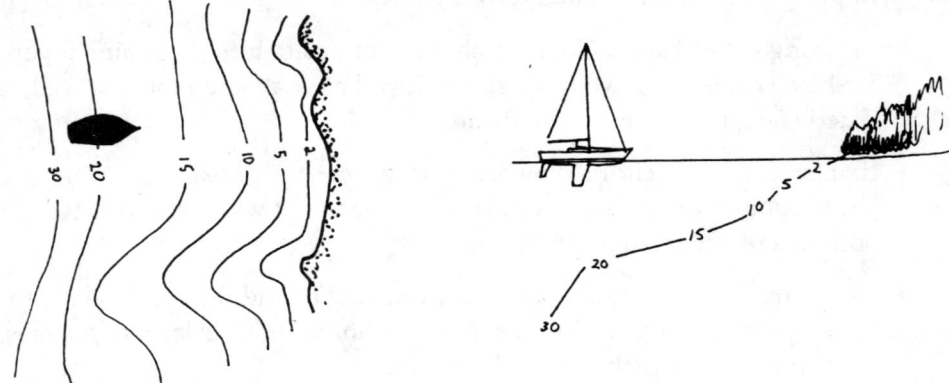

Figure 17-4 – Using the bottom contours

In reduced visibility you can use the bottom contours in conjunction with the chart to help find your way, confirm your position and keep you from going aground.

- Hoist a radar reflector into the rigging unless there is one permanently installed.
- Avoid traffic lanes and charted hazards, for example, reefs.
- Anchor in shallow water out of the way of traffic if it is feasible.

You may power or sail in fog. When powering the boat is more maneuvrable and you can maintain a constant speed, which is helpful for navigation. You are also free from the distraction of setting sails. However, it is harder to hear sound signals made by other vessels and you should stop from time to time to listen.

Chapter 18 – Coping with the Unexpected

Unexpected events can range in degree of seriousness from mere annoyances to genuine emergencies. You must know the immediate action to be taken in each instance below. Correct action taken promptly can prevent a bad situation getting worse.

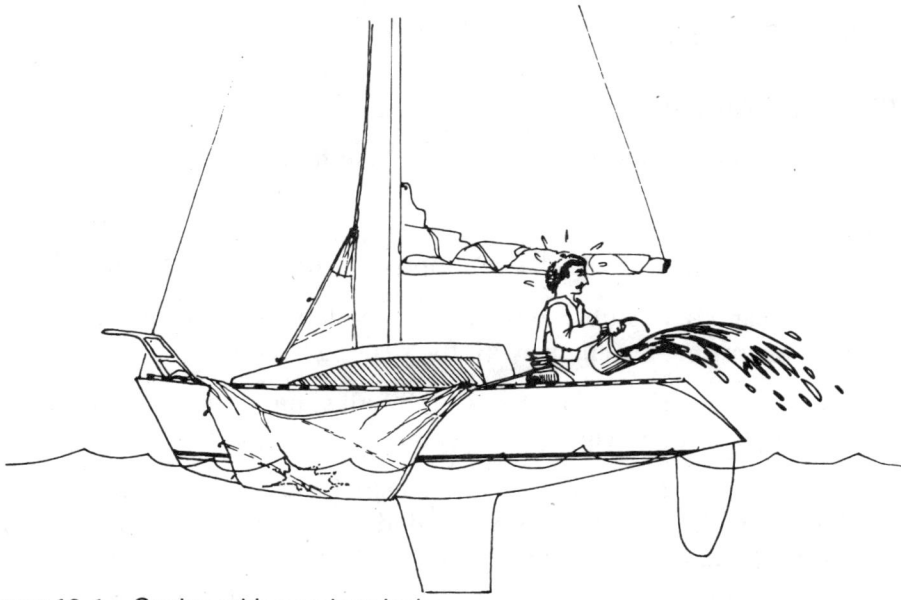

Figure 18-1 – Coping with a serious leak

SPRINGING A LEAK

IMMEDIATELY — Bail or pump to determine the source and extent of the problem.

THEN:

- Put on PFD's and ready flares in case you have to abandon ship.

- Reduce speed.

- When you have found the source of the leak, try to stop or slow it. It may well be a simple matter of closing or plugging a seacock or reclamping a loose hose. Perhaps the water tank has burst (taste the water to see if it is fresh). If the leak is near the waterline you may be able to heel the boat to the opposite side to raise the area of the leak out of the water. A more serious leak may be plugged with blankets and cushions braced against the hull with paddles or boathook. If the leak is forward of the beam, drape a sail around the bow so the water pressure caused by the forward movement of the boat will hold the sail tightly against the hull.

- If you are sinking, send a distress call on the radio and set off flares. Do not abandon ship until the last possible moment. If you are unsure of the seriousness of your situation, radio the Coast Guard, who will advise you.

- Beach the boat.

STEERING FAILURE

IMMEDIATELY — Devise other control methods.

Options to consider:

- Replace the tiller or wheel, if appropriate, with your emergency tiller.
- If the boat has an outboard motor for auxiliary power, turn it on and steer by turning the engine with the steering handle.
- A well-designed boat can be steered by adjusting the sails to create lee helm and weather helm.

To turn away from the wind, create lee helm by hardening the foresail and easing the mainsail. To turn into the wind, create weather helm by easing the foresail and hardening the mainsail. To sail a straight course, adjust the sails for a neutral helm. This method of steering can be very satisfactory and you can tack and gybe and sail on all points of sail.

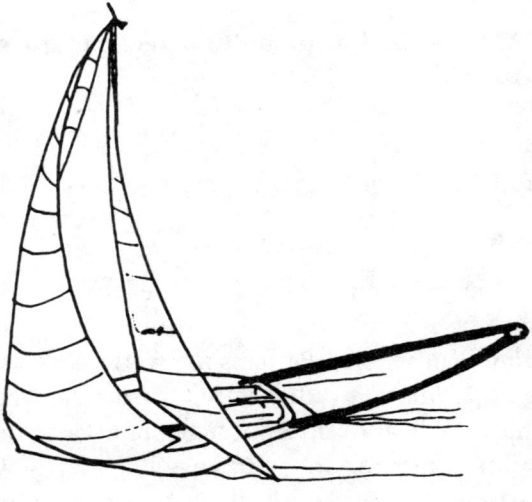

Figure 18-2 – Using a trailing weight to steer downwind

- Attach a light weight to the center of a long line. Trail the line with its ends cleated, one on each side of the stern. To steer to port shorten the line at the port cleat; to steer to starboard shorten the line at the starboard cleat. This method only works if you are sailing downwind.

If you cannot steer accurately enough to dock the boat, sail or motor to the harbour entrance and call for assistance to your berth.

GROUNDING AT ANCHOR

IMMEDIATELY — Consult the chart and tide table.

Grounding at anchor means you are enjoying life at anchor when you become aware of the boat's keel hitting the bottom.

This embarrassing state of affairs can happen when, before anchoring, you:
- do not check out the bottom contours of the anchorage
or
- do not examine the chart and read the tide table.
or
- misread the tide table.

Find out whether the tide is rising or falling. If it is rising, or will very shortly be rising, you can breathe a sigh of relief. If it is falling, see Running Aground below.

RUNNING AGROUND

IMMEDIATELY — Determine whether the crew and boat are in danger.

A boat does not have to be moving very fast for injury to the crew and major damage to the hull to be sustained when the boat comes to an abrupt stop.

THEN:

If you have hit a rock or reef hard and the boat is leaking severely or is holed, she is best left where she is until you get professional assistance. If you have run aground on sand or mud, a soft bottom, there are several methods of freeing the boat, which may be used singly or in combination:

- Motor or sail off
  If motoring off, keep an eye on the engine temperature. Overheating can mean stirred up mud or sand is blocking the cooling water intake. If sailing downwind when you run aground, a quick gybe may see you on your way again. If sailing upwind, a quick tack may do the trick.

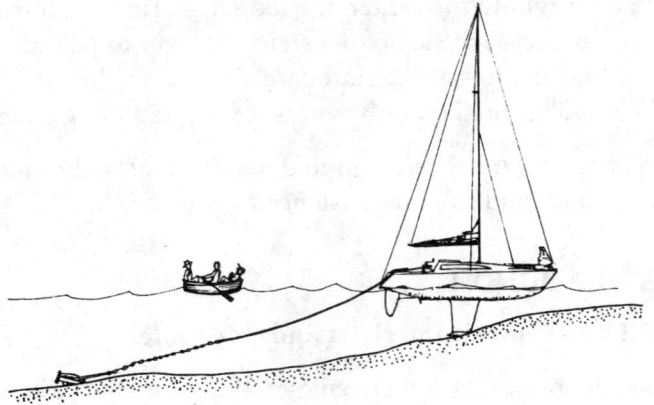

Figure 18-3 – Kedging and lightening ship

- Kedge off
  Kedging is pulling yourself off with your anchor. Row or carry your anchor out to seaward as far as you can. Lead the rode through a **chock** (guide or fairlead) to your largest winch. As you grind the winch, hopefully the boat will be pulled into deeper water.

- Heel the boat
  Heeling swings the keel off the bottom and together with kedging, powering or sailing can help you get into deep water again. Heel the boat by putting gear and crew on one side or by getting crew out onto the boom. If it is windy you may be able to heel the boat by hardening the sails. Or, extend your main halyard by attaching a line to it. Have another boat pull you over, or attach the line to a tree or other object on shore or to an anchor, and winch yourself over.

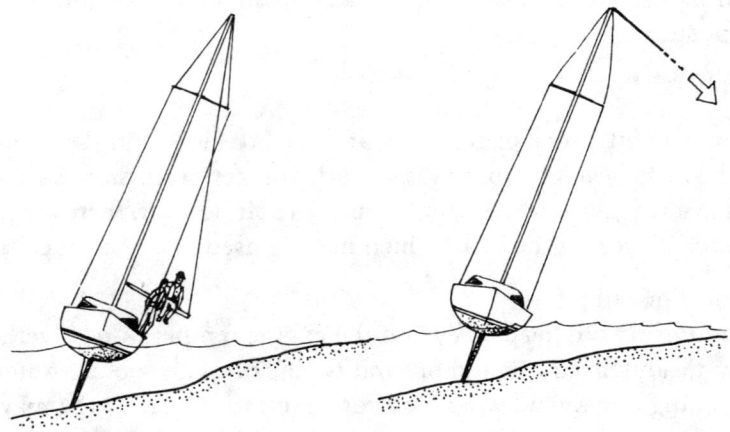

Figure 18-4 – Heeling the boat

- Lighten ship
  Have crew and heavy gear transferred to the dinghy. This may raise the keel sufficiently for you to sail or motor off.

Having another boat tow you should be a very last resort. Few pleasure boaters have the skills or gear to tow effectively or safely. Too often damage is done to one or both boats and snapping lines can injure crew. If the procedures above fail and you cannot expect a rising tide, call a commercial towing company.

If you cannot free the grounded boat and must wait for the tide to return:

- Lower and stow your sails.

- Close portlights, hatches and seacocks to prevent flooding.

- Heel the boat with its mast towards shore so that when the tide returns waves can't break into the cockpit.

- Set your anchor out to seaward as far as you can. This has two purposes — to prevent the boat from being driven farther up on shore if there are waves when the sea returns, and to provide for kedging when the boat is in sufficiently deep water again.

- If the water level drops to the point where the hull is about to touch the shore, protect it with a padding of sailbags, cushions or sleeping bags.

- When the tide returns check for leaks and damage. If you have run aground on a soft bottom chances are good there will be no harm done to the boat though you must, of course, report the fact that you ran aground if the boat is rented or chartered.

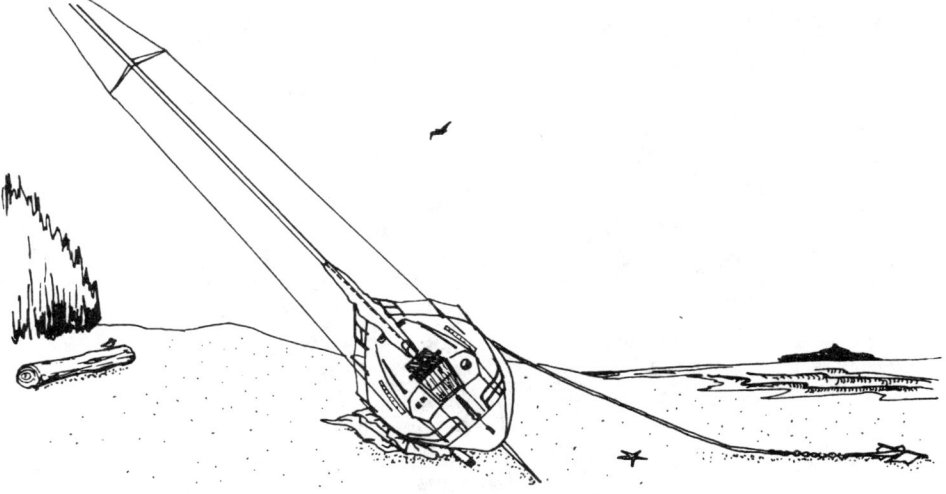

Figure 18-5 – What to do if you'll be aground for a while

FOULED PROPELLER

IMMEDIATELY — Stop the engine

THEN:

- Sail to your destination and radio for a tow in.

  or

- Sail to a calm anchorage where the water is warm. Turn the shaft manually. Try to unwind the fouled object or put a crew member over the side (with a safety harness and line to the boat) to cut away the rope, seaweed, fishing line or plastic that is wrapped around the propeller.

FAILURE OF STANDING RIGGING

IMMEDIATELY — Position the boat to reduce strain on the mast.

This means:

- If a windward shroud breaks, tack.
- If the forestay breaks, turn downwind.
- If the backstay breaks, harden the mainsheet as much as you can and simultaneously turn the boat into the wind.

THEN:

- Reduce or lower sail and attempt repair.

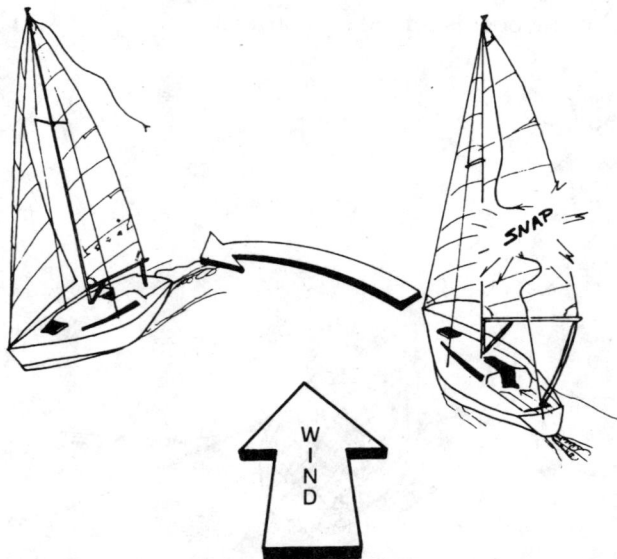

Figure 18-6 – If the standing rigging fails. Reduce strain on the mast. In this figure the backstay has broken. The immediate response is to harden the mainsheet and turn the boat into the wind.

- If you are unable to make a secure repair, motor or sail with reduced sail to a place where the rigging can be properly repaired.

BROKEN HALYARD

IMMEDIATELY — Ease the sheet.

THEN:

- Lower the sail completely and remove the broken halyard from the head of the sail. A spare halyard may be rigged ready for use.
- If there is no spare halyard, proceed under motor or the remaining sail.

DRAGGING ANCHOR

IMMEDIATELY — Increase scope (the amount of rode you have out).

THEN:

- Maintain an anchor watch to see if this has solved the problem.
- If it has not done so or you find you are too close to other boats or the shore, you will have to re-anchor.

Regular boat maintenance, careful navigation and proper anchoring techniques (see Afloat Skills of Section D) will reduce the likelihood of occurrence of the foregoing situations. You are less likely to have a fouled propeller if you practice good seamanship by checking for lines in the water before you start the engine and while motoring.

Apart from running aground, and holing the boat, or springing a major leak, the unexpected events above are not real emergencies except if they occur when you are close to a lee shore, in which case, radio for assistance.

FIRE

IMMEDIATELY — Sound an alarm and ensure crew safety.
  — Use your nearest fire extinguisher.
  — Call for a backup.

THEN:

- Assess the damage.
- Radio for assistance if required.
- Make for the nearest port.

Chapter 19 – Using the VHF Radio

Use the radio to receive weather reports. Except in an emergency it is unlawful in Canada for you to speak on the VHF radio until you have a **Radio Operator's Restricted Certificate** (Maritime Voluntary). This certificate is relatively easy to obtain and is valid for life. Contact the Department of Communications (DOC) for their study booklet. The examination is in two parts, written and oral. Alternatively, many cruising schools offer a short course in VHF radio operation, including the examination.

MAKING A DISTRESS CALL

- Turn on the radio.
- Tune to Channel 16, adjust squelch and volume if necessary.

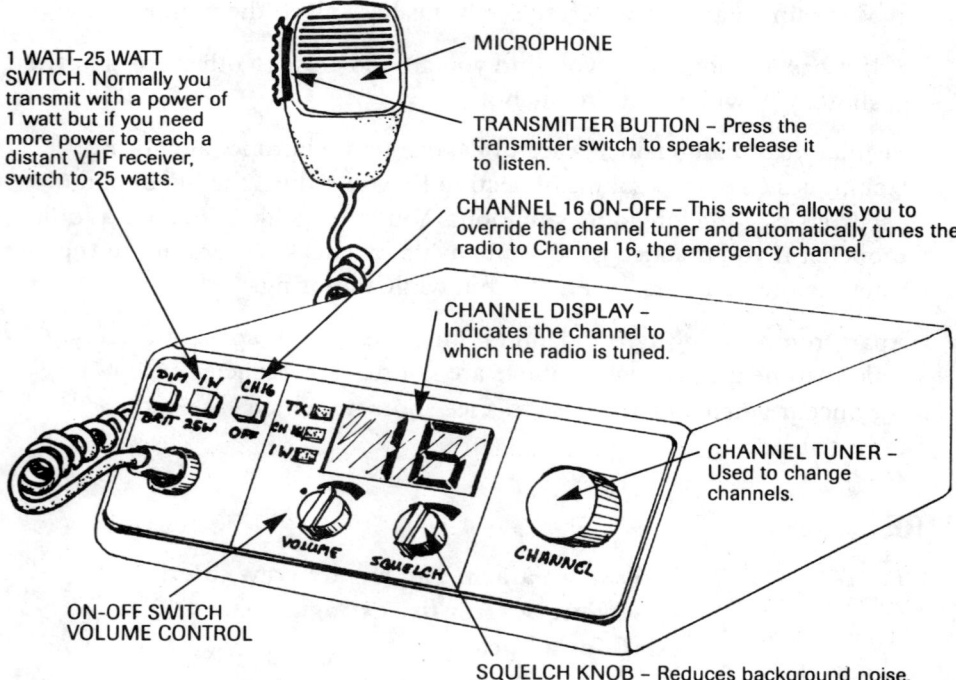

Figure 19-1 – Familiarizing yourself with the VHF Radio

Control panels vary with the model. The manufacturer's manual will assist you to identify the parts of the control panel. Look for the radio's **station license** which is required by the DOC to be in close proximity to the radio. On it you will find the boat's call sign which is used to identify your boat whenever you are making a radio transmission.

- Take the microphone in hand and depress the transmitter button.
- Transmit the following information:
- Mayday 3 times (to establish distress)
  - Name and call sign of your boat.
  - Mayday and name of your boat.
  - Position of your boat.
  - Description of your boat so it can be easily identified from sea and air.
  - Number of people aboard and any injuries.
  - Nature of your problem and the type of help you need.
  - Any information which will facilitate rescue.
  - Say "Over" to indicate you expect a reply.
- If you hear no reply after about 20 seconds, repeat the call using 25 watts power.
- Continue calling at regular intervals for as long as you can. You may be being received even if you are unable to hear a reply.

A sample distress call:
"*Mayday, Mayday, Mayday*
This is Silver Lining, Victor Golf 8724
Silver Lining, Victor Golf 8724
Silver Lining, Victor Golf 8724
Mayday Silver Lining
My position is one mile southwest of Cape Cull
My boat is a two-five* foot sailing vessel with a green cabin, green stripe on the hull and outboard motor.
We have 3 persons aboard. No injuries.
I am taking on water very fast and need pumps and assistance.
We are setting off flares and making preparations to abandon ship.
Over."

For clarity the phonetic alphabet is used on the radio. "Victor Golf" stands for "VG." You will learn the phonetic alphabet when studying for your operator's certificate . Similarly you would say "two-five" rather than "twenty-five."

The distress call MAYDAY is reserved for use only when your boat or crew is threatened by grave and imminent danger. It is the top priority radio message. The Canadian Coast Guard provides 24 hour service on Channel 16.

If you need assistance but your boat is not in grave and imminent danger, call the Coast Guard on Channel 16, identify yourself by boat name and

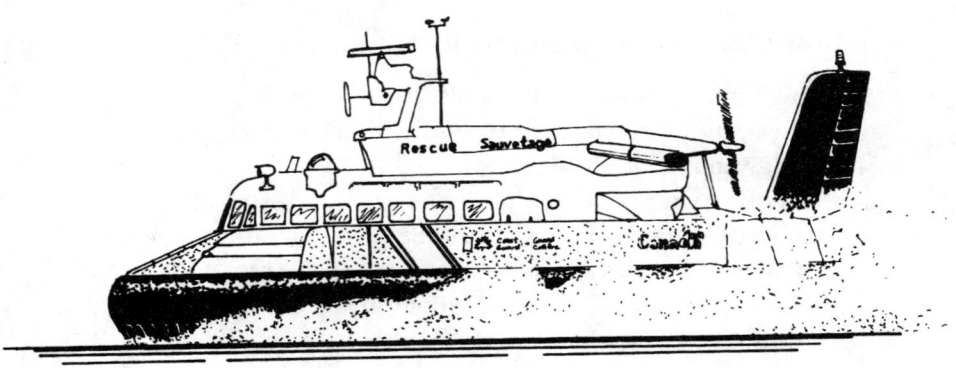

Figure 19-2 – Coast Guard assistance is available on Channel 16

call sign and say you want advice. They will ask you to switch to another channel, allowing the distress channel to remain open, and then will discuss your problem with you.

Make it a practice to monitor Channel 16. You never know when you might be the closest vessel to be able to offer assistance to someone in trouble.

SAFETY TIP:
Keep your radio tuned to Channel 16 whether or not it is turned on so it will be on the correct channel in an emergency.

SELF TEST – ANSWERS ARE ON PAGE 195.

1. Four reliable sources of weather information are:

   _____   _____

   _____   _____

2. (a) Weather forecasts are given on what VHF radio channels?

   _____

   (b) Forecasts are updated every _____ hours and include a further outlook for _____ hours.

3. (a) What is wind? _____

   (b) What causes it? _____

4. Winds for these warnings are expected to exceed:

   Small Craft Warning: _____ knots

   Gale Warning: _____ knots

   Storm Warning: _____ knots

5. List four hazards that can be associated with thunderstorms:

   _____   _____

   _____   _____

6. List 3 signs of deteriorating weather:

   _____

   _____

   _____

7. When the wind is increasing, what two criteria do you use in making the decision to reduce sail?

   _____

   _____

8. List 2 reasons why it is inefficient to sail with the boat heeled too much?

   _____

   _____

9. What is weather helm? _____
_____

10. (a) What is your lee shore? _____

    (b) Why is it dangerous? _____

11. List six actions to take in reduced visibility.

    _____   _____

    _____   _____

    _____   _____

12. To avoid grounding at anchor what two precautions do you take before anchoring? _____
_____

13. (a) Briefly list four ways to free your boat if you have run aground.

    _____   _____

    _____   _____

    (b) What is kedging? _____
    _____

14. Name the first action you should take if:

    (a) You run aground _____

    (b) Your propeller is fouled _____

    (c) A shroud breaks _____

    (d) The forestay breaks _____

    (e) Your anchor drags _____

15. (a) A distress call should be given only when _____
    _____

    (b) A distress call is made on VHF Channel _____.

    (c) List 6 pieces of information to give when transmitting a distress call.

    _____   _____

    _____   _____

    _____   _____

Safety and Basic Sailing Skills

AFLOAT SKILLS

Main Topics:
- Raising Sail
- Safe Winch Techniques
- Sail Trim
- Maneuvering Under Sail
- Coping With Stronger winds
- Lowering Sail

In the Afloat Skills part of Section B you learned to motor out to the sailing area. So let's begin these Afloat Skills under power in the sailing area, ready to raise sails. In Section A Afloat Skills you raised and lowered the sails at the dock. The procedure on the water is similar but there are differences.

Review the sailing theory in Chapters 1 and 2 before commencing with these Afloat Skills because you are now going to put the theory into practice.

> **SAFETY TIP:**
> While aboard maintain a constant level of awareness. Danger areas are the foredeck between mast and forestay, the cabin top, the companionway, and the steps to the cabin. Safer areas are the pulpit, pushpit, cockpit, and the area between the mast and shrouds.

Chapter 20 – Raising Sail

RAISING THE MAINSAIL

Whether you are under power, at anchor, or at a mooring buoy, normally the mainsail is raised first and lowered last to keep the boat under control. The mainsail is raised and lowered while the boat is head to wind so the sail won't fill while it is being raised or lowered.

PROCEDURE FOR RAISING THE MAINSAIL:

HELM:

- Motors slowly head to wind with just enough power to maintain good steerage. If at anchor or at a mooring buoy the boat will probably already be head to wind. Turn on the engine and proceed as follows.

- Commands "READY TO RAISE THE MAINSAIL."

CREW:

- Checks to make sure the halyard is attached to the head of the sail.

- Closes the companionway hatch cover.

- Removes and stows the sail ties or furling line.

- Releases the boomvang.

- Eases the cunningham or downhaul. If the gooseneck is not fixed the downhaul will have to be recleated so the gooseneck will not exit the mast slot when the sail is raised.

- Drops the mainsail halyard coil and makes sure the halyard will run free.

- Stands beside the mast and responds "READY."

- Cockpit crew uncleats and frees the mainsheet, so the sail will **luff**, and responds "READY."

> **SAFETY TIP:**
> When any sail is being raised or lowered its sheet must be free so the sail cannot fill with wind. If it fills with wind it is very difficult to raise the halyard properly because the halyard and sheet are working against each other. Always wait until the halyard has been cleated off before hardening the sheet.

HELM:

- Checks that the boat is still head to wind.

- Commands "RAISE THE MAINSAIL."

CREW:

- Raises the sail quickly. If there is a boltrope, feeds the sail into the mast slot as the halyard is raised.

- Secures the main halyard to its cleat.

Figure 20-1 – Raising the mainsail
Crewmember stands safely by the mast
Mainsheet uncleated
Helm keeps the boat head to wind
Boomvang released
Companionway hatch cover closed

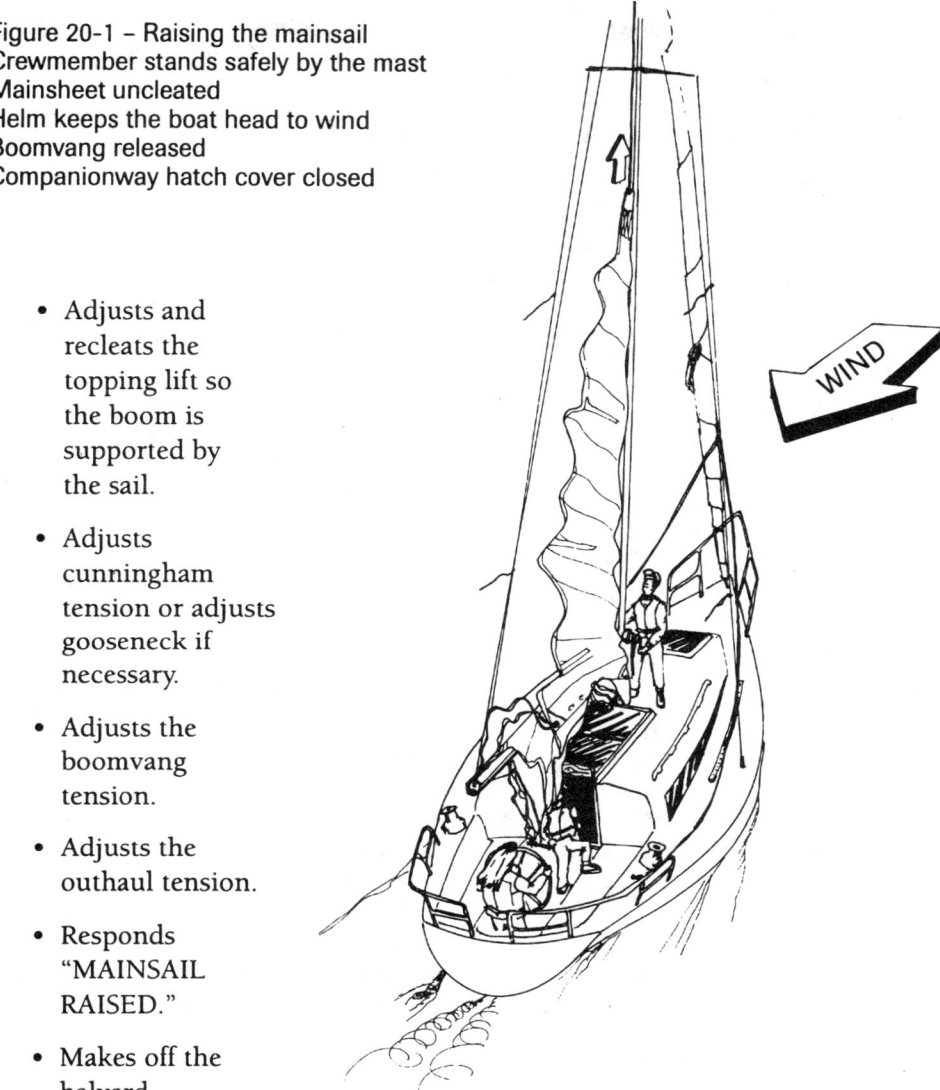

- Adjusts and recleats the topping lift so the boom is supported by the sail.

- Adjusts cunningham tension or adjusts gooseneck if necessary.

- Adjusts the boomvang tension.

- Adjusts the outhaul tension.

- Responds "MAINSAIL RAISED."

- Makes off the halyard.

HELM:

- Commands "HARDEN THE MAINSHEET."

- Bears away and sails under mainsail until ready to raise the foresail. If at anchor, raise the anchor before hardening the mainsheet; if at a mooring buoy, cast off the mooring line before hardening the mainsheet.

- Shuts off the engine. If the engine is an outboard, closes the vent on the gas tank, and raises the engine.

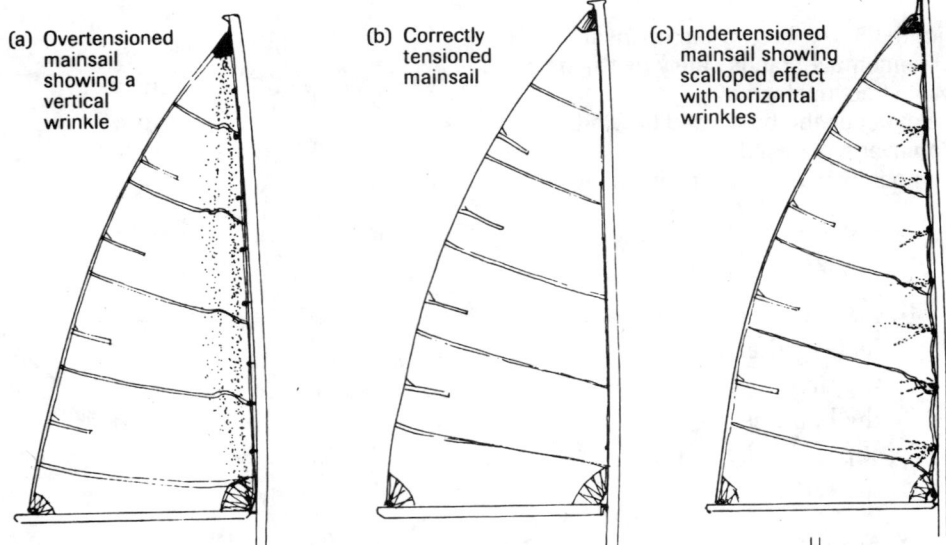

Figure 20-2 – Mainsail Luff Tension

The luff of the mainsail is tensioned by the halyard and cunningham or downhaul. A foresail luff is usually tensioned only by the halyard. Two very general rules for tensioning the luff of a sail are:

1. Increase luff tension as the wind increases. The luff should be tensioned so there are neither horizontal nor vertical wrinkles in the luff when the boat is sailing. Horizontal wrinkles indicate too little tension while vertical wrinkles indicate too much tension.

2. Tension the luff when sailing upwind; ease tension when reaching and running.

The rules for tensioning the outhaul are similar. In light winds the boomvang should be very lightly tensioned. Increase the tension as the wind strength increases. Finer points of achieving optimum sail shape for each wind and sea condition are taught in the *Advanced Cruising Standard*.

> **SAFETY TIP:**
> When working along the boom make sure the mainsheet has been hardened and cleated and the companionway hatch cover closed.
>
> When working at the mast, position yourself between the mast and the shrouds. You can lean against the shrouds for support. If you need to work using both hands, hook your arm around a shroud.

RAISING THE FORESAIL

When raising the foresail on a boat with the halyard cleat on the mast, position the boat so the foresail halyard is to windward. Most foresail halyard cleats are on the port side of the mast, which means the boat should be on a port tack when the sail is raised. The crewmember raising the sail will then be safely on the windward side and, when the sail is raised, it will blow to leeward away from the crewmember.

If the foresail halyard is controlled from the cockpit, the foresail may be raised on either tack.

The following procedure assumes the foresail halyard cleat is on the port side of the mast.

HELM:

- Puts the boat on a port tack, closehauled.
- Commands "READY TO RAISE THE FORESAIL."

CREW:

- Goes forward on the windward side (port side in this instance).
- Makes sure the foresail halyard is able to run free.
- Attaches the halyard shackle to the head of the foresail.
- Unties the foresail bag. Grabs the bag by the bottom and moves aft, thus releasing the sail and trailing it aft. Checks that the sheets are clear of foredeck cleats and fittings.
- Secures the sailbag and stands by the foresail halyard on the port side of the mast.
- Responds "READY."
- The cockpit crew releases the windward sheet and makes sure it can run freely, then releases the leeward sheet, removes the slack, and takes one wrap clockwise around the winch.
- Cockpit crew responds "READY."

HELM:

- Commands "RAISE THE FORESAIL."

CREW:

- Quickly raises the foresail, tensions the luff and cleats off the halyard.
- Responds "FORESAIL RAISED."

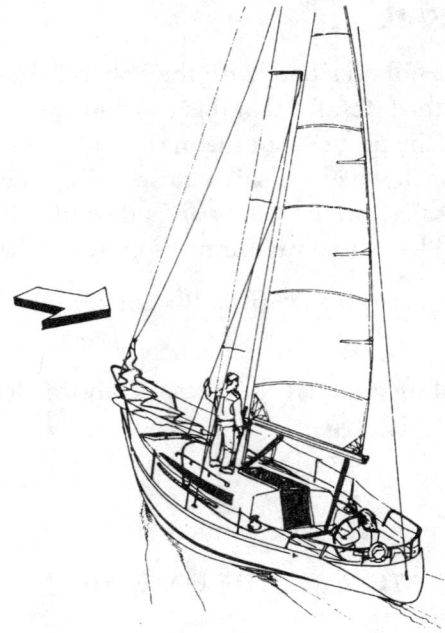

Figure 20-3 – Raising the foresail, closehauled on port tack

- Makes off the halyard.
- Returns to the cockpit on the windward side.

HELM:

- Commands "HARDEN THE FORESAIL."

CREW:

- Hauls in the sail, cleats the leeward sheet, flaking the end of the sheet neatly.

UNFURLING THE ROLLER FURLING FORESAIL

HELM:

- Puts the boat on a closehauled course on either tack.
- Commands "UNFURL THE FORESAIL."

SAFETY TIP:
When sailing, work the windward side of the boat. Keep low on the windward side when transiting the foredeck between mast and forestay. Never move or walk behind the leeward side of the boom or sail; if the sheet should inadvertently let go you may be knocked overboard.

CREW:

- Uncleats the windward sheet and makes sure it can run freely.

- Uncleats the furling line leaving one turn on the cleat and makes sure it will run.

- Uncleats and hauls on the leeward sheet while the furling line is eased. During the unfurling the furling line should be kept under light tension to maintain control so that the sail does not unfurl with a snap and the furling line does not foul on the drum.

- Cleats off and coils the furling line.

- Hauls in the sail, cleats the leeward sheet, flaking the end of the sheet neatly.

SAFE WINCH TECHNIQUES

Winches work by mechanical advantage and friction. The more turns on a winch, the more friction there is. A winch should have its drum covered by line prior to using the handle. A winch allows crew to control a large force, such as a genoa full of wind, with relatively small effort.

Since there can sometimes be very high strain on halyards and sheets, there are safety precautions you must take while using a winch:

- Place wraps on the winch in a clockwise direction, the direction in which the drum revolves.

- Place each wrap **above** the previous one.

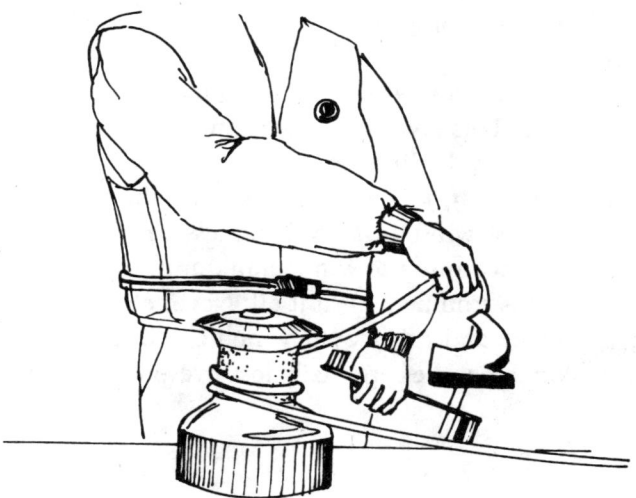

Figure 20-4 – Placing wraps on a winch safely.

- Use only one hand when placing wraps on the winch.
- Keep your fingers at least several inches away from the winch.
- Stand behind the winch if you are hauling in a sheet or other line, so you are away from the line with the strain on it.
- Do not hold a line between the winch and sail.

TO HARDEN A SHEET:

- Pull the sheet till taut with one wrap on the drum. More than one wrap initially may result in an *override* (jammed wraps) which can be difficult to clear.
- Haul in the sheet briskly, hand over hand, tossing the excess behind you, until the line becomes taut again.
- Holding the *tail* (the line on your side of the winch) firmly, place two or three more wraps on the winch.
- Harden again until you can pull no more. For maximum advantage, the drum must be well covered with wraps.
- Hold the tail firmly with one hand, insert the winch handle into the drum with the other hand. Insert the winch handle by grasping it near the lock, if fitted, so you can work the lock with your thumb, thus allowing the winch handle to be cleanly inserted into the drum.
- Crank in a clockwise direction with one hand, while keeping tension on the tail with the other. If the sheet is under high strain get another crewmember to *tail* (pull on the line) for you while you crank with both hands.
- If the last few inches prove too much for you to crank in, there are two solutions:
  - If the winch is a two-speed winch, begin cranking the handle anticlockwise. This gives more mechanical advantage though it takes longer to bring in the line.
  - Ask the helm to *luff up* (turn the boat into the wind) momentarily so there will be less wind in the sail and less strain on the sheet. While the boat is turned into the wind, crank until the sheet is hauled in.
- When the sheet is trimmed, cleat it off. Never cleat off a sheet with a half hitch. Unlock and remove the winch handle and stow it in its pocket. Winch handles are easily lost overboard and are easy to trip over.

If the winch is a self-tailing winch, after you have all the wraps on and have hauled in the sheet by hand as much as you can, wind the sheet over the guide and around the top of the winch between the plates. Give a sharp yank on the line to set it in the **self-tailer.** Insert the winch handle and begin cranking. You do not have to hold the tail as you crank.

EASING A SHEET:

To cast off a sheet **rapidly:**

- Uncleat the sheet.

Figure 20-5 – Casting off a sheet rapidly

- Pull straight up on the tail so the line unwraps itself from the winch.

- Cast off the tail, making sure it runs freely.

To ease a sheet **gradually:**

- Uncleat the sheet.

- Keep tension on the tail with the right hand. Put the heel of your left hand over the wraps, keeping your fingers back to prevent injury.

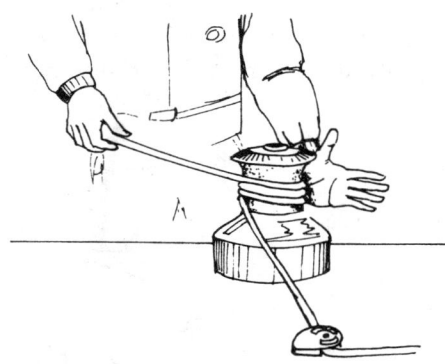

Figure 20-6 – Easing a sheet gradually

- Ease the tail with one hand while steadying the coils against the drum with the heel of the other.

TO CLEAR AN OVERRIDE:

When a winch is jammed with overriding turns of the line, the only way to clear the override is to get slack on the part of the line that is under strain. The easiest way to do this, if the line is a sheet, is to turn the boat further into the wind and clear the override while the strain on the line is reduced.

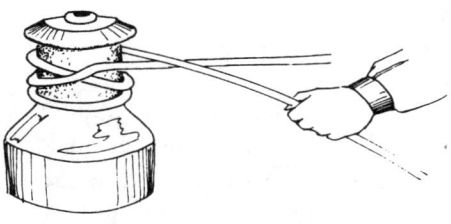

Figure 20-7 – A winch override

Chapter 21 – How a Boat Sails

HOW SAILS WORK

It is easy to understand how a boat sails downwind on a broad reach or a run. The wind presses on the sails and pushes the boat along. If you turn your back to the wind on a blowy day and hold an open umbrella in front of you, it will tug you along!

What is less obvious is how a boat can sail upwind, closehauled, and across the wind on a close or beam reach. This works because the sail generates lift, as does an airplane's wing, to which sails are often compared. When a sail is sheeted in, the air flowing past its curved surfaces is diverted from a straight line path. Over the hollow windward side of the sail, the air slows down and a higher pressure area develops. At the same time, the air flowing over the bulging leeward side speeds up and its pressure falls. This difference in pressure results in a force acting to leeward on the sail. The umbrella, if held upright on a windy day, will try to lift you from the ground because of the same effect.

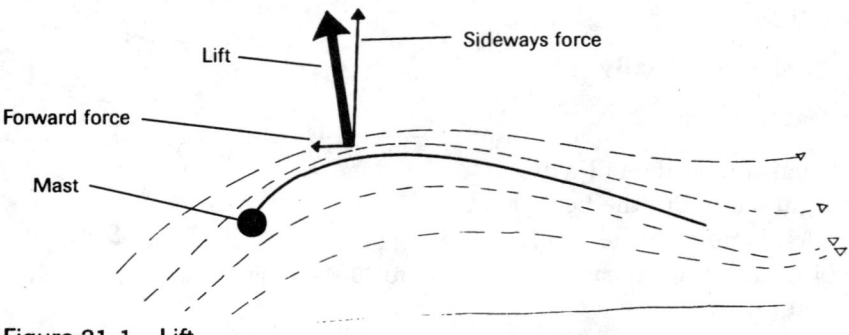

Figure 21-1 – Lift.

The force has both sideways and forward components, the resultant of which is LIFT, as shown in Figure 21-1.

THE KEEL'S JOB

Without the keel as an appendage the boat would be blown primarily sideways, also known as 'making leeway'. As many 15th century nautical adventurers discovered, without deep keels, going to windward was impossible, thus making the run down the tradewinds the preferred route.

The good news is that as a boat tries to make leeway, the keel, being foil shaped like the sail, also produces lift while it impedes the boat's drift to leeward.

Thus with both the sails and the keel providing lift, a modern keelboat is able to sail to windward along the forward components of the combined lifts. To maximize the effectiveness of your boat on a windward course, the correct trimming of the sails is essential.

SAIL TRIM

To trim or set your sails is to adjust the sails with the sheets and other controls to take best advantage of the wind. **Trim is concerned with sail shape and the angle of the sail relative to the wind direction**. You have dealt with the adjustment of luff tension, outhaul and boomvang, all of which affect sail shape. Now you will use the sheets to trim the sails to their best angle to the wind for each point of sail. A general rule is to let the sail out until it luffs, then pull it in until it stops luffing.

To trim your sails for maximum performance you must know where the wind is coming from. The boat should have telltales fixed to the shrouds and backstay. A masthead fly, a small windvane at the top of the mast, is also extremely helpful. Telltales blow downwind whereas the arrow on the fly points into the wind. Your sails should have pairs of ticklers on either side of the foresail luff to give you information about the horizontal flow of air over each side of the sail.

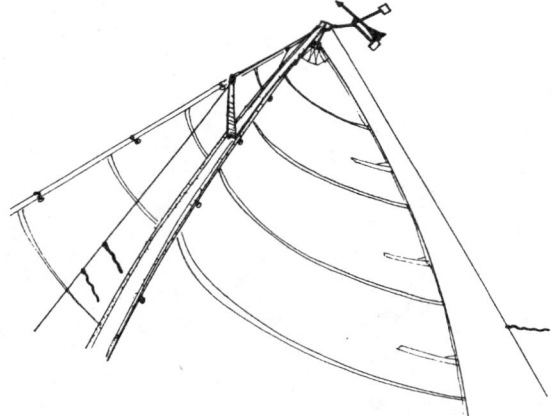

Figure 21-2 – The masthead fly, as seen from the windward deck.

The wind you see acting on your telltales, **ticklers** or masthead fly is the apparent wind. Although you can get a good idea where the true wind is coming from by looking about you, you cannot trim your sails accurately using the true wind, as shown in Figure 17-1, because it can be quite different in both strength and direction with respect to the apparent wind.

SAIL TRIM FOR CLOSE HAULED, CLOSE REACH AND BEAM REACH

Each sail should be trimmed so the air divides over both sides of the sails, flows smoothly and remains attached all the way across the sail, as shown by boat A in Figure 21-3. This will ensure the maximum lift. If the sail is not sheeted in enough, as shown by boat B, the airflow is broken-up at the luff of the sail, and the sail is luffing. If the sail is sheeted in too far, the air next to the leeward side of the sail prematurely breaks away into turbulence and eddies; the sail **stalls** as boat C shows.

Of the two evils, it is more damaging to performance to have the sails sheeted in too much because a stalled sail wants to tip the boat rather than drive it forward. Rely on the maxim, "When in doubt, let it out."

Your keys to proper trim are the ticklers on the foresail and the luff of the mainsail.

The foresail tickler on the windward side gives an early warning of an impending luff. The tickler on the leeward side indicates when the sail is

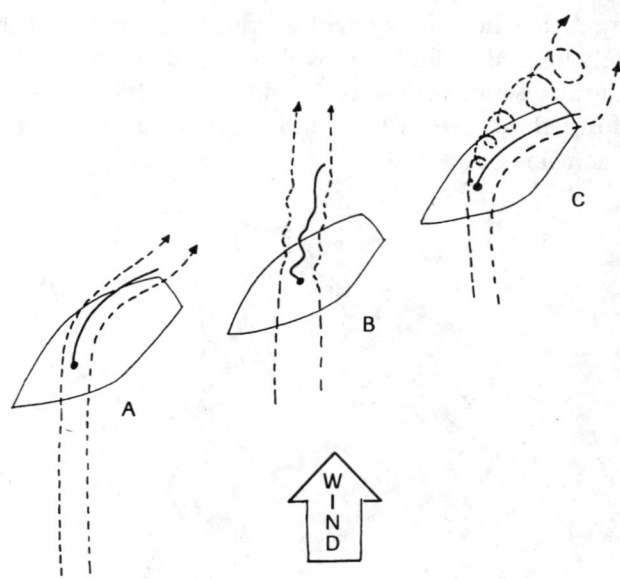

Figure 21-3 – Principles of Sail trim

Each sail should be trimmed so the air divides over both sides and flows smoothly and remains attached all the way across the sail.

stalled. Trim is correct (Figure 21-4b) when both ticklers are streaming aft. When the windward tickler drops or flutters, (Figure 21-4a) the sail is about to luff and you must either harden the sheet or bear away so the windward side of the sail gets more wind flowing over it. When the leeward tickler drops, (Figure 21-4c) the air flowing over the leeward side is breaking away and you must either ease the sheet or head up so the leeward side of the sail gets more wind flowing over it.

Although there are no ticklers on the luff of the mainsail it is easy to see when the sheet is not hardened enough because the sail will begin to luff. The most common error with the mainsail is in hardening it too much. The sail looks firm even when stalled. Keep checking to see if you can ease the sheet a little without causing luffing.

If the mainsail is fully battened, you may not see the luff shaking, but you will see the whole sail curl. Watch the leech or leech ticklers instead of the luff.

Closehauled is the only point of sail on which the helm must steer to the sails as trimmed by the crew. Once the sails are hardened close to the centerline of the boat, you are sailing as close to the wind as possible. The foresail is hardened until the after part of the sail is a few inches outside

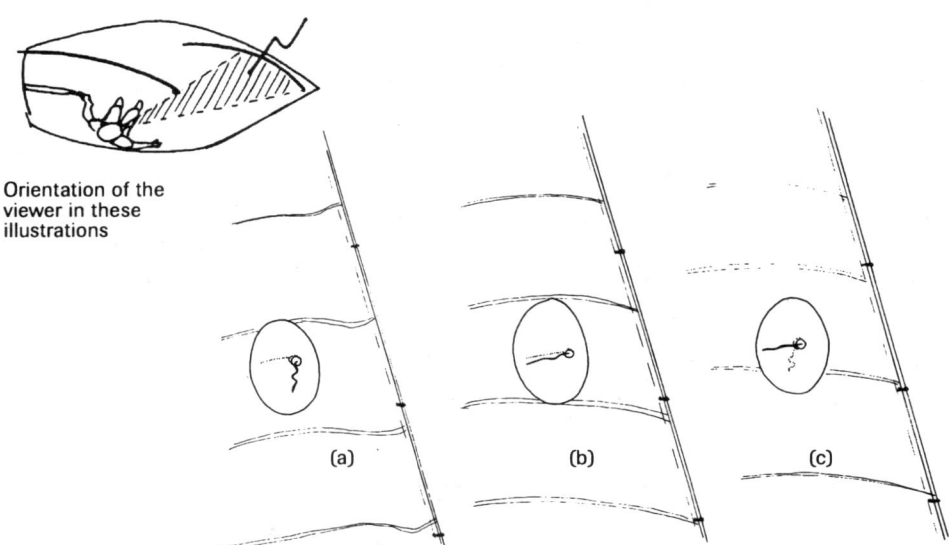

Orientation of the viewer in these illustrations

(a) (b) (c)

Figure 21-4 (a),(b),(c) – Using the foresail telltales or ticklers for proper trim.

In these views from the cockpit, the windward ticklers are shown as solid lines, the leeward ticklers as dotted lines.

Figure 21-4 (a) – The windward tickler has dropped, indicating an impending luff.

Figure 21-4 (b) – Both ticklers are streaming aft. The sail is trimmed correctly.

Figure 21-4 (c) – The leeward tickler has dropped, indicating the sail has stalled.

the spreader. If you harden the sail so it touches the spreader, the spreader will eventually chafe a hole in the sail.

No wind is absolutely steady in strength and direction, though some winds are steadier than others. **To steer well closehauled the helm must concentrate on keeping both foresail telltales streaming aft so the boat is making the best progress possible.** This will result in a zig zag course through the water as you head up and bear away to follow the telltales.

On the reaches the helm holds the desired course and the crew keeps the sails trimmed to any changes in the wind.

When closehauled, close reaching and beam reaching, trim your foresail first and then the mainsail. i.e. working from the bow of the boat aft.

SAIL TRIM FOR BROAD REACH AND RUN

On a broad reach or a run your method of trimming the sails will change because, with the wind pushing from behind, the sails are stalled, with masses of eddies on their leeward side. This is one of the reasons downwind sailing is slower, given the same wind conditions and sails you used upwind. **Your goal now is simply to present as much sail area to the wind as possible.**

Wind deflected off the mainsail can cause the shroud telltales to be inaccurate for giving wind direction. Use the backstay telltale or the masthead fly.

When sailing downwind the foresail telltales no longer function properly. On a broad reach the foresail sheet is eased until it begins to luff, then hardened just until the luffing stops. On a run the foresail is trimmed perpendicular to the wind.

On a broad reach or a run the mainsheet is eased until the boom is perpendicular to the wind or, on a run, as nearly perpendicular as the position of the shrouds permit.

SAIL TRIM		
POINTS OF SAIL	**FORESAIL**	**MAINSAIL**
Closehauled	Telltales streaming aft	Harden just until luffing stops
Close reach	Telltales streaming aft	Harden just until luffing stops
Beam reach	Telltales streaming aft	Harden just until luffing stops
Broad reach	Harden just until luffing stops	Perpendicular to the wind
Run	Perpendicular to the wind	Perpendicular to the wind

Chapter 22 – Maneuvering Under Sail

HEADING UP AND BEARING AWAY

Sail across the wind so the wind is blowing over the beam of your boat. Harden both sails until they just stop luffing.

HEADING UP:

Turn the helm so your boat's bow turns a little closer to the wind. To alter course toward the wind is **heading up**. To head up with a tiller-steered boat, turn the tiller to leeward (Think: "Towards the boom, towards the wind.") To head up with a wheel-steered boat, turn the wheel towards the wind. To notify the crew, announce "HEADING UP" as you turn the helm.

BEARING AWAY:

Turn the helm so your boat's bow turns downwind so the boat is sailing with the wind on the beam again. To alter course away from the wind is **bearing away**. To bear away with a tiller-steered boat, turn the tiller to windward (Think: "Away from the boom, away from the wind.").

To bear away with a wheel-steered boat, turn the wheel away from the wind. To notify your crew, announce "BEARING AWAY" as you turn the helm.

SLOWING AND STOPPING

Your sailboat has no brakes and cannot be slowed or stopped when it is sailing downwind on a broad reach or a run because you cannot get the wind out of the sails. You must use the wind to your advantage to slow or stop the boat.

SLOWING:

There are two ways to slow your boat:

- **Head up so the sails will luff and drive will be reduced**. When you have slowed to the desired speed, resume your course. Head up as needed to adjust your speed. Announce "HEADING UP" or "BEARING AWAY" as appropriate.

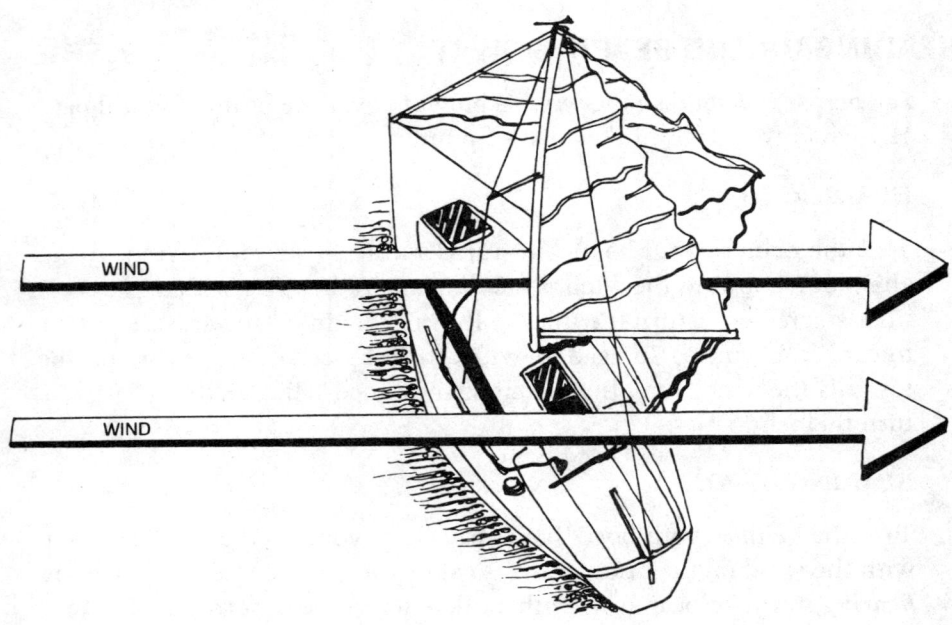

Figure 22-1 – Ease sheets completely to stop your boat while on a close reach.

- **Maintain your course and ease the sails until they luff**. To resume speed, harden the sails again. Ease the sails as needed to adjust your speed. Your commands are "EASE THE SHEETS" and "HARDEN THE SHEETS."

STOPPING:

There are two ways to stop your boat:

- **Turn your boat head to wind and ease the sheets completely so the sails luff (cannot fill)**. The boat will glide to a stop, though it will not stay head to wind for long. This maneuver is useful for stopping the boat quickly. It is used when anchoring and picking up a mooring buoy. The command is "HEADING UP, RELEASE THE SHEETS."

- **Turn your boat to a beam reach or close reach position and ease the sheets completely**. The boat will slow, stop and stay stopped, though it will make a little leeway. This maneuver is useful if you wish to leave the helm unattended briefly. It is used in crew overboard situations. The command is "RELEASE THE SHEETS."

Note: In each case above the sail is in line with the wind and luffing. Only the position of your boat in relation to the wind is different.

POINTS OF SAIL

The **points of sail** are the courses (directions or headings) sailed in reference to the apparent wind direction. Your sail trim must be correct for your point of sail or your boat will not move well.

While closehauled, beam reach and run are fairly precise courses, there are an infinite number of courses you may sail when close reaching or broad reaching. A close reach is any course between closehauled and a beam reach; a broad reach is any course between a beam reach and a run.

In light and moderate winds a close reach is the fastest point of sail.

A beam reach is the only point of sail on which speeds when travelling reciprocal (opposite) courses will be equal. For this reason it is often useful in crew overboard situations and search patterns.

Sailing on a run carrying the mainsail on one side and the foresail on the other is sailing **wing and wing**. Your boat is presenting all her sail area to the wind. This requires concentration by the helm to prevent an accidental gybe.

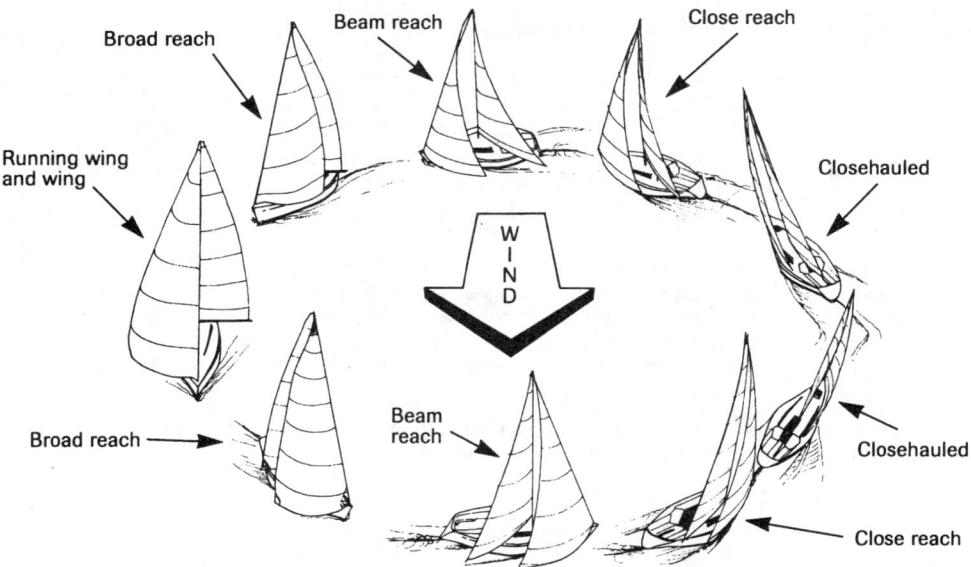

Figure 22-2 – Learning the points of sail by sailing in a circle.

No one can give you a "recipe" that always works for getting from a set departure point to, for example, the lighthouse across the bay. Today you may be able to reach across to it. Tomorrow the wind may have changed so you may have to sail closehauled to get there. On yet another day you may run down to it. You trim your sails in relation to the wind direction of the present.

Procedure for sailng the points of sail from closehauled to a run

Procedure	Command	Change course to approximately	Crew	Helm
To sail closehauled	"Harden sheets for closehauled"	45° off wind direction	Trims for closehauled	Steers to tell-tales on the foresail
To move from closehauled to a close reach	"Ease sheets for a close reach"	50° – 85° off wind direction	Trims so foresail telltales are streaming aft and the mainsail just stops luffing — maintains watch on sail trim and adjusts as necessary	Maintains course
To move from a close reach to a beam reach	"Ease sheets for a beam reach"	90° off wind direction		
To move from a beam reach to a broad reach	"Ease sheets for a broad reach"	95° – 175° off wind direction	Trims foresail until luffing stops and boom is perpendicular to the wind — maintains watch on sail trim and adjusts as necessary	
To move from a broad reach to a run	"Ease sheets for a run"	Gradual course change to 180° off wind direction	Foresail will not fill because it is blanketed by the mainsail — boom is perpendicular to the wind	Steers carefully directly downwind, avoiding sailing by the lee (see Chapter 23)
To run wing and wing	"Gybe the foresail"	No course change	Eases leeward sheet of foresail while hardening windward sheet and trims foresail perpendicular to the wind on the windward side of the boat	

When bearing away through the points of sail from closehauled to a run, preface commands with "Ease sheets..." because the farther off the wind your boat sails the farther out her sails are trimmed. Conversely, when heading up from a run through the points of sail to closehauled, preface commands with "Harden sheets..." Return on the same tack, working up the table, to the closehauled course on which you began.

You can sail these courses on the opposite tack as a mirror image of what you have just done, but first, you must learn to change tack by tacking or gybing.

Chapter 23 – Tacking and Gybing

TACKING

Tacking, or *coming about,* is changing tack by steering the boat through head to wind from closehauled on one tack to closehauled on the opposite tack, a turn of about 90°.

HELM:

- Checks that there are no vessels or obstructions nearby and to windward.

- Sights abeam and to windward (approximately 90°) to estimate the course after tacking.

- Commands "READY ABOUT" and waits for crew response, while maintaining a closehauled course.

CREW:

- Crew on the leeward side uncleats the leeward foresail sheet but does not ease it.

- Crew on the windward side puts one wrap on the windward winch and snugs up the sheet until no slack remains.

- All crew respond "READY", although the mainsheet trimmer can take a well earned rest because the mainsail flops to the opposite side of the boat by itself during the tack.

HELM:

- Makes a final check for traffic.

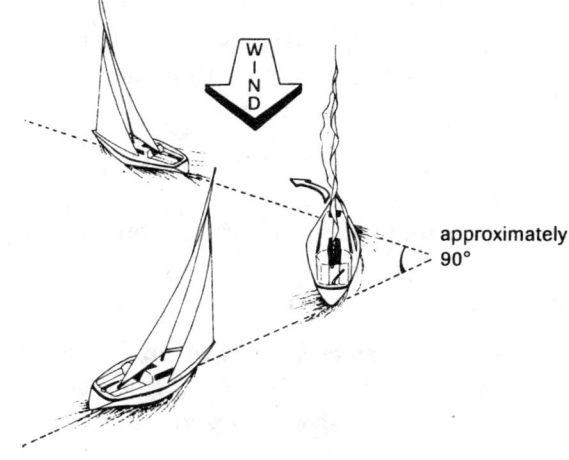

Figure 23-1 – Tacking

- Commands "HELMS-ALEE" and simultaneously begins to steer through head to wind to the new course.

CREW:

- Crew holds leeward sheet until the foresail collapses, then rapidly removes the sheet from the winch and casts the sheet off completely, making sure it can run freely.
- Crew holding the new leeward sheet (former windward sheet) trims the sheet rapidly for the new closehauled course. Good timing is important and can save muscle and winch power.

HELM:

- Begins straightening out the helm as the bow passes through head to wind in order to stop the turn when the closehauled course on the new tack is reached.
- Until the foresail is trimmed, sails on the mainsail alone.
- As soon as the foresail is trimmed, returns to steering by the foresail luff telltales.

The secret to tacking well is to maintain the boat's speed right up to the moment you say "HELMS-ALEE". A common error is the helm anticipating the tack from the moment of saying "READY ABOUT." The boat is steered too close to the wind, the sails luff, boat speed drops and steerage is reduced. You must be able to steer through the tack so the boat does not stop in irons nor oversteer past closehauled on the new tack.

IN AND OUT OF IRONS

Most frequently your boat gets caught in irons when you lose steerage during the tacking maneuver. Inexperienced helming and/or poor timing in the handling of the foresail sheets is usually responsible. When the water is rough and you choose the wrong moment to tack into large waves your boat can also be caught in irons.

A little patience together with a little knowledge will have you quickly out of irons. After the boat has come to a stop head to wind it will be only a moment or two before the wind starts pushing the boat astern. To sail off on your new tack all you need do is apply your knowledge of how to steer when the boat is moving astern.

1. **If the boat is tiller-steered, pull or push the tiller towards the direction you want to go. If the boat is wheel-steered, turn the wheel away from the direction you want to go.**

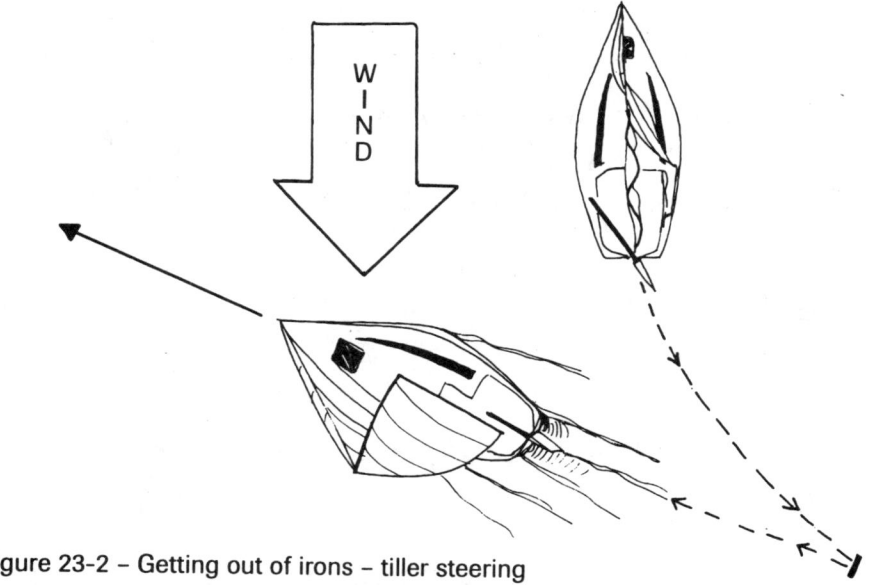

Figure 23-2 – Getting out of irons – tiller steering

Push the tiller in the direction you want to go. Hold the clew of the foresail out to the windward side on the desired tack.

2. Hold the clew of the foresail out to the windward side on the desired tack. The wind on the foresail will push the bow to leeward.

3. Hold the helm to the appropriate side until the bow is headed in the desired direction and the mainsail has filled with wind.

4. Adjust the helm, trim the foresail sheet on the leeward side, and sail away.

THE GENTLE GYBE

Gybing is changing tack while sailing downwind. Emphasis, while gybing, must be on control. If you do not maintain control you could have an accidental gybe.

Gybing is quite different from tacking. To gybe you change the sails from one side of the boat to the other while maintaining an almost straight course. During tacking the mainsail looks after itself, but during gybing the mainsail must be handled with care.

The gybe is initiated with the boat on a run and the boat remains on a run throughout the gybing procedure. It is essential for the helm to concentrate on steering straight downwind and on giving commands.

GYBING:

HELM:

- Steers the boat gradually down to a run, watching for the collapse of the foresail.
- Commands "GYBE THE FORESAIL."

CREW:

- Gybe the foresail. The boat is now running **wing and wing**.

HELM:

- Commands "READY TO GYBE THE MAINSAIL."

CREW:

- All except the mainsheet trimmer respond "READY." Thus the helm is assured that all crewmembers are aware of the impending gybe.
- The mainsheet is quickly hardened to center the boom, but the sheet is not cleated. Mainsheet trimmer responds "READY."

HELM:

- Makes a **very slight** alteration of course to turn the boat sufficiently for the wind to push the boom across the boat's centerline.
- Calls "GYBE-HO" as the mainsail crosses the centerline.
- Corrects the helm promptly to maintain course and prevent the boat pivoting and heading up to a reach.

CREW:

- As soon as the mainsail crosses the centerline the mainsheet trimmer rapidly, but with control, eases the mainsheet for a run.

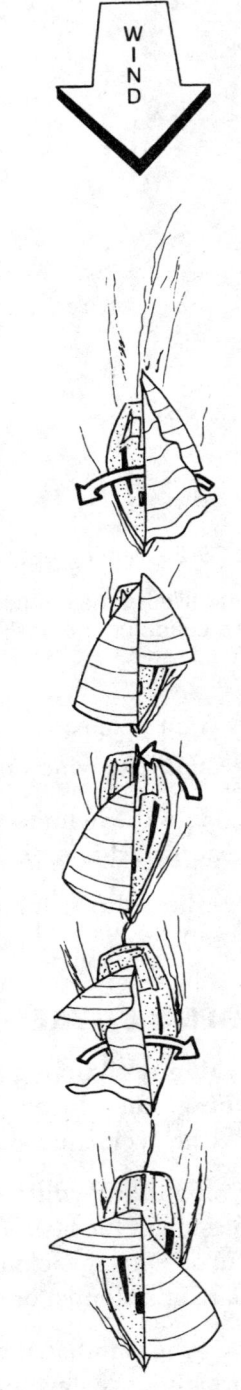

Figure 23-3 – Performing the gybe

When you have completed the gybe you are still on a run. If you wish to remain on a run you will want to gybe the foresail again.

Note: A gybe has not been completed until the mainsail has been gybed because it is the side on which the mainsail is being carried that determines the tack.

After you have mastered the gentle gybe you may wish to try gybing from a broad reach to a broad reach. You might choose to do this if you want to change course as you gybe. For example, you may have to gybe around a buoy at a bend in a channel. Maintaining control during a reaching gybe is more difficult because:

- hardening the mainsheet is more work as the apparent wind is stronger than when the boat is on a run.

- while the sheet is being hardened considerable weather helm is created, making steering more demanding.

- the gybe is more violent and helm correction must be well timed and sufficient to prevent the boat from rounding up to a beam reach.

In strong winds and rolly seas you may wish to avoid gybing if you are doubtful that you can gybe in a controlled manner. This might be because the boat is short of crew, or the crew or yourself are inexperienced. In this case simply head up through the points of sail to closehauled, tack, then bear away to a run on the new tack. Do not pause at each point of sail. Command "HARDEN SHEETS FOR CLOSEHAULED," give the normal command for tacking and as the tack is completed, command "EASE SHEETS FOR A RUN."

When you want to change tack you have the option of tacking or gybing. Most often you will base your decision on which is the shortest way around the sailing circle from your present point of sail to your intended point of sail on the opposite tack.

SAILING BY THE LEE

When you are sailing with the wind blowing over the same side of your boat as the mainsail is being carried, you are sailing by the lee. You have turned past a run dead downwind to a course that is a broad reach on what should be the opposite tack. Since you have not changed tack by gybing the mainsail, the wind may do it for you by getting behind the mainsail and slamming it across the boat in an accidental, uncontrolled gybe, much as the wind slams a door shut. In a strong wind an accidental gybe can be dangerous, resulting in crew injury, or crew knocked overboard, or damage to the rigging.

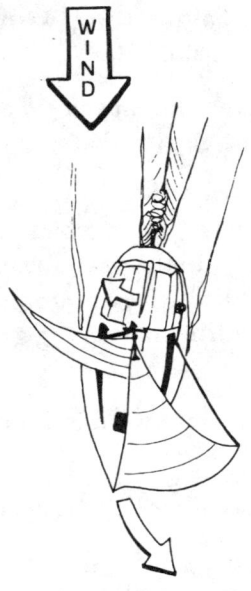

Figure 23-4 – Sailing by the Lee

If you find yourself sailing by the lee, avoid an accidental gybe by:

- On a tiller-steered boat, moving the tiller towards the boom.
- On a wheel-steered boat, turning the wheel away from the boom.

You can avoid an accidental gybe by always turning gradually onto a run and by keeping a close eye on your backstay telltale or masthead fly whenever you are running.

If you have difficulty recognizing when you are sailing by the lee, ask your instructor to demonstrate during a light wind lesson.

PRACTICE, PRACTICE, PRACTICE!

Practice maneuvering under sail until you are able to work with your crew as a team. The following exercises are helpful and fun. Be sure to use proper commands as you maneuver.

- Sail in a large circle, pausing briefly on each point of sail. Include a tack and a gybe where appropriate.
- Sail upwind and downwind in a figure eight pattern, rounding convenient objects or especially set marks.

SAFETY TIP:

When the boat is sailing downwind make it a practice to keep your head low while moving about, just in case an accidental gybe should be caused by a sudden wind shift or a momentary lapse of attention on the part of the helm. Why? To avoid head injury and possibly being knocked overboard.

Keep your hands off the boom while gybing. This is ineffective and unsafe in a keelboat.

- Pick a destination to windward and work your way upwind to it in a series of tacks.
- Run a distance downwind making a series of controlled gybes.
- If there is another school boat nearby, take turns playing Follow the Leader.

Chapter 24 – Coping with Stronger Winds

HEAVING TO

Heaving to is primarily a heavy weather technique used for riding out strong winds. However, it can also be useful in any situation where the crew needs a rest or the boat needs to be stabilized for cooking, reefing, repairs or navigation.

Before heaving to:

- Make sure you have enough **sea room**. Sea room is sufficient space to perform an intended maneuver without running into obstructions such as reefs, shallows or anchored vessels. You will not be stopped when hove-to, but making some headway and considerable leeway.

- Avoid heaving to with the genoa. Change to a jib or, if you have roller furling, furl the genoa to jib size. A genoa will be chafed by the spreader and shrouds, and will cause the boat to make more headway than a jib.

- If possible, arrange to heave to on the starboard tack so you will be the stand-on vessel over port tack sailboats as well as powerboats.

TO HEAVE TO:

HELM:

- Sails a closehauled course, preferably on a port tack.

- Commands "READY TO HEAVE TO."

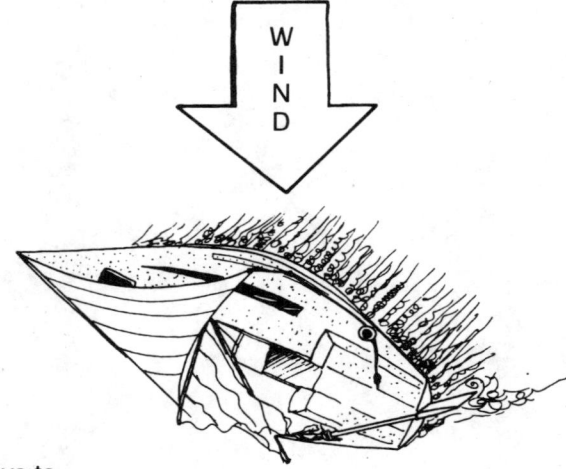

Figure 24-1 – Hove to

Foresail is cleated on windward side. Tiller is lashed to leeward.

CREW:

- Responds "READY." The boat is tacked without changing the foresail to the new leeward side.

HELM:

- Commands "HEAVING TO."
- Turns the boat past head to wind.
- Eases mainsheet.
- Waits until the boat loses way.
- Lashes tiller to leeward or wheel to windward.
- Maintains a lookout.

After you have performed this maneuver you are **hove-to**. The wind blowing on the foresail is pushing the bow to leeward while the helm is acting to push the bow to windward. **With foresail and helm working in opposition an equilibrium is maintained.**

Boats vary in the ease with which they can heave to. Some boats have to be coaxed. Faster, racier boats may continue to move at a good speed after the tack, thus maintaining steerage. When you lash the tiller or lock the wheel this type of boat will simply tack back onto the previous tack. If you find this to be so, take the way off the boat by luffing past closehauled and temporarily easing the mainsheet. Once boat speed is under about a knot you can lash the tiller to leeward or lock the wheel to windward and gradually harden the mainsheet until luffing stops.

When hove to, ideally your bow will be heading about 60° off the wind. The mainsheet offers some control over the boat's attitude to the wind. The more you harden the mainsheet the more weather helm you will have and the further into the wind the bow should point.

Some boats will heave to by themselves if the helm is left unattended while the boat is closehauled, a very desirable situation so far as safety is concerned.

To get out of the hove to position, release the foresail sheet, center the helm, and wait until the boat begins to move forward. Then set your

> **SAFETY TIP:**
> *In rough weather when it becomes hazardous working on deck, wear your safety harness and make sure it is at all times hooked to a strongpoint on the boat.*

course and trim the sails and you are off again. The other option is to gybe out of the hove-to position by bearing away and gybing onto the opposite tack.

A FISHERMAN'S REEF

If the wind is gusty you may find yourself in a situation where between gusts the boat sails well but during gusts is overpowered. This problem can be solved by having the mainsheet trimmer standing by to quickly ease the mainsheet during each gust so the main luffs and to harden it as the gust diminishes. The boat thus drives through the gusts on the foresail alone. This maneuver is called a **fisherman's reef.**

If the wind is steadier and the boat is overpowered all or most of the time, you need to reduce sail.

REEFING THE MAINSAIL

Shortening sail by taking in a reef is easier to do sooner than later if the wind is building. Hopefully you will have practiced reefing at the dock before you have to do it in earnest, and will have checked that the reefing system is fully operational.

Jiffy or slab reefing is currently the most favoured system. It is so named because you can put in a reef in a jiffy. After practice a crew working as a team should be able to reef in about one minute.

You may put in or **shake out** (undo) a reef while closehauled or hove-to. The advantage of reefing while closehauled is that you continue sailing towards your destination as you put in the reef; the disadvantage is that the boat is heeling and sailing into the waves. The advantage of reefing while hove to is that you will be working on a more stable platform; the disadvantage is that you will give up a little ground to leeway. If you are singlehanding, sailing alone, reefing while hove to is the preferred method.

For safety, reef with the boat on starboard tack. Because many boats have the main halyard and reefing controls on the starboard side the crew will be working to windward. You will also be the stand-on vessel over powerboats and port tackers.

Tension the luff of the sail before tensioning the foot with the leech reefing line. Premature tensioning of the leech reefing line during reefing can force the boltrope out of the mast slot and can damage the sail.

After reefing, excess sailcloth should be **loosely** rolled and tied so you don't stress or pinch the sail. You are only tidying up.

PROCEDURE FOR REEFING THE MAINSAIL:

HELM:

- Puts the boat on a starboard tack, closehauled or hove to.
- Commands "READY TO REEF THE MAINSAIL."

CREW:

- Closes the hatch cover.
- Releases the boomvang.
- Eases the cunningham or downhaul. Secure the gooseneck if necessary.
- Tensions and recleats the topping lift.
- Drops the main halyard coil and uncleats the halyard, keeping one turn of the halyard around the cleat.
- Responds "READY".
- Cockpit crew releases the mainsheet and responds "READY."

HELM:

- Commands "REEF THE MAINSAIL."

CREW:

- Eases the main halyard while pulling the luff down until the luff cringle can be placed in the reefing hook at the gooseneck or the luff reef line has been tensioned and secured. The luff cringle has now become the new tack of the sail.
- Retensions and cleats the halyard.
- Tensions the leech reef line. (this brings the cringle down to the boom to be the new clew, and flattens the shortened sail).
- Eases the topping lift.
- Responds "MAIN REEFED."

HELM:

- Hardens the mainsheet.

CREW:

- Tensions and cleats the boomvang.
- Makes off the halyard.

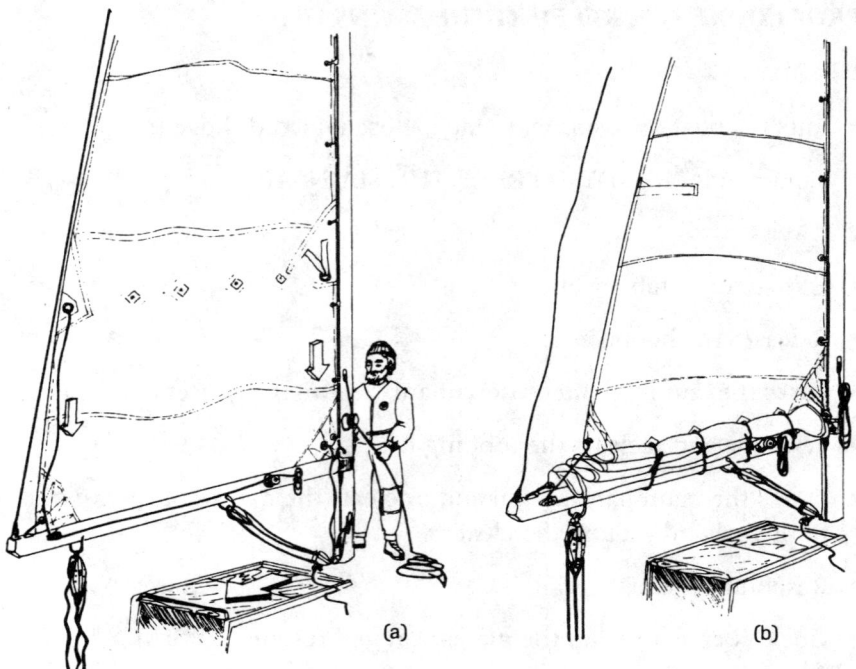

Figure 24-2 – Reefing the Mainsail

(a) The sail is ready to be reefed.

Hatch closed
Released boomvang
Tensioned topping lift
Eased cunningham
Halyard uncleated
Eased mainsheet
Crew "READY"

(b) The reef is completed.
Luff cringle on the reefing hook
Halyard tensioned and secured
Leech reef line tensioned
Topping lift eased
Boomvang re-tensioned
Mainsheet re-tensioned

- On the way aft to the cockpit, ties excess sailcloth loosely at the reefing points with reef knots, being careful not to distort the shape of the sail.

SHAKING OUT THE REEF

This procedure is almost the reverse of putting in a reef.

HELM:

- Puts the boat on a starboard tack, closehauled or hove-to.
- Commands "READY TO SHAKE OUT THE REEF".

CREW:

- Closes the hatch cover.

- On the way forward, unties the reef ties.
- Releases the boomvang.
- Tensions and cleats the topping lift.
- Responds "READY."
- Cockpit crew releases the mainsheet and responds "READY."

HELM:

- Commands "SHAKE OUT THE REEF."

CREW:

- Releases the leech reefing line.
- Uncleats the main halyard and eases it slightly so the luff cringle can be removed from the gooseneck, or releases the luff reef line.
- Tensions and re-cleats the main halyard.
- Eases and re-cleats the topping lift.
- Tensions and cleats the cunningham, the downhaul and adjusts the gooseneck if necessary.
- Responds "REEF SHAKEN OUT."

HELM:

- Commands "HARDEN THE MAINSHEET."

CREW:

- Tensions and re-cleats the boomvang.
- Makes off the halyard.

Procedure for reefing down to the second or third reef points is the same.

Some foresails have reef points and can be reefed in much the same way.

SAFETY TIP:
Though the mainsheet must be completely eased during reefing and shaking out a reef, it must be hardened to closehauled position to give you support when you are working along the boom tying or untying the reef ties.

Chapter 25 – Lowering Sail

The sail closest to the wind, the foresail, is lowered first to assist in maintaining control of the boat with the mainsail. We will continue to assume that the foresail halyard cleat is on the port side of the mast.

LOWERING THE FORESAIL

HELM:

- Puts the boat on a port tack, closehauled.
- Commands "READY TO LOWER THE FORESAIL."

CREW:

- One crew goes forward on the windward side with the sailbag to the pulpit and kneels on one knee on the windward side of the forestay.
- A second crewmember moves to the port side of the mast, drops the halyard coil, uncleats the halyard, keeping a turn around the cleat and makes sure the halyard is free to run.
- Cockpit crew uncleats the foresail sheet and stands ready to ease it.
- All crew respond "READY."

On a small boat or if short handed, one crewmember can control and lower the foresail by taking the halyard around the cleat and moving forward to the pulpit with the halyard.

HELM:

- Commands "LOWER THE FORESAIL."

CREW:

- The crew at the mast lowers the halyard while the crew in the pulpit pulls the sail down. The cockpit crew maintains control of the clew while the sail is being lowered so the sail does not fall into the water.
- The crew in the pulpit removes the halyard from the head of the sail, shackling it to the pulpit or mast ring.
- The crew on the halyard snugs up and cleats the halyard.
- Both crew flake the foresail along the deck, flat-folding it forward from the clew to the forestay, leaving the sheets to one side. The sailbag is worked over the folded sail, enclosing it right to the hanks. The drawstring is tightened and the bag is secured.

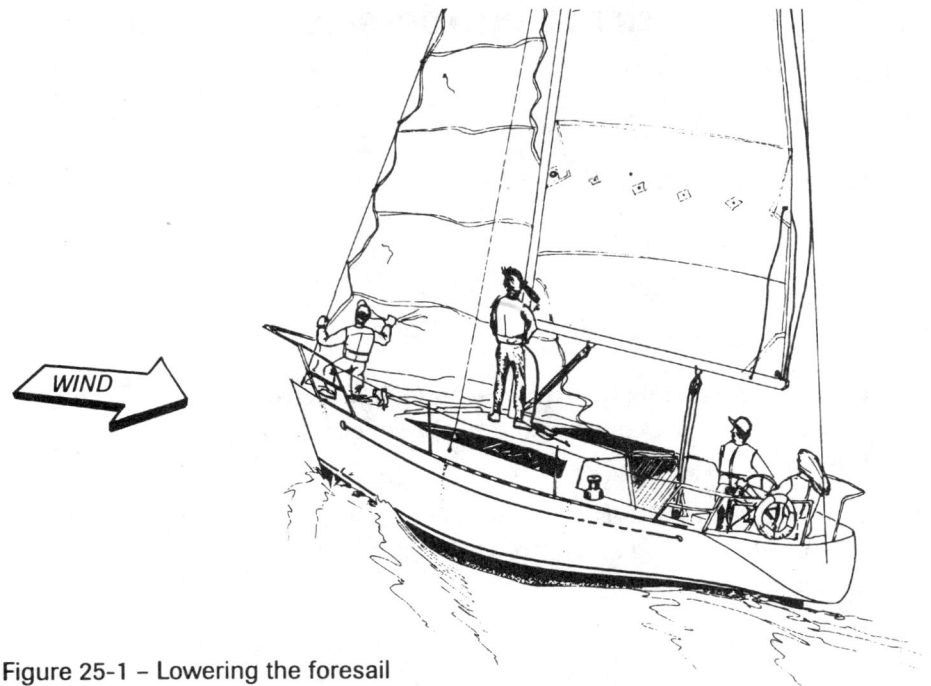

Figure 25-1 – Lowering the foresail

- Crew advises "FORESAIL SECURED."
- Makes off the halyard.
- Snugs up and cleats the sheets, leaving the figure eight knots in the ends and makes sure no lines are trailing over the side.

The foresail and sheets are not removed and stowed below until the boat is at the dock or at anchor or at a mooring buoy. If the foresail is in the way for anchoring, swing the bag up so it rests against the pulpit. Both sails must always be ready for use in case of engine failure.

> **SAFETY TIP:**
> When in the pulpit, work on one knee for steadiness and to protect your back, with the other foot flat on the deck.
>
> When lowering the foresail, hook your elbow around the forestay so you can be secure while using both hands to lower the sail.
>
> When working on the foredeck, folding the sail or stowing it in its bag, face the sea so you can anticipate the motion of the boat or the likelihood of taking a wave over the bow.

FURLING THE ROLLER FURLING FORESAIL

HELM:

- Puts the boat on a closehauled course.
- Commands "FURL THE FORESAIL."

CREW:

- Uncleats the furling line and makes sure it will run freely.
- Uncleats the leeward sheet.
- Hauls on the furling line while keeping light tension on the sheets. Furling should be continued until the sheets are wrapped a couple of times about the sail.
- To furl in strong winds, ease the sheets first or the sail may unfurl completely, creating a dangerous situation if you release the furling line first.
- Cleats and coils the furling line.
- Tidies the sheets, cleating them loosely.

LOWERING THE MAINSAIL

When the mainsail is lowered the boat must be head to wind for control and to keep the sail from filling with wind.

HELM:

- Turns on the engine and motors slowly head to wind with just enough power to maintain good steerage.
- Commands "READY TO LOWER THE MAINSAIL."

CREW:

- Closes the hatch cover.
- Releases the boomvang.
- Eases the cunningham or downhaul and adjusts the gooseneck if necessary.
- Tensions and re-cleats the topping lift.
- Drops the main halyard coil and uncleats the halyard, keeping one turn of the halyard around the cleat and making sure the halyard is free to run.

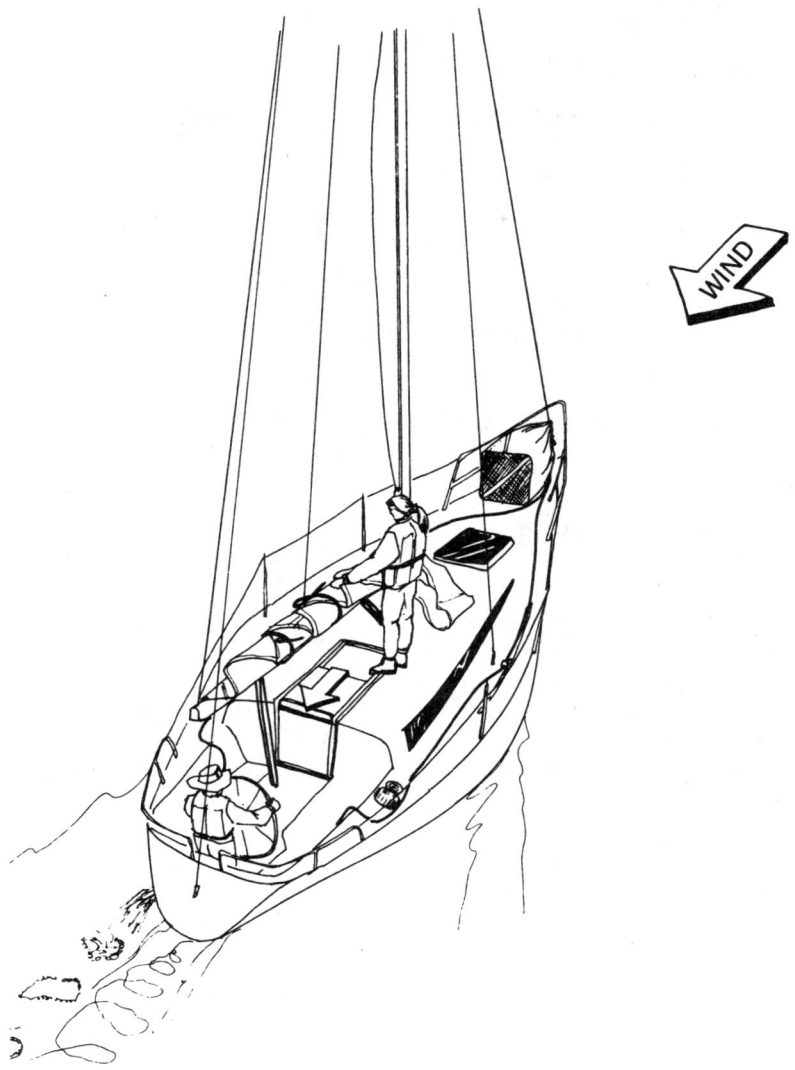

Figure 25-2 – Lowering and Flaking the Mainsail

- Responds "READY."
- Cockpit crew releases the mainsheet and responds "READY."

HELM:

- Checks that the boat is still head to wind.
- Commands "LOWER THE MAINSAIL."

CREW:

- Eases the main halyard and pulls the sail down quickly
- Hardens and cleats the mainsheet as soon as the sail is down.
- Cleats off the halyard.
- Flakes the sail neatly, making sure the battens lie parallel to the boom.
- Secures the sail along the boom with sail ties or furling line.
- Adjusts boomvang, topping lift and mainsheet so the boom is horizontal. Recleats each.
- Advises helmsman "MAINSAIL SECURED."

HELM:

- Steers desired course.

CREW:

- Makes off halyard.
- Coils the mainsheet.

The main halyard is not removed from the head of the sail and the sail cover is not put on until the boat is at dock, again in case of engine failure.

SECTION D:
NAVIGATION AND SEAMANSHIP

Ashore Knowledge for this section consists of navigation, the art of safe passage-making using charts, publications and instruments, which are mostly electronic. There are two principal types of navigation. Coastal Navigation, applying to inland and coastal waters, is concerned with the use of land-based or inshore (close to shore) reference points for determining the boat's position. Celestial navigation is practiced by sailors making ocean passages who determine their boat's position by reference to the sun, moon and selected stars and planets.

Seamanship is a catch-all word relating to all the abilities needed by a professional or amateur seaman. It involves navigating, maintaining and handling a vessel, experience, competence, judgement and common sense.

The ability to anchor a boat securely and to handle a crew overboard situation successfully are two aspects of seamanship explored in the Afloat Skills.

ASHORE KNOWLEDGE

Main Topics:
- Reading a Chart
- Aids to Navigation
- The Tide and Current Tables

Chapter 26 – Reading a Chart

A chart differs from a map in that it emphasizes and provides more detail on water features (e.g. depths, hazards, type of seabed) and places less emphasis and provides fewer details on land features except those useful for navigation (e.g. lighthouses, bridges, land contours). A remarkable amount of information is included on a chart.

The Canadian Hydrographic Service (CHS), publishes approximately 1000 official charts covering the navigable waters of Canada. Charts and publications used for navigation may be purchased in marine stores and **chandleries** (marine hardware stores) or directly from the CHS.

Figure 26-1 – The Title Block

Each chart has both a number and a title. In this section of a title block:

- The scale of the chart is 1:40 000 meaning that one distance unit on the chart represents 40,000 such units on the surface of the earth.

- The projection is Mercator, the most common projection used for charts in the middle latitudes of the earth.

- The units of measurement for depths of water are metres as are the units of measurement for elevations on land and clearances, (eg. bridge clearances).

Carefully inspect the title block of each chart you use, because the information given regarding scale, projection and units of measurement differs from chart to chart.

MEASURING DISTANCE

The way you measure distance on a chart depends on the projection as stated in the title block. Unfortunately it is not possible to represent part of the earth's spherical surface on a flat piece of paper without there being at least some distortion. The larger the part of the earth's surface represented on a chart, the greater the distortion.

Distance on a Mercator chart is measured along the latitude scale at the side of the chart.

On a Polyconic chart distance is measured on the distance scale provided.

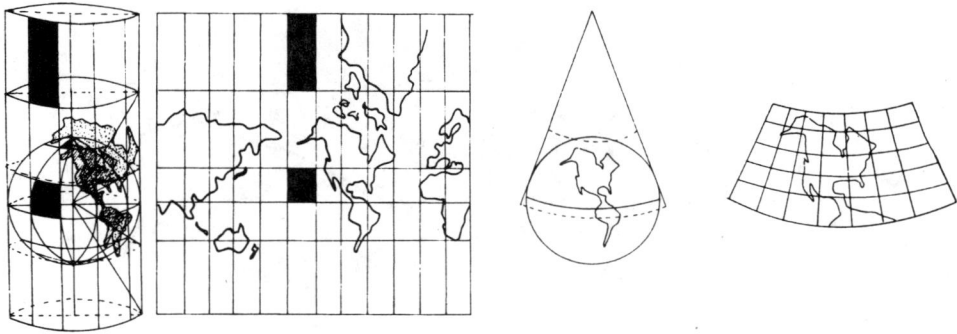

Figure 26-2 (a) Mercator Projection (b) Polyconic projection

Figure 26-2 (a) Mercator Projection
A map or chart made from a projection such as this is a Mercator projection. Latitude and Longitude lines are straight lines. Distortion increases the further away from the Equator because the Longitude lines don't converge at the poles.

Figure 26-2 (b) Polyconic Projection
A projection made using a number of cones is a polyconic projection. The lines of Longitude converge at the poles and the lines of Latitude curve away from the Equator.

On a Mercator chart the measurement of distance along the latitude scale at the side of the chart is based on the fact that **one minute of arc on a Great Circle equals one nautical mile.** Each Meridian of Longitude together with its corresponding Meridian of Longitude on the opposite side of the earth is a Great Circle because, if you could slice the earth in two through these meridians, the earth would be divided into two equal parts. The latitude scale on each side of your chart lies along a Meridian of Longitude which is part of a Great Circle. If this is confusing, think of a tall building in which you can take an elevator from one floor (Parallel of Latitude) to another floor (another Parallel of Latitude) with the elevator shaft being the Meridian of Longitude.

Distances on charts are expressed in nautical miles, unless otherwise stated. **The nautical mile is equal to 1852 meters or 6076 feet.** This is a little longer than the **statute** (land) mile of 1610 meters or 5280 ft. When you are wearing your sailing hat, refer to nautical miles simply as "miles."

Sixty nautical miles is equal to one degree of latitude. If you lived on the fiftieth Parallel of Latitude you would be 3000 nautical miles (multiply 60 x 50) north of the equator.

A *cable* is .1 (one tenth) of a nautical mile, or about 200 meters (600 ft.)

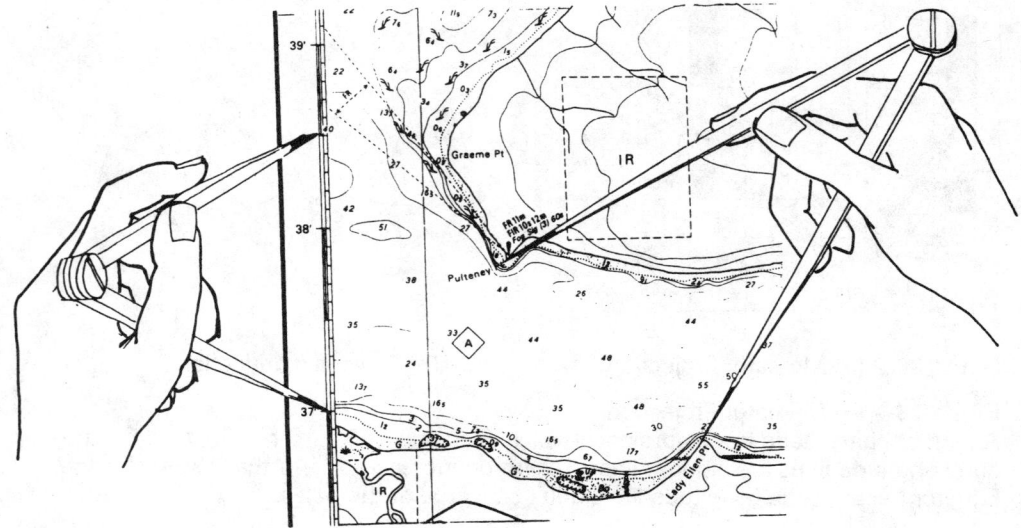

Figure 26-3 – Measuring distance using the latitude scale.
The distance between Pulteney Point and Lady Ellen Point is 1.5 nautical miles

Dividers are used to measure distance on a chart. If you are measuring a distance longer than the span of your dividers, set the dividers to a convenient span and step the dividers between the two places. If there is a small step at the end, add it to distances stepped off by the dividers to arrive at the total distance. For best accuracy, measure on the part of the scale that is on the same latitude as the area of interest.

Never measure distance along the scales at the top and bottom of the chart. The meridians converge at the poles and one degree equals 60 miles only at the equator.

DEPTHS AND HEIGHTS

The units used for *soundings* (depths) are stated in the title block. On metric charts the legend METRIC/METRIQUE set in large type and printed in magenta colour is displayed in the border of the chart. The Canadian Hydrographic Service (CHS) is issuing new charts in metric units. During the transition period depths are expressed in the following ways on Canadian charts:

- Metres and decimetres (tenths of metes).

- Fathoms and feet (a fathom is six feet).

- Feet.

- Fathoms and fractions of fathoms on a few older charts.

Chart datum is the plane of reference, or baseline, for soundings and is stated in the title block. Chart datum is the low water plane to which are referenced the depths of water over features permanently covered by the sea and the elevations of those features which are periodically covered and uncovered. Very occasionally low water can be expected to fall below chart datum.

The significance of chart tints is:

- Tan — Land which under normal circumstance is not covered by water.

- Green — The green tint between the high and low water lines identifies drying areas. In tidal waters this is foreshore that covers and uncovers with the change in tidal height. When the tidal height coincides with chart datum the green tinted area is dry.

- Blue — The blue tint emphasizes the shallow water areas. The extent of the blue tint can vary. Normally a full blue tint (the deeper blue) is shown between chart datum and 5 meters, 18 feet, or 3 fathoms depth. The lighter blue normally shows depths between 5–10 metres, 18–36 feet or 3–6 fathoms.

- White — White indicates deeper water. To determine depth consult the contour lines on the white area of the chart.

While figures in the blue and white areas of a chart indicate depths below chart datum, underlined figures on drying areas or in brackets against drying features are elevations <u>above</u> chart datum. (Memory aid: Think of the underline as the datum line, with the number being <u>above</u> the line).

> **SAFETY TIP:**
> When in doubt as to how to interpret a depth or elevation figure on a chart, always assume the worst case to be true. Assuming the worst case scenario is standard operating procedure for the prudent navigator.

ROCKS, WRECKS AND OTHER NASTIES

Chart No 1: Symbols, Abbreviations, Terms explains the symbols, abbreviations and terms used on charts published by the CHS. Learn to recognize the common symbols and abbreviations. Consult *Chart No. 1* whenever you come across an unfamiliar symbol or abbreviation.

Figures 26-4 to 26-7 are excerpts from *Chart No. 1*. On the left side of each is the current symbology as per the "International Chart

Rocks			Roches
10		Rock which does not cover, with elevation Roche qui ne couvre pas, avec altitude	
11		Rock which covers and uncovers, with drying height Roche qui couvre et découvre, avec sonde découvrante	
12		Rock awash at chart datum Roche à fleur d'eau au zéro des cartes	
13		Dangerous underwater rock of 2m (6 ft) or less Roche dangereuse submergée de 2m (6 pi) ou moins	

Figure 26-4 – Symbols for rocks.

Wrecks		SNS/SCNS c	Épaves
24		Wreck showing any portion of hull or superstructure Épave montrant une portion de la coque ou superstructure	
25	Mast/Mât	Wreck, masts visible Épave, mâts visibles	Masts/Mâts
28		Dangerous wreck, depth unknown Épave dangereuse, profondeur inconnue	

Figure 26-5 – Wrecks

Submarine cables			Câbles sous-marins
30.1		Submarine cable Câble sous-marin	
30.2		Submarine cable area Zone de câbles sous-marins	

Submarine pipelines		SNS/SCNS a-c	Conduites sous-marines
40.1	Oil/Pétrole Gas/Gaz (see/voir Note)	Oil or gas pipeline Oléoduc ou gazoduc	Oil/Pétrole Gas/Gaz
43	Obstn	Diffuser, crib (depth known) Diffuseur, caisson (de profondeur connue)	

Figures 26-6 – Submarine Cables and Pipelines – The presence of a submarine (submerged) cable and pipeline may be indicated by a sign as well as the symbol on the chart. Do not anchor in a submarine cable or pipeline area.

A crib is an underwater structure, often made of wood, with rock in the middle as a foundation e.g. the foundation for a daybeacon.

Types of seabed			SNS/SCNS a-1	Genres de fond marin	
1	S	Sand Sable		S	s
2	M	Mud Vase		M	m
3	Cy	Clay Argile		Cy	Cl cl
4	Si	Silt, Ooze Limon, Boue, Fange		Si	Oz oz
6	G	Gravel Gravier		G	g
9	R	Rock, Rocky, Shingle Roche, Rocheux, Galets		R	r Rk Rky Sn shin
13.1	Wd	Weeds Herbes marines		Wd	Wds
13.2	〰️	Kelp Varech		〰️	

Figure 26-7 – Types of Seabed – When choosing an anchorage you want to know the type of seabed (bottom) because each style of anchor is designed to hold best in a certain type or types of seabed.

Specifications" of the International Hydrographic Organization (IHO). On the right is the symbology appearing on CHS charts.

Apart from rocks, wrecks, submerged cables, cribs, shallow areas and kelp, other navigation hazards you may encounter include:

- uncharted rocks, reefs and shoals (shallow areas)
- strong currents
- objects in the water. For example:
  - floating synthetic rope and floating plastic may foul your propeller.
  - fishing floats or nets.
  - logs and deadheads (logs which have become so water-logged that they are almost entirely submerged. A deadhead usually assumes a vertical position with its upper end awash or just below the surface, making it extremely difficult to see).
- fishing vessels with outlying gear
- tugs with long tows
- failure of an aid to navigation. For example:
  –a buoy missing or out of position
  –a light that is not working

Chapter 27 – Aids to Navigation

Aids to navigation are devices or systems *external* to a vessel which are provided to help a mariner determine position or course, to warn of dangers or obstructions, or to advise the location of the best or preferred route. The Canadian Coast Guard, part of the Department of Transport, is responsible for the provision of aids to navigation in major Canadian waters. The Canadian Coast Guard publication The *Canadian Aids to Navigation System* explains the system in detail. The *Safe Boating Guide* also contains some information on aids to navigation.

Aids to navigation may be floating (such as buoys) or fixed (such as lighthouses), and may be lighted or unlighted. Only lights, buoys, and daybeacons are presented here.

A reference card on the subject is available from the Canadian Yachting Association.

LIGHTS

Lights may be:

- Fixed: A light which is continuous, steady and constant in colour.
- Rhythmic: flashing in a rhythm of single or grouped flashes.
- Alternating: rhythmic and showing light of alternating colours.

The flash characteristic of a light denotes either a specific aid to navigation or a type of aid. The colour and flash characteristic is printed in abbreviated form on the chart adjacent to the light symbol. If the light characteristic is not followed by an abbreviation for a colour, the light is a white light. For example, FlG means "flashing green" whereas Fl means "flashing white".

A flashing light (Fl) flashes once every 4 seconds. A quick flashing light (Q) flashes every second. A very quick flash (VQ) is 120 flashes per minute.

In Figure 28-5 on page 173 the light on Licka Point is a quick flashing white and red alternating light (QWR); the Cracroft Point light is flashing red (FlR).

Figure 27-1 – The symbol for a light.

On a standard chart lights are shown in magenta. A number of important chart features are represented in the colour magenta.

Lightstations such as lighthouses are fixed structures equipped with a light and are located in prominent positions. The flash characteristics of a light identifies a light station. No two lightstations in an area will have lights with the same colour and flash characteristic.

Other fixed lights warn of shallow areas or obstructions, or guide the mariner safely into harbour.

The light symbol is frequently added to the symbol for a buoy to indicate on the chart that the aid is a lighted aid. At night the colour and flash characteristic of a buoy indicate its type and function.

Many lights have sun switches that turn the lights off in daylight.

The *List of Lights, Buoys and Fog Signals* is published for four geographic regions of Canada. Each volume lists by number every lighted aid to navigation in the region together with a detailed description of the aid.

LATERAL AIDS TO NAVIGATION

The Canadian aids to navigation system is a combined Lateral-Cardinal system. Be able to recognize and interpret the aids for both. Lateral aids may be either buoys or fixed aids. Lateral aids indicate the location of hazards and of the safest or deepest water by indicating the side on which they are to be passed. The key to correct interpretation of lateral aids is knowing the **upstream direction**.

The upstream direction is the direction taken by a vessel when proceeding from seaward, towards the headwaters of a river, into a

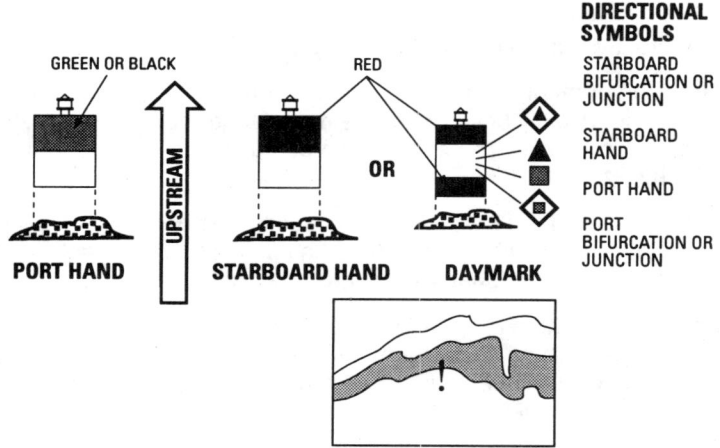

Figure 27-2 – Lateral System – Fixed Aids – Lighted

harbour, or with the flood tide. **In general the upstream direction is in a southerly direction along the Atlantic coast, in a northerly direction along the Pacific coast** and in an easterly direction along the Arctic Coast. In some waters the upstream direction is indicated on the charts by the use of lines and arrows.

When proceeding in the upstream direction, starboard hand aids are kept to starboard (to your right) and port hand aids are kept to port (to your left). In the Americas and Japan the colour red is associated with starboard hand aids and the colour green with port hand aids. Colours are reversed elsewhere in the world. Always check local publications. Shape is also significant. Pointed shapes (red triangles, or cones point up) are associated with starboard hand aids; flat topped shapes (green squares and flat topped buoys) are associated with port hand aids. Diamond shapes are associated with **bifurcation** (junctions).

When proceeding downstream the situation is reversed. Starboard hand aids are kept to port (to your left) and port hand aids are kept to starboard (to your right).

STANDARD DAYBEACONS

PORT HAND — BLACK OR GREEN
PORT BIFURCATION / JUNCTION
UPSTREAM
STARBOARD BIFURCATION / JUNCTION
STARBOARD HAND — RED

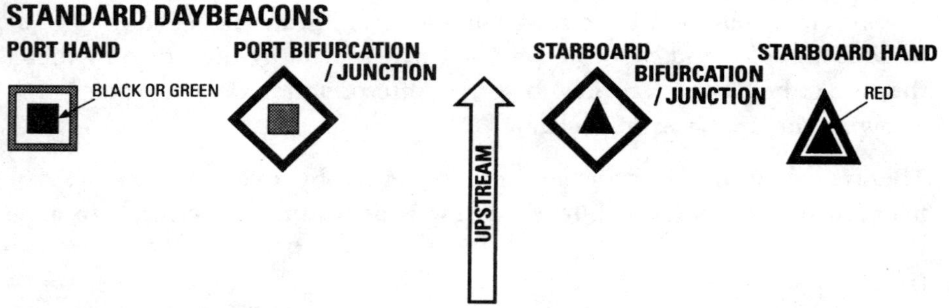

Figure 27-3 – Lateral System – Fixed Aids – Unlighted

Daybeacons are used primarily to assist the mariner during daylight hours, and are usually unlit. Reflective material on the daybeacons improves the ability to identify them at night with the aid of a searchlight.

When proceeding upstream the port hand daybeacon must be kept on the boat's port (left side) the starboard hand daybeacon must be kept on the boat's starboard (right side).

A bifurcation daybeacon with a red triangle should be left on the boat's starboard (right) side, thus the preferred channel is to the left. A bifurcation daybeacon with a green square should be left on the boat's port (left) side, thus the preferred channel is to the right.

BUOYS

The shape and/or colour of a buoy and the colour and flash characteristic of its light indicate its function.

The standard buoy shapes are cylindrical (can), conical, pillar, spar and spherical. The tall, lighted, pillar buoys are used in main traffic areas. The smaller, less expensive, usually unlit can, conical, spar and spherical buoys are placed in areas of lesser traffic.

Because the colour of a buoy may be altered by rust or fouling by birds, it is helpful to be able to identify the function of a buoy by its shape. Unlit starboard hand buoys all have pointed tops (conical and starboard spar buoy; and starboard bifurcation buoy). Unlit port hand buoys all have flat tops (can and port spar buoy; and port bifurcation buoy). A spherical shape indicates that the buoy is marking the center of a channel or safe water.

The use of **topmarks** (a shape or shapes on top of a buoy) as an additional means of daytime buoy identification is, at the time of publication, restricted to the isolated danger buoy and cardinal buoys in ice-free conditions. Topmarks, being very susceptible to damage are not used in Canada to the extent that they are in other parts of the world because of our harsh environmental conditions.

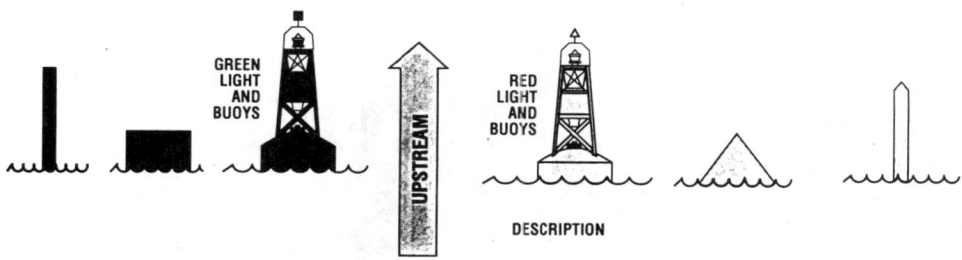

Figure 27-4 – Lateral system – Port and Starboard Hand Buoys

SAFETY TIP:
The correct interpretation of aids to navigation can be difficult. Always refer to your chart to confirm the location of safe water.

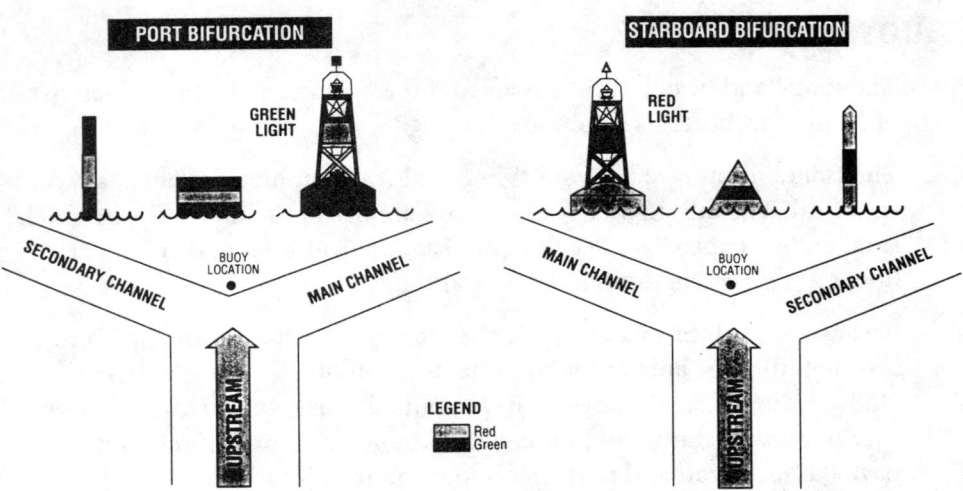

Figure 27-5 – Lateral System – Port and Starboard Bifurcation Buoys

These buoys mark the point where a channel divides.

The dominant colour on a starboard bifurcation buoy is the top colour, red, thus when proceeding upstream it should be kept on the boat's starboard hand, meaning that the preferred channel is to the left.

The dominant colour on a port bifurcation buoy is the top colour, green, thus it should be kept on the boat's port hand, meaning that the preferred channel is to the right.

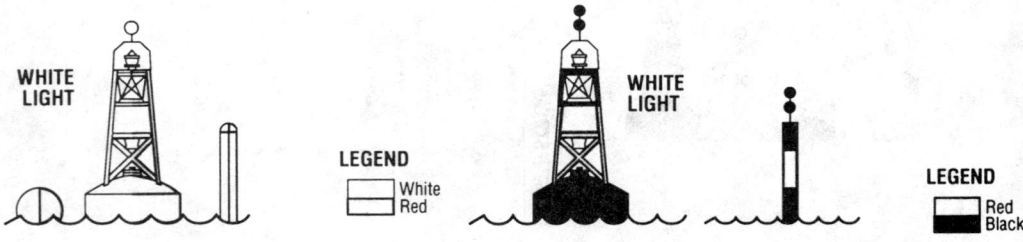

Figure 27-6 – Lateral System – Fairway Buoy

A fairway buoy indicates safe water and is used to mark channel entrances and channel centers. It may be passed on either side but should be kept to port (left) when proceeding in either direction.

Figure 27-7 – Lateral System – Isolated Danger Buoy

This buoy marks an isolated danger which has safe water all around it. Consult your chart for the dimensions and depth of the danger.

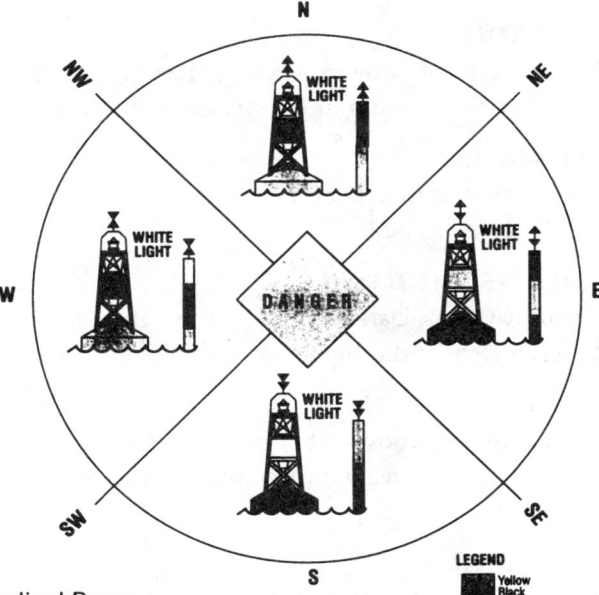

Figure 27-8 – Cardinal Buoys

Cardinal aids indicate the location of hazards and of the safest or deepest water by reference to the four cardinal points of the compass. There are four cardinal buoys, North, South, East and West, which are positioned so that the safest or deepest water is to be found to the named side of the buoy. (eg. to the north of a north cardinal buoy). This keeps the buoy between you and danger.

If a cardinal buoy does not carry a light it is normally spar shaped with topmarks as shown, although other shapes may be used.

The following are classified as special buoys:

CAUTIONARY:
A yellow cautionary buoy marks dangers such as firing ranges, underwater pipeline, race courses, seaplane bases and areas where no through channel exists. A cautionary buoy may also be used as a traffic separation marker, in which case it has lateral significance and is treated as a fairway buoy (ie. kept on your port side when proceeding in either direction). Consult your chart to determine the specific danger being marked.

ANCHORAGE:
A yellow anchorage buoy marks the perimeter of designated anchorage areas. Consult the chart for water depth.

MOORING:
An orange and white mooring buoy is used for mooring or securing vessels. A vessel may be secured to such a buoy.

INFORMATION:
A white information buoy displays information such as locality, marina, campsite, etc. within the orange square.

CONTROL:
A white control buoy indicated speed limits, wash restrictions, etc. Obey the restriction illustrated within the orange circle.

 **KEEP-OUT:**
A white and orange keep out buoy marks areas in which boats are prohibited.

 **SCIENTIFIC (ODAS):**
A yellow Ocean Data Acquisition System buoy collects meterological and other scientific data.

 **DIVING:**
A white diving buoy with a red flag with a diagonal white stripe marks an area where scuba or other such diving activity is in progress.

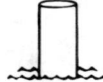 **SWIMMING:**
A white swimming buoy marks the perimeter of swimming areas. It may not be charted.

Chapter 28 – The Tide & Current Tables

The Canadian Tide and Current Tables are published in six volumes and two composite volumes to cover all tidal waters in Canada. Buy the right volume for your area.

The Tide Tables provide predicted times and heights of the high and low waters associated with the vertical movement of the tide. These tables are necessary for obtaining the depth of water under the keel or over a shoal, and for anchoring.

The Current Tables provide predicted times for **slack water** (when there is little or no horizontal flow of water) and the times and velocities of maximum current, all of which are associated with the horizontal movement of the tide. This information is needed for efficient navigation. It is required when navigating narrow passes or channels that have strong current and for safety when the wind is against the current causing steep waves (tide rips).

The tides are caused by the gravitational attraction of the sun and the moon. The attractions of these two celestial bodies causes large bulges in the sea affecting both sides of the earth as shown in Figure 28-2. Because the moon is closer to the earth the moon's gravitational attraction is stronger and has a much greater influence on tides.

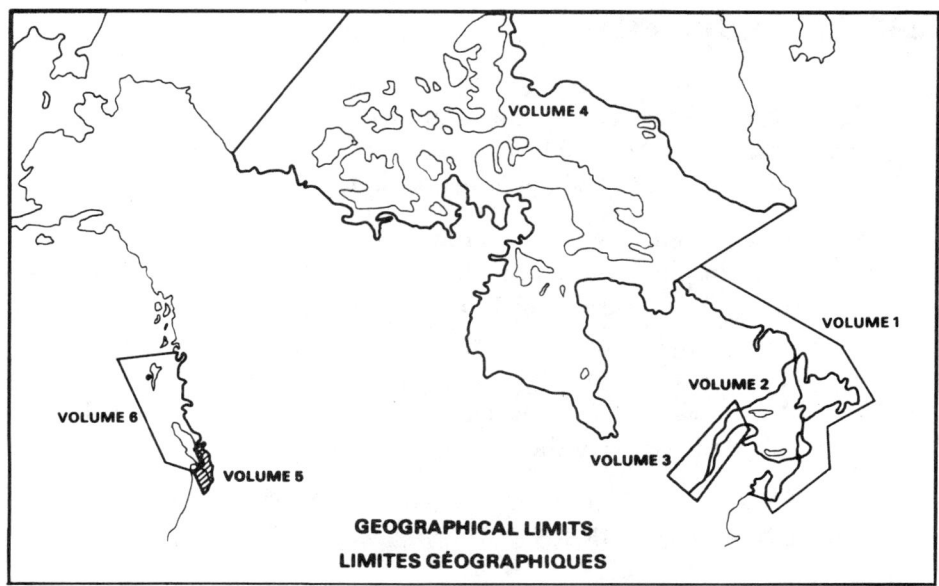

Figure 28-1 – Tide table coverage areas
This map shows the geographical limits of the various volumes of the Canadian Tide and Current Tables.

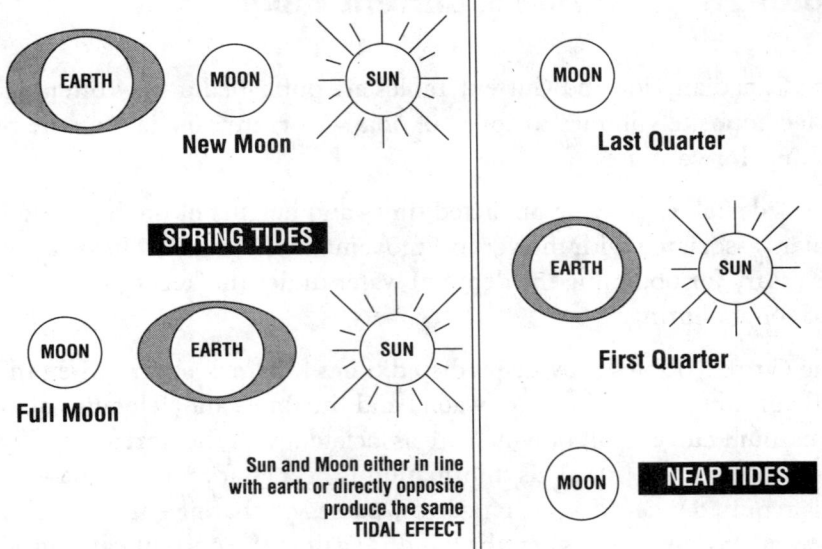

Figure 28-2 – Tidal forces

Meteorological conditions can cause differences between the predicted and the observed tide. These differences are mainly the result of barometric pressure changes and strong, prolonged winds. Currents are particularly sensitive to the effects of wind. The times of slack water can be advanced or retarded considerably by strong winds.

READING A TIDE TABLE

Reference ports are those for which predictions are published in the form of daily tables of times and heights of high and low waters. Some locations have two high tides and two low tides during a 24 hour period, others have only one high tide and one low tide daily.

When the tide is flooding, the water level is rising; when it is ebbing the water level is dropping. When the tide has risen to its high level there is a short period called the *stand of the tide* when there is no change in water level. After it has fallen to its low level there is another stand. The daily highs and the daily lows are seldom equal in height. The difference between a high water and low water or between a low water and a high water is called the *range* of the tide.

TO DETERMINE THE HIGH AND LOW TIDES FOR POINT ATKINSON, AUGUST 3RD, 1992:

1. Find the daily tide tables for July, August and September for Point Atkinson as shown in Figure 28-3. Use the book's Table of Contents, or thumb through the book until you come to the appropriate page. The

POINT ATKINSON PST Z+8 **TIDE TABLES**

1992

JULY-JUILLET							AUGUST-AOUT							SEPTEMBER-SEPTEMBRE						
Day	Time	Ht /ft	Ht /m	Jour	Heure	H /pi	H /m	Day	Time	Ht /ft	Ht /m	Jour	Heure	H /pi	H /m	Day	Time	Ht /ft	Ht /m	Jour	Heure	H /pi	H /m
1 WE ME	0425 1150 1920	14.0 .3 15.6	4.3 .1 4.8	16 TH JE	0045 0520 1220 1935	10.4 12.6 3.1 14.8	3.2 3.8 .9 4.5	1 SA SA	0110 0635 1300 1945	7.9 13.6 3.6 15.8	2.4 4.1 1.1 4.8	16 SU DI	0115 0650 1255 1925	7.6 12.5 5.9 14.3	2.3 3.8 1.8 4.4	1 TU MA	0215 0850 1415 2005	4.1 13.4 8.8 14.8	1.2 4.1 2.7 4.5	16 WE ME	0140 0825 1350 1915	4.6 13.2 9.3 13.5	1.4 4.0 2.8 4.1
2 TH JE	0040 0525 1235 1955	10.5 13.8 .9 15.9	3.2 4.2 .3 4.8	17 FR VE	0125 0610 1250 2000	9.8 12.4 3.8 14.8	3.0 3.8 1.2 4.5	2 SU DI	0200 0740 1345 2015	6.8 13.1 5.3 16.7	2.1 4.0 1.6 4.8	17 MO LU	0150 0740 1325 1950	6.9 12.3 6.9 14.2	2.1 3.7 2.1 4.3	2 WE ME	0310 1005 1510 2040	4.0 13.2 10.0 14.3	1.2 4.0 3.0 4.4	17 TH JE	0220 0920 1435 1945	4.3 13.1 10.1 13.3	1.3 4.0 3.1 4.1
3 FR VE	0135 0630 1320 2030	9.7 13.3 2.1 15.9	3.0 4.1 .6 4.8	18 SA SA	0200 0655 1320 2025	9.2 12.1 4.7 14.7	2.8 3.7 1.4 4.5	3 MO LU	0255 0850 1430 2050	5.9 12.5 7.2 15.6	1.8 3.8 2.2 4.8	18 TU MA	0225 0830 1400 2010	6.3 12.2 8.0 14.1	1.9 3.7 2.4 4.3	3 TH JE	0405 1130 1620 2125	4.2 13.1 11.0 13.6	1.3 4.0 3.4 4.1	18 FR VE	0305 1030 1530 2020	4.1 13.3 10.8 13.1	1.2 4.0 3.3 4.0
4 SA SA	0230 0735 1405 2105	8.8 12.6 3.7 15.9	2.7 3.8 1.1 4.8	19 SU DI	0240 0745 1355 2045	8.5 11.7 5.8 14.8	2.6 3.6 1.8 4.5	4 TU MA	0350 1010 1520 2130	5.2 12.2 8.9 16.2	1.6 3.7 2.7 4.6	19 WE ME	0305 0930 1440 2040	5.8 12.0 9.1 13.9	1.8 3.7 2.8 4.2	4 FR VE	0500 1305 1750 2215	4.5 13.3 11.5 12.8	1.4 4.1 3.5 3.9	19 SA SA	0400 1150 1645 2105	4.0 13.3 11.3 12.8	1.2 4.1 3.4 3.9
5 SU DI	0330 0845 1450 2140	7.7 11.9 5.6 15.8	2.3 3.6 1.7 4.8	20 MO LU	0320 0840 1425 2110	7.9 11.3 7.0 14.5	2.4 3.4 2.1 4.4	5 WE ME	0450 1155 1620 2210	4.7 12.2 10.4 14.6	1.4 3.7 3.2 4.5	20 TH JE	0350 1045 1525 2105	5.3 12.0 10.2 13.7	1.6 3.7 3.1 4.2	5 SA SA	0605 1420 2320	4.7 13.6 12.2	1.4 4.1 3.7	20 SU DI	0500 1310 2215	3.9 13.6 12.4	1.2 4.1 3.8
6 MO LU	0435 1010 1535 2220	6.6 11.4 7.5 15.6	2.0 3.5 2.3 4.8	21 TU MA	0405 0945 1500 2135	7.2 11.1 8.2 14.3	2.2 3.4 2.5 4.4	6 TH JE	0550 1340 1740 2255	4.4 12.7 11.5 14.0	1.3 3.9 3.5 4.3	21 FR VE	0445 1220 1630 2145	4.8 12.2 11.2 13.5	1.5 3.7 3.4 4.1	6 SU DI	0715 1510 2050	4.8 13.9	1.5 4.2	21	0610	3.9	1.2
7 TU MA	0535 1200 1635 2300	5.6 11.4 9.4 15.3	1.7 3.5 2.9 4.7	22 WE ME	0450 1110 1545 2205	6.4 11.1 9.5 14.1	2.0 3.4 2.9 4.3	7 FR VE	0655 1505 1920 2350	4.1 13.4 12.0 13.4	1.2 4.1 3.7 4.1	22 SA SA	0545 1400	4.7				0005 0605 1200 1805	6.2 13.1 6.9 13.8	1.9 4.0 2.1 4.2	28 MO LU	0015 0650 1230 1805	3.3 14.5 8.3 14.8	1.0 4.4 2.5 4.5
8 WE ME	0635 1355 1750 2340	4.6 12.0 10.9 14.8	1.4 3.7 3.3 4.5	23 TH JE	0540 1255 1645 2240	5.6 11.4 10.7 13.9	1.7 3.5 3.3 4.2	8 SA SA	0750 1600 2050	3.9 12.7 6.7				4.6 2.0		SU DI				MO LU			
9 TH JE	0730 1525 1920	3.8 13.0 11.8	1.2 4.0 3.6	24	0635 1440	4.6				1.3 4.3 4.4	SA SA	0540 1200 1820	14.0 4.4 15.4	4.3 1.3 4.7	14 MO LU	0035 0650 1235 1825	5.5 13.2 7.7 13.8	1.7 4.0 2.3 4.2	29 TU MA	0015 0745 1315 1840	2.8 14.5 9.3 14.4	.9 4.4 2.8 4.4
			4.7						0045 0605 1225 1905	8.3 12.7 5.0 14.3	2.5 3.9 1.5 4.4	30 SA SA	0040 0640 1240 1855	5.5 13.9 5.9 15.4	1.7 4.2 1.8 4.7	15 TU MA	0105 0735 1310 1850	5.0 13.2 8.5 13.7	1.5 4.0 2.6 4.2	30 WE ME	0140 0845 1410 1915	2.8 14.5 10.1 13.9	.9 4.4 3.1 4.2
								31 FR VE	0020 0535 1215 1910	9.0 13.9 2.2 15.6	2.7 4.2 .7 4.8	31 MO LU	0130 0745 1330 1930	4.6 13.7 7.4 15.2	1.4 4.2 2.3 4.6								

Figure 28-3 — A typical tide table

This shows part of the page of the daily tide tables for the reference port Point Atkinson for the months of July, August and September, 1992: Each date is listed with the abbreviation for the day of the week in English and French. The first column to the right of the date and day is time. All times in the Canadian Tide & Current Tables are given in Standard Time and are based on the 24 hour clock. The letters PST at the top of the page indicate that times for Point Atkinson are in Pacific Standard Time. On a 24 hour clock 0000 h (hours) is midnight and 1200 h is noon. One in the afternoon, for example, is 1300 h and 10:45 p.m. is 2245 h.

The second, shaded column is the height of the tide in feet and the third column is the height of the tide in metres.

SAFETY TIP:
Check both chart and tide table before docking, anchoring or tying to a mooring buoy. Make sure you will have sufficient water depth during the entire time you will be there. Do not assume that docks or mooring buoys are always in deep water. Many sailors have found out that it is not so.

tide tables are in the first part of the daily pages section and are followed by the current tables. Both are listed geographically from south to north and/or in order from seaward.

2. On Monday, August 3rd, 1992:

Line 1: at 0255 (2:55 a.m.) PST there is a low tide of 5.9 ft. or 1.8 m.

Line 2: at 0850 (8:50 a.m.) PST there is a high tide of 12.5 ft. or 3.8 m.

Line 3: at 1430 (2:30 p.m.) PST the tide has fallen to the second low of the day which is a height of 7.2 ft. or 2.2 m.

Line 4: At 2050 (8:50 p.m.) PST the higher of the two high tides is 15.6 ft. or 4.8 m.

3. **When Daylight Time is in effect, one hour is added to Standard Time to calculate Daylight Time.** August 3rd falls within the Daylight Time period. One hour is added to the Pacific Standard Time given for tidal heights on that date to arrive at Pacific Daylight Time (PDT).

To find the depth of the water in a specific location, add the height of the tide to the depth shown on the chart. On August 3rd, for instance, if the charted depth in your location at 2150 PDT is 7 m, you would add 4.8 m to get a water depth of 11.8 m.

Occasionally a low tide will fall below tidal or chart datum (0.0 m or 0.0 ft.) in which case tidal height will be preceded by a minus sign. Tidal heights preceded by a minus sign are subtracted from the charted depth to determine water depth.

READING A CURRENT TABLE

The times of slack water and of maximum current as well as rates of maximum current at the reference current stations are predicted and **tabulated as daily tables**. The ***turn*** or ***slack*** is the interval when the speed of the current is very weak. These terms refer to the period of reversal between ebb and flood currents. The **ebb current** is the horizontal movement of water associated with a **falling tide**. The **flood current** is the horizontal movement of water associated with a **rising tide**. The time of slack water seldom coincides with the stand of the tide.

TO DETERMINE THE DIRECTION AND RATE OF CURRENTS AT DODD NARROWS, AUGUST 6TH, 1992:

1. Find the daily current tables for Dodd Narrows for July, August and September, 1992.

2. On Thursday, August 6th, 1992:

DODD NARROWS PST Z+8 — **1992** — CURRENT TABLES

JULY–JUILLET

Turns Day	Turns Time	Maximum Time	Maximum Rate/kn	Renverse Jour	Renverse Heure	Maximum Heure	Maximum Vit/n
1		0035	+4.6	16		0120	+3.9
	0320	0635	-8.1		0405	0715	-6.4
WE	1025	1300	+8.8	TH	1040	1335	+7.4
ME	1715	2025	-5.4	JE	1730	2030	-5.2
	2320				2355		
2		0125	+5.0	17		0200	+4.0
	0420	0725	-8.1		0445	0755	-6.2
TH	1110	1345	+8.9	FR	1110	1410	+7.2
JE	1755	2110	-5.8	VE	1755	2100	-5.3
3	0010	0215	+5.1	18	0025	0240	+4.1
	0515	0820	-7.7		0530	0840	-5.7
FR	1155	1430	+8.7	SA	1145	1435	+7.0
VE	1835	2155	-6.2	SA	1825	2125	-5.6
4	0105	0315	+5.2	19	0105	0325	+4.2
	0620	0920	-7.0		0620	0930	-5.1
SA	1240	1525	+8.2	SU	1220	1510	+6.5
SA	1915	2245	-6.4	DI	1850	2150	-5.8
5	0155	0425	+5.3	20	0140	0415	+4.4
	0720	1020	-6.1		0710	1020	-4.3
SU	1330	1620	+7.3	MO	1300	1550	+5.8
DI	2000	2330	-6.4	LU	1925	2225	-5.9
6	0250	0530	+5.6	21	0220	0505	+4.7
	0835	1125	-5.1		0810	1120	-3.7
MO	1430	1720	+6.1	TU	1345	1630	+4.9
LU	2045			MA	1955	2300	-6.0
7		0015	-6.2	22	0305	0555	+5.1
	0345	0635	+5.9		0915	1220	-3.2
TU	0955	1235	-4.2	WE	1445	1725	+3.9
MA	1535	1830	+4.9	ME	2035	2345	-5.9
	2130						
8		0110	-5.9	23	0350	0640	+5.5
	0440	0740	+6.2		1035	1330	-3.0
WE	1120	1405	-3.7	TH	1600	1835	+3.0
ME	1655	1940	+3.8	JE	2120		
	2215						
9		0210	-5.6				
							+5.6
						0625	-8.6
			+7.4	TH	1010	1250	+8.8
ME	1700	2010	-5.0	JE	1645	2000	-6.1
	2315				2300		
				31		0110	+6.1
					0415	0715	-8.3
				FR	1055	1325	+8.8
				VE	1720	2045	-6.6
					2350		

AUGUST–AOUT

Turns Day	Turns Time	Maximum Time	Maximum Rate/kn	Renverse Jour	Renverse Heure	Maximum Heure	Maximum Vit/n
1		0200	+6.4	16		0205	+5.3
	0515	0810	-7.8		0515	0825	-5.8
SA	1140	1415	+8.5	SU	1125	1355	+6.7
SA	1800	2125	-6.8	DI	1740	2035	-6.0
2	0035	0255	+6.4	17	0020	0240	+5.6
	0610	0910	-6.9		0600	0910	-5.3
SU	1225	1500	+7.7	MO	1200	1430	+6.2
DI	1840	2210	-6.8	LU	1805	2055	-6.3
3	0125	0355	+6.3	18	0050	0320	+5.7
	0710	1010	-5.9		0650	1000	-4.6
MO	1315	1600	+6.6	TU	1240	1505	+5.5
LU	1920	2250	-6.5	MA	1835	2130	-6.4
4	0215	0500	+6.3	19	0130	0405	+5.9
	0820	1115	-4.9		0740	1045	-4.0
TU	1410	1655	+5.2	WE	1330	1555	+4.4
MA	2000	2335	-6.2	ME	1910	2205	-6.3
5	0310	0605	+6.2	20	0210	0450	+6.0
	0940	1220	-4.1		0845	1150	-3.5
WE	1525	1805	+3.9	TH	1430	1650	+3.3
ME	2045			JE	1950	2255	-6.0
6		0030	-5.7	21	0300	0545	+6.0
	0405	0710	+6.2		0955	1300	-3.4
TH	1100	1340	-3.6	FR	1550	1805	+2.4
JE	1650	1920	+2.9	VE	2040	2355	
	2135						
7		0130	-5.3	22			
	0500	0830	+6.2				
FR	1215	1525	-3.8				
VE	1815	2030					
	2235						
8							
							-8.3
						1225	+8.5
					1605	1930	-6.9
					2240		
				29		0055	+7.4
			-6.5		0415	0700	-8.0
		1310	+7.1	SA	1035	1300	+8.3
	1650	2000	-5.3	SA	1645	2010	-7.2
	2315				2320		
15		0130	+5.1	30		0140	+7.5
	0435	0740	-6.3		0505	0800	-7.3
SA	1055	1330	+7.0	SU	1120	1345	+7.8
SA	1715	2015	-5.6	DI	1720	2055	-7.2
	2345						
				31	0005	0230	+7.4
					0600	0905	-6.6
				MO	1205	1430	+6.8
				LU	1800	2130	-7.0

SEPTEMBER–SEPTEMBRE

Turns Day	Turns Time	Maximum Time	Maximum Rate/kn	Renverse Jour	Renverse Heure	Maximum Heure	Maximum Vit/n
1	0050	0325	+7.2	16	0010	0235	+7.1
	0700	1000	-5.8		0630	0945	-4.9
TU	1255	1525	+5.5	WE	1230	1440	+4.7
MA	1835	2205	-6.6	ME	1755	2050	-6.7
2	0135	0425	+6.8	17	0045	0320	+7.1
	0800	1055	-5.0		0720	1035	-4.4
WE	1400	1635	+4.2	TH	1320	1530	+3.7
ME	1915	2250	-6.1	JE	1830	2125	-6.4
3	0225	0525	+6.5	18	0130	0410	+6.9
	0915	1200	-4.3		0820	1135	-4.1
TH	1515	1745	+3.0	FR	1430	1630	+2.7
JE	2000	2345	-5.5	VE	1915	2215	-5.8
4	0320	0630	+6.2	19	0220	0505	+6.6
	1030	1320	-3.9		0930	1235	-4.0
FR	1645	1855	+2.3	SA	1550	1800	+2.1
VE	2100			SA	2020	2335	-5.3
5		0050	-5.0	20	0325	0615	+6.3
	0420	0755	+5.9		1040	1345	-4.2
SA	1140	1450	-4.0	SU	1715	1935	+2.3
SA	1810	2005	+2.3	DI	2135		
	2215						
6							
		1920	-5.8	DI	1605	1935	-7.5
	2240				2255		
13		0105	+6.4	28		0120	+8.4
	0425	0730	-6.2		0500	0810	-6.8
SU	1035	1300	+6.4	MO	1105	1320	+6.6
DI	1630	1930	-6.2	LU	1640	2010	-7.4
	2310				2335		
14		0130	+6.7	29		0200	+8.1
	0505	0815	-5.8		0550	0900	-6.3
MO	1110	1325	+6.0	TU	1155	1410	+5.6
LU	1655	1950	-6.6	MA	1715	2045	-7.1
	2340						
15		0200	+7.0	30	0015	0250	+7.8
	0545	0900	-5.4		0640	0945	-5.8
TU	1145	1400	+5.5	WE	1245	1505	+4.5
MA	1720	2010	-6.8	ME	1755	2115	-6.6

88 + FLOOD/FLOT DIRECTION 335 TRUE/VRAIE - EBB/JUSANT DIRECTION 155 TRUE/VRAIE

Figure 28-4 – A typical current table

This shows part of the page of the daily current tables for the reference current station Dodd Narrows for the months of July, August and September 1992. Each date is listed with the abbreviation for the day of the week in English and French. The first column to the right of the date and day gives the time of the turn (slack), the second column in bold print gives the time of maximum current flow together with the direction and rate in knots of the maximum current. The current directions are indicated by + when the flow is from the ocean moving inland (flood tidal stream) and by a – when the current flow is back towards the ocean (ebb tidal stream). At the bottom of the page the flood and ebb tidal stream directions are given in degrees true (ie. with reference to true north as opposed to magnetic north). Tidal streams and currents are described by the direction in which they flow.

Line 1: At 0030 PST the current is ebbing at a maximum rate of 5.7 knots. Then it slows.

Line 2: At 0405 PST there is slack water at the turn and then the current begins to flood. At 0710 PST the current is flooding at a maximum rate of 6.2 knots. Then it slows.

Line 3: At 1100 PST the current turns to ebb. At 1340 PST it has reached its maximum rate of 3.6 knots. The current then slows.

Line 4: At 1650 PST there is slack water at the turn. The current then begins to flood and by 1920 PST it has reached its maximum speed of 2.9 knots.

Line 5: By 2135 PST the current is turning again.

All the times above are converted to PDT by adding one hour to PST.

In summary, the current flows in one direction until it reaches a maximum speed, then it slows and eventually turns in the opposite direction. At the turn there is a period of slack water before the current picks up speed. The times of the turns (the time column printed in regular print) are the safest times to transit a pass with strong currents.

At the time of the turn there is a safe "time window" when the current is slack or very slow. The length of time the current is stopped, or very slow, depends on the speed that the current will be moving at the next time of maximum flow, because the faster the current will flow at maximum, the faster it will pick up speed after the turn. A conservative rule of thumb is:

- If the current will be more than 6 knots at maximum it is safe to start through the pass any time between 15 minutes before the time of the turn to 15 minutes after it.
- If the current will be 3–6 knots at maximum it is safe to start through the pass any time between 30 minutes before the time of the turn to 30 minutes after it.
- If the current will be less than 3 knots at maximum it is safe to start through the pass one hour before the time of the turn to one hour after it.

On a larger boat with a diesel engine you can stretch these time windows a bit, but do beware, when wind and current oppose each other, the rough seas can be a hazard.

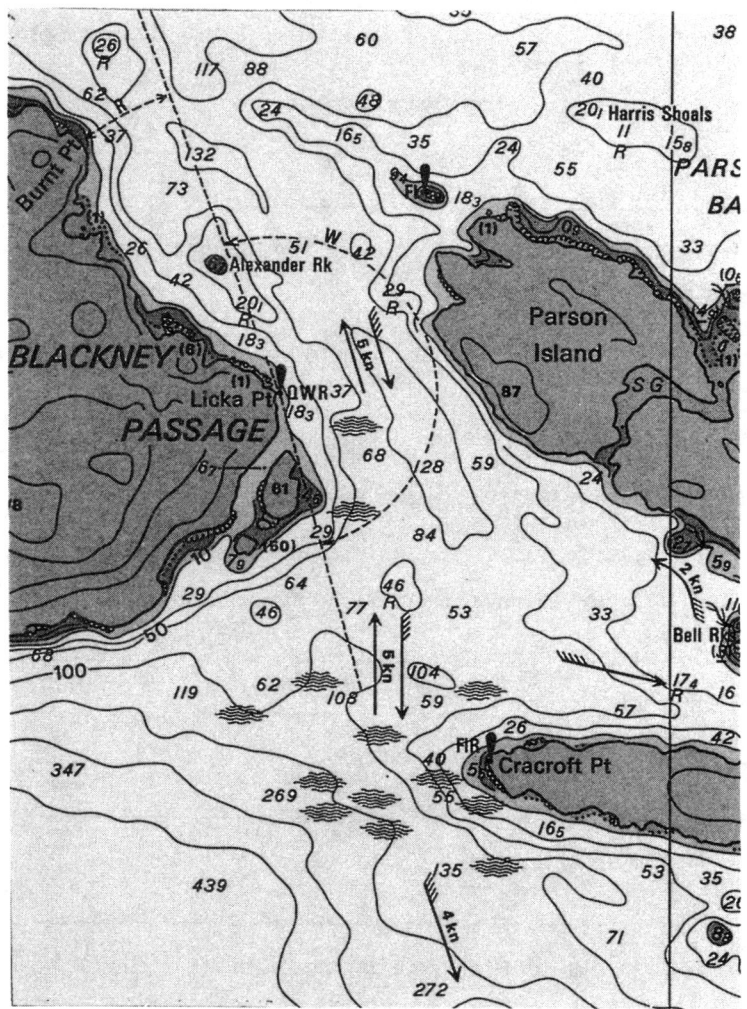

Figure 28-5 – Chart Illustrating Current Direction

In this chart section of Blackney Passage a number of chart symbols pertaining to current can be seen. The arrows with 4 feathers on one side indicate the direction of the flood current. Two of the flood stream arrows have above them a maximum rate in knots. Usually the rate will be less than that shown. The arrows without feathers indicate the direction of the ebb current. The rate between arrows applies to both. Most of the time the current rate will be less than 5 knots.

Off Licka and Cracroft Points there are a number of groups of short, closely spaced wavy lines. These are symbols for tide-rips.

SELF-TEST — ANSWERS ARE ON PAGE 196

1. List three pieces of information to look for in the title block of a chart.

   _____

   _____

   _____

2. (a) Which imaginary set of lines circling the earth are Great Circles?

   _____

   (b) How do the Great Circles relate to the measurement of distance on a chart?

   _____

   (c) How do you measure distance on a Polyconic chart?

   _____

   (d) How do you measure distance on a Mercator chart?

   _____

   (e) How long is a cable? _____

3. (a) What is meant by "chart datum"?

   _____

   (b) What is tidal datum?

   _____

   (c) How do chart datum and tidal datum relate to each other?

   _____

4. (a) What does the green tint on a chart indicate?

   _____

   (b) What do underlined figures on drying areas or in brackets against drying features signify?

   _____

5. Give the number of the symbol or abbreviation for:

   (a) a rock awash at chart datum _____

   (b) a dangerous underwater rock of 2m (6 ft) or less. _____

   (c) a wreck showing any portion of hull or superstructure. _____

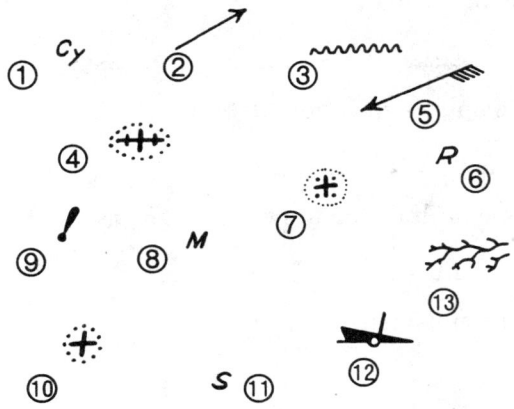

(d) a dangerous wreck, depth unknown _____

(e) a submarine cable _____

(f) a clay seabed _____

(g) a mud seabed _____

(h) a rocky seabed _____

(i) a sandy seabed _____

(j) kelp _____

(k) a light _____

(l) ebb stream direction _____

(m) flood stream direction _____

6. (a) What is the "upstream" direction in the lateral aids to navigation system?

_____

_____

(b) In North America the colour _____ is associated with port hand aids and the colour _____ is associated with starboard hand aids.

7. (a) How do the shapes of unlit buoys in the lateral aids to navigation system differ between starboard hand buoys and port hand buoys?

_____

(b) A port bifurcation daybeacon has what colour and shape in the middle of the diamond?

_____

(c) What colour is a cautionary buoy?

_____

(d) Describe or draw the topmark on an east cardinal buoy.

_____

(e) Describe an isolated danger buoy.

_____

(f) Cardinal buoys are positioned so that the safest or deepest water is to be found where?

_____

8. (a) On July 19, 1992 what was the time and height of the lowest tide? Give the time in Pacific Daylight Time. Use Figure 28-3.

_____

(b) If at that time the charted depth at your location was 18 feet, what would the depth of the water be? Give your answer in feet. Use Figure 28-3.

_____

9. On Friday, Sept. 18, 1992 what was the rate and time of the maximum current at Dodd Narrows. Give your answer in PDT. Use Figure 28-4.

_____

10. For Thursday, Sept. 17, 1992 list the times of slack water and give the earliest and latest times you should start through the pass. Give your answer in PDT. Use Figure 28-4.

EARLIEST	SLACK WATER	LATEST
_____	_____	_____
_____	_____	_____
_____	_____	_____
_____	_____	_____

11. Identify symbols in chart section below:

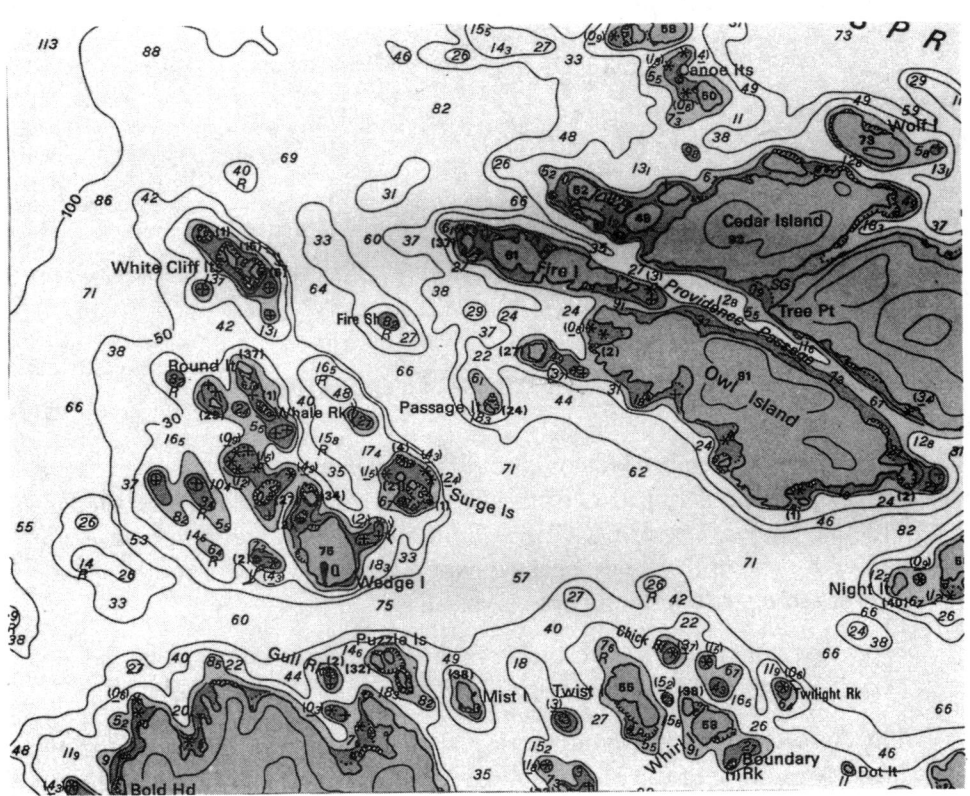

Figure 28-6 – Diagram for Question #11 – In this section of chart find one or more symbols for each of the following: (Units are metric).

a) A rock awash at chart datum. _____

b) A dangerous underwater rock of 2m (6 ft.) or less. _____

c) A rock which covers and uncovers. _____

d) A non-dangerous rock of known depth. _____

e) A rock which does not cover. _____

f) A sand and gravel foreshore. _____

g) Kelp. _____

NAVIGATION AND SEAMANSHIP

AFLOAT SKILLS

Main topics:
- Crew Overboard Procedures
- Recovery Techniques
- Anchoring
- Ground Tackle
- Scope
- Selecting an Anchorage
- Anchoring Procedure
- Weighing Anchor

Chapter 29 – Crew Overboard Procedures

When a crew member falls overboard it is always a serious matter. Take strict precautions to prevent this event which so often ends in tragedy. Practice crew overboard (COB) drill often, and especially each time you sail on an unfamiliar boat, because you must know before someone falls overboard exactly how the boat responds.

A person can fall overboard under many possible circumstances. Both experienced and inexperienced sailors alike may fall overboard.

The circumstances, the competence of the crew remaining aboard and the maneuverability of the boat are factors in the choice of the method used to return to the crew overboard (COB). The likelihood of successfully reaching and then recovering a COB depends on practicing an effective technique and sheer good luck.

EFFECTIVE TECHNIQUES

In recent years considerable work has gone into researching crew overboard procedures. Various methods have been tried under controlled conditions and case histories have been reviewed.

The majority of research groups agree on actions that are elements of an effective method of return to a COB. These are:

- **Raise an immediate alert:**
  The instant there is a COB the person who sees the person fall overboard shouts loudly "CREW OVERBOARD" to alert all on board. This person is the spotter.

The duties of the spotter are:
(1) to keep their eyes on the COB and arm pointed at the COB continuously until the COB is safely secured to the side of the boat.
(2) to assist the helm to return to the COB by keeping the helm informed of the location of the COB without obstructing the helm's view.

Do not change the spotter because the COB can be lost from view in the process. The head of a person in the water is extremely difficult to keep in sight, even in very small waves. Once the COB is lost from view the chance of sighting the COB again is drastically reduced. Additional spotters may be designated if they can see the COB and are not essential for other duties.

- **Throw buoyant object(s) to the COB.** Immediately the call "CREW OVERBOARD" is heard, throw flotation to the person in the water. This can be a PFD, lifebuoy, buoyant cushion or the crew overboard pole and lifebuoy assembly*, although some researchers believe that by the time the COB pole and lifebuoy are deployed the boat will have travelled too far from the COB for these to qualify as immediate flotation. Others recommend throwing over all easily accessible buoyant items, littering the wake to assist in marking the area.

* The COB pole, lifebuoy and light are linked together and are deployed as a unit. The heaving line is a separate item.

- **Stay in close proximity to the COB while maneuvering for the return.** Not only is there the danger of losing sight of the COB, but time is critical. A person in cold water and suffering from the shock of immersion very quickly becomes unable to assist in his or her own recovery. Also, it is a comfort for the COB to see the boat nearby.

- **Tack, rather than gybe, when maneuvering for the return.** The boat has already lost the services of one crewmember. Others may be standing up, trying to see the COB. A gybe at such a time, especially in rough weather, is likely to be a wild and uncontrolled maneuver of tangled lines and general confusion. In the process another person may be injured or knocked overboard.

- **Approach the COB from downwind so you can stop the boat.** A close reaching approach is best. A close reaching approach offers the opportunity to control the boat's speed.

SAFETY TIP:
Stay near the COB.

- **Make sure the boat is almost stopped as you arrive by the COB.** If boatspeed is more than about one knot, the COB may be unable to grasp a thrown heaving line. If the boat continues on at speed after the COB is secured to the end of the heaving line, the COB may drown while being towed.

- **Keep the COB on the boat's windward side as you approach.** There are several reasons for this:
  - A cruising boat is too small to provide a safe lee (shelter) for the COB. If the COB is to leeward there is a danger of the COB getting under the boat or being injured by the boat.
  - A closer approach can be made with the victim to windward. The helm can usually better judge the approach and so steer more accurately.
  - The COB will automatically turn his or her back to the wind, waves, and spray to make breathing easier. The COB can see better to leeward and so has a better chance of seeing the boat's approach and of grasping a heaving line.

THE TRIANGLE METHOD

1. The spotter alerts all on board by shouting "CREW OVERBOARD!"

2. The spotter or other crew throw buoyant object(s) to the COB and shouts "ARE YOU OK?"

3. Upon hearing the alert the skipper/helm **immediately** puts the boat onto a beam reach on the same tack, (the success of the maneuver depends on the immediacy of this course change) and commands "EASE SHEETS" (or "HARDEN SHEETS" if sailing downwind) FOR A BEAM REACH." The skipper/helm does not wait for the crew to ease or harden sheets before making the course change.

4. A check is made of the COB's condition.

5. The boat is sailed no further away from the COB than is necessary to effect the maneuver.

6. Skipper or helm commands "READY ABOUT. HARDEN SHEETS. HELMS-A-LEE." The crew hardens the sheets as the boat heads up so speed will be maintained through the tack.

> **SAFETY TIP:**
> Attach a whistle to your PFD. Make sure it is the kind that works when wet. If you do go overboard you can raise the alarm.

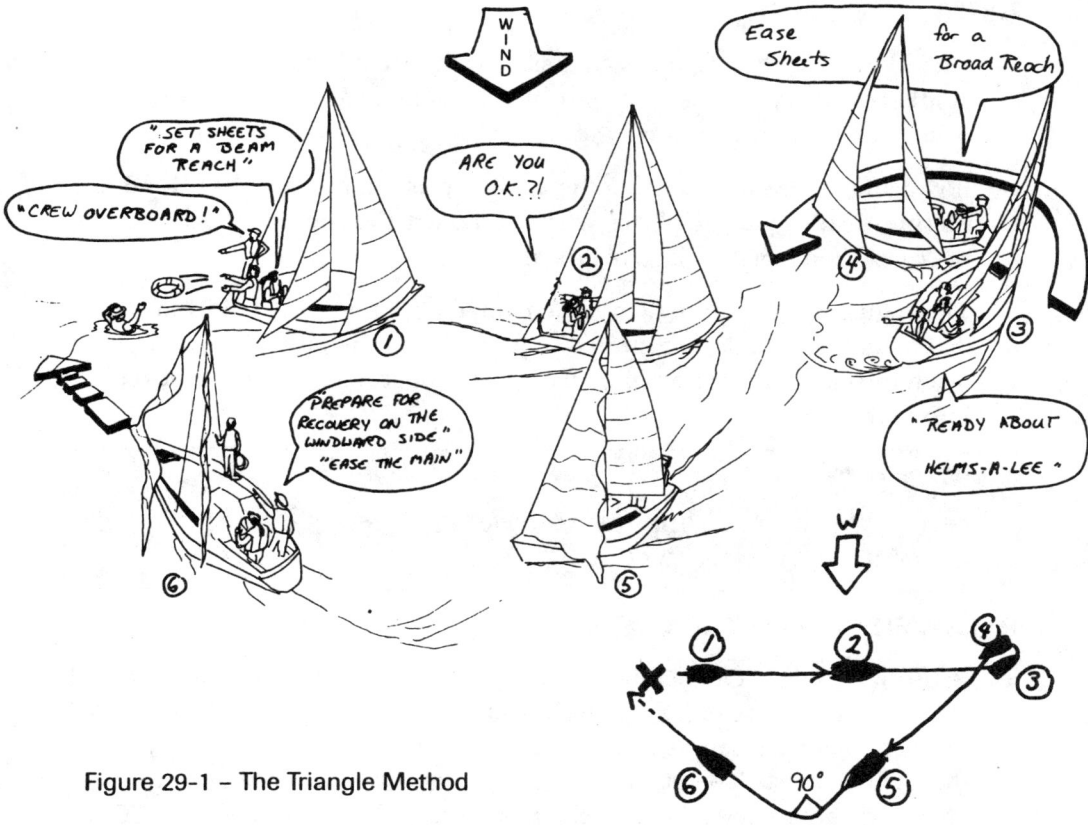

Figure 29-1 – The Triangle Method

7. After the bow passes through the eye of the wind skipper or helm commands "BEARING AWAY, EASE SHEETS FOR A BROAD REACH."

8. The boat is sailed on a broad reach, its speed controlled by the sheet trimmer(s) luffing or hardening the sail under the direction of the skipper or helm, until the boat is in a position where it can turn to approach the COB on a close reach. The crew readies the heaving line on the windward side.

9. The boat heads up to a close reach. The jib sheet is released and speed is controlled by the mainsheet to arrive with the COB on the windward side with a speed less than 1 knot.

10. The heaving line is thrown to the COB. If possible the COB secures self with a bowline (made from the bitter end of the heaving line) under the arms.

11. The COB is pulled to the boat and secured to the side of the boat while preparations are made to recover the COB from the water. The COB must be secured to the boat so he or she cannot drift away. The COB is pulled out of the water as far as possible before being secured, to minimize hypothermia.

USING THE ENGINE

Should you use the engine as an assist? There are no rules, only guidelines, and you must use your own judgement and do whatever you have to do to return **promptly** to the COB.

If you are under sail and using the engine to assist, **beware that there are no lines trailing in the water when you start the engine,** which is often the case when a person falls overboard.

The engine must be in **neutral** when you coast up to the COB from downwind, so you do not injure the person with the propeller. After you reach the COB turn the engine off so it cannot accidentally be knocked into gear.

> **SAFETY TIP:**
> Sheets overboard may wrap the propeller and prevent you from motoring or sailing back to the COB.

RECOVERY FROM THE WATER

Returning to the COB is only half the battle. Because of the high freeboard (height of the boat's hull from deck to waterline) of a cruising boat, recovery of a COB can be even more of a problem than maneuvering to the COB. Success depends upon the recovery equipment available to the crew, their ability to use it, and the mental and physical state of the COB. It is common for a person who falls overboard to be injured by the boom or by falling against the hull. Cold water quickly renders a COB unable to help himself or herself. It is important to act quickly and to be successful on the first or second attempt at recovery before the crew and COB exhaust their strength.

Assuming the COB is uninjured, wearing a PFD, and able to help, methods of recovery from the water are:

1) A boarding ladder. A ladder can be dangerous in a rolling sea.

2) Make a bowline in the end of line or sheet, lower into the water, and wrap the other end around a winch, leaving enough slack for the COB to get a foot or knee into it. The main halyard may also be attached to the COB to assist.

3) If the boat is towing a rubber dinghy the COB may be able to climb into it and be assisted aboard from there. Partial deflation of the dinghy facilitates entry by the COB.

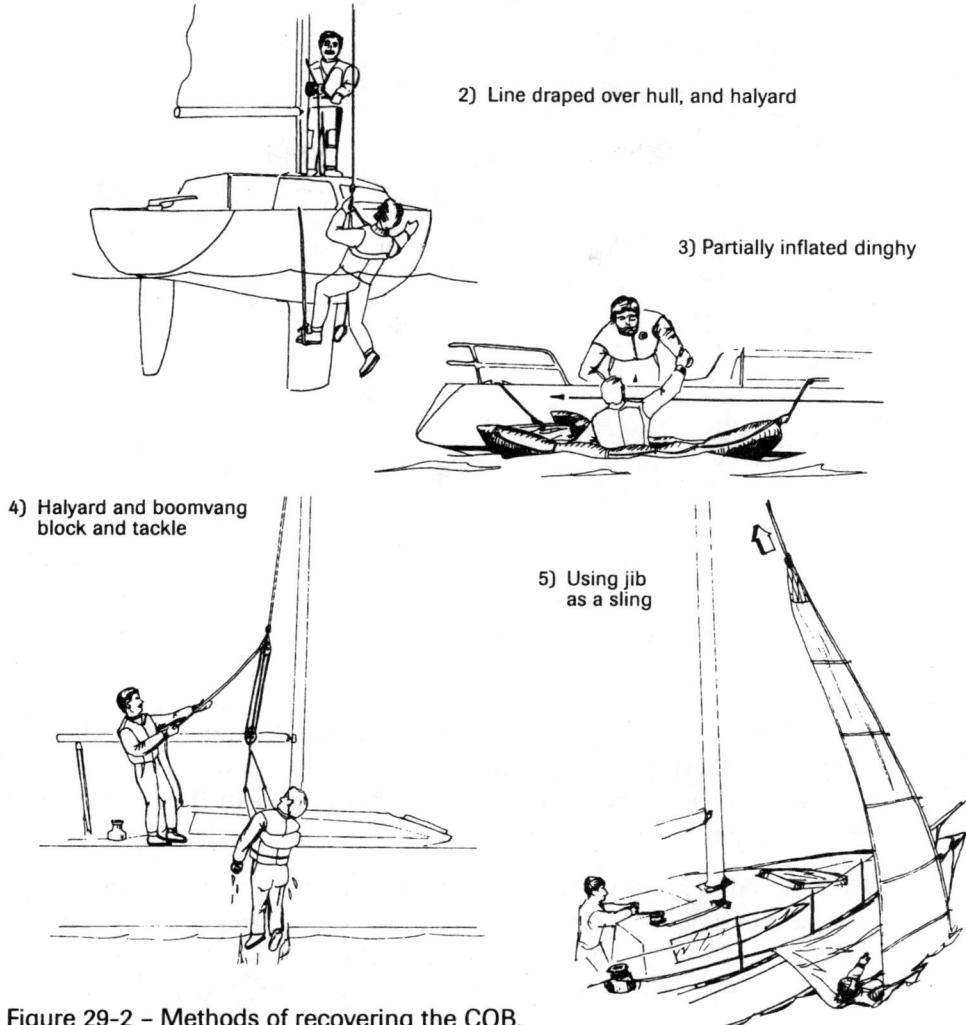

Figure 29-2 – Methods of recovering the COB.

4) Detach the boomvang and use it as a block and tackle on the end of the main halyard. Lower the tackle and attach one end to the COB. Then raise the halyard and pull on the bitter end of the tackle line. In the case where the boomvang is not easily detached use the main halyard alone.

5) Use the jib lowered over the side as a sling. The tack should be lashed to the toe rail and the clew sheeted hard. Where possible injured COB's should be lifted horizontally.

Do not, under any circumstances, practice returning to a COB by putting a real person into the water. For practice, two fenders tied together makes a good COB. They are easily retrieved with the boathook.

You can increase your chances of dealing successfully with a COB emergency by developing your boat handling skills generally and by

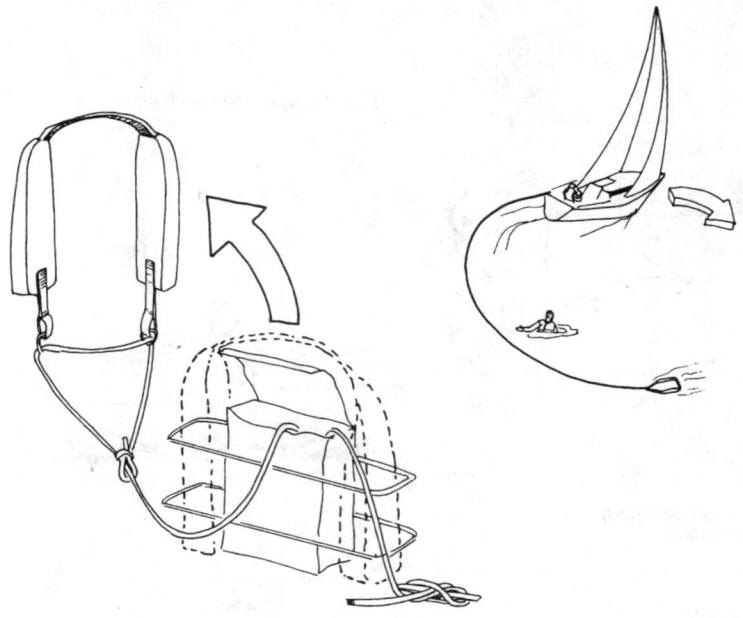

Figure 29-3 – A collar with buoyant line that can be attached to the pushpit for COB recovery.

practicing one or two methods until your response is automatic and you are successful every time. The drills themselves help to hone your sailing skills and teach you to control your speed. Try out the drills in light winds at first, with the COB "falling over" on each point of sail.

Don't be afraid to insist on taking time out to practice with your crew. Make it into a timed game of skill in which everyone rotates duties and gets a turn at the helm. On occasion, when the crew is trained, toss an object overboard without warning, shout "THIS IS AN EXERCISE – CREW OVERBOARD!" and go below. Start your stopwatch. You may be surprised to see how long it takes for the crew to rescue "you".

When anchored in calm, shallow, warm water, try out some recovery methods, keeping in mind that in a real-life situation recovery will be much more difficult. Before you put anyone in the water, make sure you have a boarding ladder.

SAFETY TIPS:

If you are skipper, do not pocket the engine key after you turn the engine off, in case you fall overboard. Keep the key in an accessible place in the cockpit and make sure every crewmember knows where it is.

Instruct your crew if they should fall overboard to face the boat and give the International Signal "I'm OK," by raising one arm making a circle to the top of the head.

Chapter 30 – Anchoring

The first few times you anchor, especially overnight, you may be anxious wondering how such a small item as your anchor can possibly hold the boat in place. Perseverance in learning to anchor well frees you from the worry of wondering whether a marina will have dock space when you arrive and affords quiet and privacy. Also, the "Anchor Hotel" is very inexpensive.

Anchoring is a skill that requires practice. Methods of anchoring vary with the location and the particular circumstances. For example, if a harbour is very small, the boats will set bow and stern anchors, so they can be closely spaced. There are entire books devoted to the topic of anchoring.

The standard method of anchoring under power, using one anchor, is presented here. To be successful you need a knowledge of **ground tackle** (anchoring equipment), the ability to select a good anchorage and a strictly adhered-to anchoring routine.

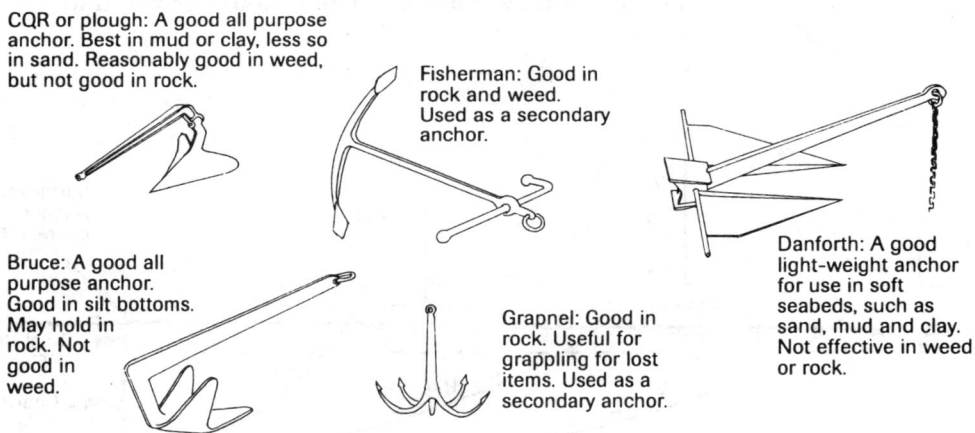

CQR or plough: A good all purpose anchor. Best in mud or clay, less so in sand. Reasonably good in weed, but not good in rock.

Fisherman: Good in rock and weed. Used as a secondary anchor.

Danforth: A good light-weight anchor for use in soft seabeds, such as sand, mud and clay. Not effective in weed or rock.

Bruce: A good all purpose anchor. Good in silt bottoms. May hold in rock. Not good in weed.

Grapnel: Good in rock. Useful for grappling for lost items. Used as a secondary anchor.

Figure 30-1 – Anchors

The most common anchors for cruising boats are; Danforth, CQR or Plough, and Bruce.

GROUND TACKLE

Ground tackle must be adequate for the size of the boat. Tables regarding anchor weights and breaking strengths of line are to be found in chandleries and books on cruising.

The anchor rode on most small cruising boats consists of a short length of chain (3–15m, 10–50ft.) and a long length of line.

The chain is attached to the anchor ring with a shackle. The shackle pin should be wired to the shackle with monel or stainless steel wire to prevent the shackle from opening accidentally.

Chain in the anchor rode serves several purposes:

- It increases the holding power of the anchor by keeping the pull on the anchor horizontal. An anchor works like a plough. The more horizontal the pull, the better it holds.

- It serves as a shock absorber by causing the rode to sag, which lessens the sudden loading caused when the boat rises and falls on the waves. This adds to the effective weight of the anchor because the chain is raised rather than the anchor shank.

- It keeps the rode from chafing on rocks or sharp surfaces on the seabed.

The line used in an anchor rode is usually nylon because of its strength and elasticity. Minimum length of line for a 20–30 ft. cruising boat is 50m (150 ft.). 65-80 m (200-250 ft.) is better if it is practical to carry it. If the line is attached to the chain with a shackle, the pin should be wired to the shackle.

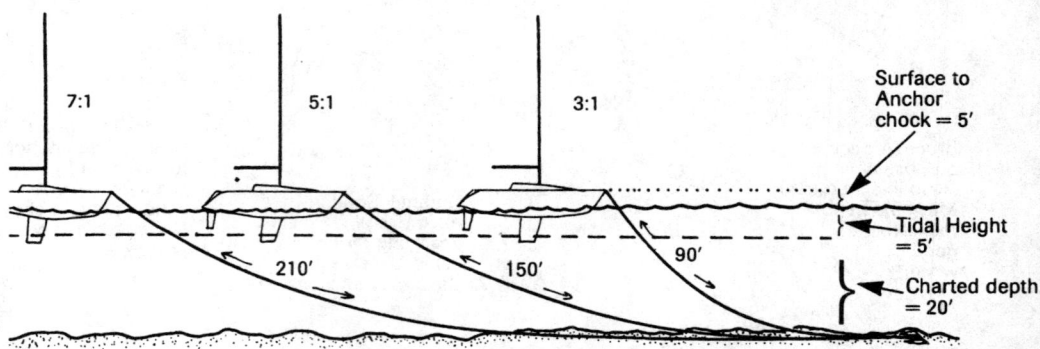

Figure 30-2 – Scope

The scope depends on whether you are anchoring in the daytime or at night and on the weather.

For a **lunch stop** scope should be 3:1. For **overnight** in calm weather scope should be 5:1. For **rough weather** scope should be 7:1 or more. Be guided by the maxim, "When in doubt, let it out."

You want to anchor for the night in a spot where the depth on the chart is 20ft. If the maximum tidal height during your stay will be 5ft., you have a total depth of 25ft. Then add the height from the water to your anchor chock (allow 5ft). This is a total of 30ft. Multiply 30ft. times 5 to get 150ft. for 5:1 scope.

The DOT required equipment list calls for a minimum rode of 15m. A rode of only 15m would be very inadequate for a cruising sailboat.

The bitter end of the rode must be permanently secured to the boat to prevent losing your ground tackle overboard. If it is not, secure it to a strong deck cleat on the bow.

SCOPE

Scope is the ratio of the length of the rode deployed to the total depth of the water measured from the deck to the bottom. The total depth of the water is the charted depth plus allowance for tidal range for the duration of your stay. **The more scope, the better the holding power of the anchor.**

Selecting an Anchorage

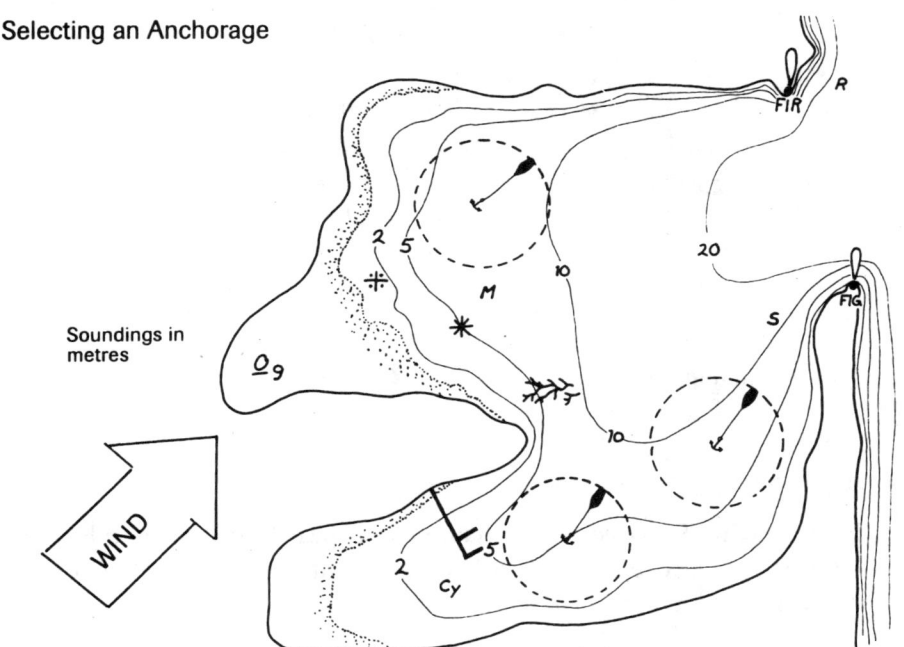

Figure 30-3 – Selecting an overnight anchorage

Prerequisites for a secure overnight anchorage:

- Shelter from strong winds and waves and out of the way of traffic. Do not anchor on a lee shore or in an anchorage that is likely to soon become a lee shore.

- Adequate total water depth. The depth must be sufficient after allowing for change(s) in tidal height. Allow at least 1 metre of water under your keel. Do not anchor in water so deep you cannot lay out sufficient scope if the weather deteriorates.

- Suitable type of seabed for the type of anchor you are using.

- Room to swing after you have laid out the recommended scope. Make sure you cannot swing into other boats, shallow water or obstructions. Account for the swinging circles of other boats near you.

ANCHORING PROCEDURE

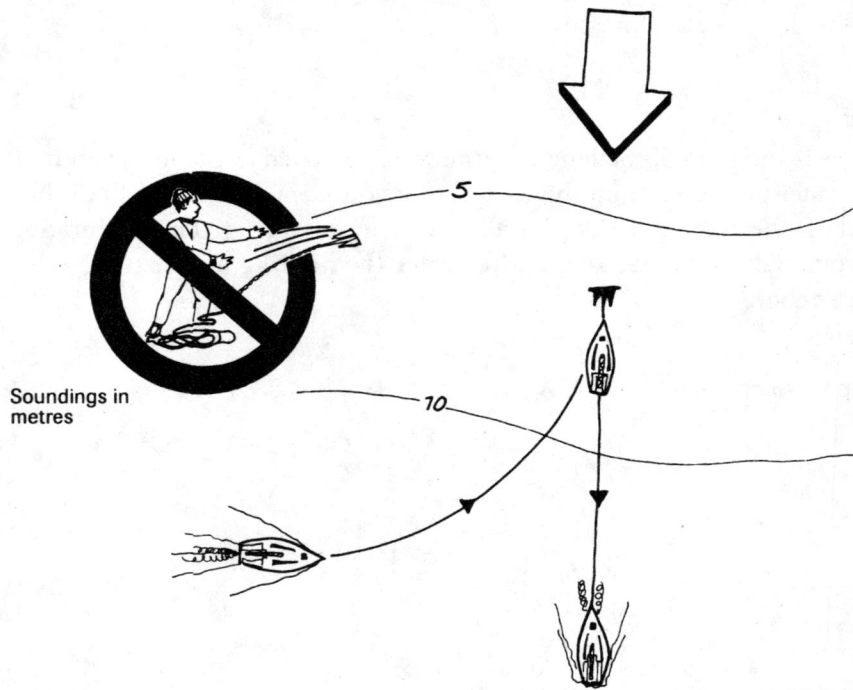

Figure 30-4 – Anchoring procedure

Before anchoring:

- **Get a weather forecast.** Avoid having your peaceful evening followed by a hasty departure in the middle of the night because your anchorage has turned into a windy lee shore.

- **Check the chart and tide table** for the type of seabed and the depth for the duration of your stay. Note how steeply the seabed shelves (you want a gently shelving bottom) and whether there are any hazards to avoid.

- **The foresail should be lowered and bagged in the usual manner, and the foresail bag pushed up into the pulpit to clear the foredeck.**

- The mainsail may be lowered and furled before beginning the anchoring procedure or you may opt to anchor with the mainsail raised (the mainsheet must be completely eased) and lower and furl the mainsail when the boat settles to her anchor.

HELM:

- Turns on engine and depthsounder.
- Commands "READY TO LOWER THE ANCHOR".

CREW:

- Goes forward and readies the anchor for lowering. This includes making sure the bitter end of the rode is secured to the boat and that the rode is free to run.
- Responds "READY".

HELM:

- Turns into the wind, coming to a stop head to wind in the anchoring location.
- Commands "LOWER THE ANCHOR".
- Notifies crew of the depth so the crew knows what scope to lay out.

The scope is not laid out at this time because if the rode is dropped on top of the anchor it will foul the anchor. When giving the depth, the helmsman must know whether the sounder has been calibrated to the bottom of the keel or to the bottom of the hull (when in doubt, assume the worst case). Often the chart will not show enough depth readings for you to know exactly what the depth will be. In this situation the helm will motor in slowly to a suitable depth and then notify the crew of the reading.

If you sail with a regular crew, arrange a set of hand signals for anchoring. Otherwise, station a crewmember amidships to relay commands and responses. Sound carries extremely well over water and you do not want to provide entertainment for those already in the anchorage, especially if something goes wrong.

CREW:

- Lowers the anchor, under control, to the seabed. Crew handles the anchor and rode so as to protect the bow from damage and so as to protect their backs. Notifies helm when the anchor is on the bottom.

HELM:

- Puts the engine in reverse and motors astern slowly.

CREW:

- Lays out the recommended scope as the boat moves astern.

- Notifies the helm when all the rode has been paid out and is cleated off to a large cleat on the bow.

HELM:

- When the rode comes taut, runs the engine in reverse at half throttle for about half a minute while watching abeam to see when the boat stops. This is to set the anchor, ie, dig it into the seabed. Often you can feel the anchor set. The wheel or tiller will jerk suddenly.

CREW:

- Feels the anchor rode while the engine is at half throttle. Just as you can feel movement through a fishing line, so you can feel what is happening to the anchor. If the anchor is setting, the rode just ahead of the boat will rise out of the water and become very taut, perhaps quivering. If the anchor is not setting, it can be felt bumping over the bottom.

If, after half a minute to a minute the anchor is not set, you will have to re-anchor. You will be disappointed but it is better than dragging anchor in the night or when you are ashore.

When the boat has settled to her anchor:

- Shut off the engine and lower and furl the mainsail (if appropriate).
- Take bearings so you will know if the anchor drags. Lighted aids are best for this but there may be none available. A simple visual bearing (for example, of a tree lined up against a corner of a house) may be the best you can do. Two bearings are better than one.
- If anchoring for the night, display your all-round white light.
- If, when anchored, the weather should turn nasty, increase scope.

WEIGHING ANCHOR

To **weigh anchor** is to raise it.

HELM:

- Orders mainsail raised (if desired). The mainsheet must be completely eased until the anchor is up, or the boat will sail over the anchor.
- Turns on the engine.
- Commands "READY TO WEIGH ANCHOR."

CREW:

- Makes preparations to raise the anchor. This includes removing the half hitch and figure eight from the cleat, but keeping a full turn around the cleat.

- Responds "READY."

HELM:

- Commands "RAISE THE ANCHOR."

CREW:

- Raises the anchor, flaking the rode neatly. If the wind is strong (or backs are weak) the helm, guided by the crew, motors gently towards the anchor to take the strain off the rode. The rode is hauled in until the anchor line runs vertical. At this point the boat should be stopped.

- The crew breaks out (lifts) the anchor and notifies the helm that the anchor is off the bottom so the helm can take any evasive action necessary to avoid other boats or shallow water.

- The crew finishes raising the anchor (taking care with boat finish and backs) and stows and/or secures it. If the anchor is coated with mud or clay, it will have to be washed off before it is stowed.

HELM:

- Motors away slowly until anchor is secured.

SECTION E:
WHAT NEXT?

Congratulations on completing the CYA Basic Cruising Standard, which is valid for life. You have a foundation to build on. Now you need to practice, practice, practice the Afloat Skills to make you as perfect as you are going to get. Take this book with you to assist in your review.

Many schools provide an opportunity for you to continue sailing and developing your boat handling skills by offering day rentals and adventure cruises. Some offer the **CYA Basic Keelboat Racing Standard**. Racing is fun and an excellent skill builder. You may wish to join a cruising, sailing or yacht club.

Increase your knowledge by attending lectures and reading books and magazines about sailing and cruising and watching some of the numerous sailing videos. Obtain first aid, CPR and radio operators' certificates. Take a course on weather or diesel engines. There is always more to know, which is one of the attractions of sailing.

As you browse through your newly acquired logbook you will see that there are six more CYA Cruising Standards. They are:

- **Intermediate Cruising Standard**

The Intermediate Cruising Standard is a live aboard Standard in which you take part in a cruise of at least 48 hours, learning to operate all the systems and equipment aboard a cruising boat of 25–35 feet. Your sailing skills receive further development; you learn to fly a cruising spinnaker, and you extend your navigation skills by practicing entry into an unfamiliar harbour or anchorage. **The CYA recommends that you hold the Intermediate Standard before you begin chartering.** Before you take a course leading to the Intermediate Standard, it is a good idea to have experience as skipper during a number of day sails and to have applied the knowledge and thoroughly mastered the skills of the Basic Standard.

- **Coastal Navigation Standard**

This theory Standard is also highly recommended before you begin chartering. Many students take a course leading to this Standard in the winter after they have completed the Basic Standard. They then take a course leading to the Intermediate Standard the following spring or summer.

- **Advanced Cruising Standard**

The Advanced Standard is for those who have had chartering or cruising experience as a skipper. Day and night navigation are practiced intensively in a course leading to this Standard. You are taught to dock, anchor, and moor to a buoy under sail. (It is a great confidence builder to know you can cope without an engine — all engines fail eventually).

- **Celestial Navigation Standard**

In a theory course leading to this Standard you learn to navigate by the sun, moon, planets and stars in preparation for ocean passage-making, though frequently people take such a course out of general interest.

- **Advanced Navigation**

It's the objective of this Standard to present the theory and practice necessary to navigate using electronic instruments and radar, and learn passage planning techniques for advanced sailing.

- **Offshore Standard**

In a course leading to this Standard you make an ocean passage, practicing your celestial navigation skills as you voyage.

Your Logbook lays out the minimum requirements for the awarding of each Standard. Use your Logbook as a study guide for the more advanced Standards. Record in your Logbook your rentals, charters and other sailing related experience and certifications to provide evidence of your experience to rental or charter agencies. If you own your own boat you may be able to arrange for a discount on your insurance if you hold CYA's Learn to Cruise certifications.

The CYA Cruising Standards are highly regarded and are recognized throughout North America and in many other countries. Cruising boats are available for charter in numerous parts of the globe. When you are ready to begin chartering, **flotilla cruising** in which you skipper a chartered boat but travel in company with a group of boats and leader, may help bridge the gap until you are confident enough to **bareboat** charter on your own. (A bareboat charter is one in which there is no hired skipper).

With your Basic Cruising Standard you have opened the door to adventure and perhaps a new way of life. Cruising can be social or it can be means of escape. There is camaraderie and a sense of community among sailors. They enjoy cruising with friends and family and making new friendships while cruising. As a group they are protective of the environment, enjoying nature without littering or disturbing sea life.

As you talk to other sailors, attend boat shows and read about cruising, your own special dream will reveal itself. You may want to set sail for isolated villages and coves in less travelled areas of our own country. Or you may imagine yourself anchored off a white sand, palm fringed beach, watching the sun set over a tranquil turquoise sea. Whatever your dream, go for it.

ANSWERS TO SELF TESTS

SECTION A: *(page 32)*

1. Pushpit 3
   Stanchion 10
   Spreaders 2
   Forestay 8
   Outhaul 15
   Topping lift 6
   Boomvang 17
   Genoa 5
   Reef points 12
   Cringles 14
   Clew 7
   Jiffy/slab reefing 9
   Pintle 1
   Gudgeon 16
   Chainplate 18
   Gooseneck 4
   Turnbuckle 20
   Cleat 13
   Tang 19
   Shackle 11

2. (a) Leeward
   (b) Leeway
   (c) In irons
   (d) Tacking (coming about)
   (e) Heading up

3. to plug holes in hull; secured to through hulls

4. Broad reach E
   Beam reach D
   Closehauled B
   Run A
   Close reach C

5. A

6. B

7. Safety of the crew and the boat

8. 4 years

9. If the weather is rough
   If you are singlehanding
   On deck at night

10. (a) No
    (b) Maybe
    (c) Yes
    (d) Yes
    (e) No
    (f) No

SECTION B: *(page 65)*

1. A gives way to: B,C
   B gives way to: C
   C gives way to: No one
   D gives way to: A,B,C,E,F,H
   E gives way to: A,B,C
   F gives way to: A,B,C,E
   G gives way to: A,B,C,D,E,F,H
   H gives way to: A,B,C,E,F
   Boat C will be first to pick up the balloon.

2. Not at anchor, or made fast to the shore, or aground.

3. There is none.

4. Power-driven vessels; reciprocal or nearly reciprocal courses.

194

5. Sunset to sunrise; visibility is restricted.
6. Port sidelight (red); starboard sidelight (green); sternlight (white).
7. As for sail, plus masthead light (white)
8. Methane   Head or holding tank
   Hydrogen   Batteries
9. Electrocution
10. Slow down and keep well clear.
11. Do not apply warmth to arms and legs, give alcohol, massage or treat roughly.
12. Stay as still as possible.
    Keep clothing on.
    Assume HELP position.
13. Head/neck; sides of chest; groin.
14. Shivering; numbness of hands and feet.

SECTION C: (page 115)

1. VHF radio; telephone; commercial radio stations; newspapers; television; airport weather office; polling the weather office facsimile.
2. (a) 21B; 83B; WX1; WX2; WX3   (b) 6; 24
3. (a) Air set in motion horizontally to equalize air temperature and barometric pressure between one location and another
   (b) uneven heating of the earth by the sun
4. 20 knots; 34 knots; 47 knots
5. Violent gusty winds; squalls; lightning; heavy rain or hail; decreased visibility; waterspouts
6. Cirrus cloud; halo around sun or moon; backing wind
7. Excessive heel; strong weather helm
8. The boat makes a lot of leeway; excess rudder must be applied to sail in a straight line
9. The tendency of a boat to turn to windward
10. (a) The shore to leeward of your boat
    (b) You could be blown onto it and shipwrecked
11. Determine your position; turn on navigation lights; turn on depth sounder; slow down; post a lookout; make sound signals; hoist radar reflector; avoid traffic and charted hazards; anchor if feasible
12. Consult chart and tide table
13. (a) Motor or sail off; kedge off; heel the boat; lighten ship
    (b) Pulling the boat with the anchor
14. (a) Determine whether the crew and boat are in danger
    (b) Stop the engine
    (c) Tack
    (d) Turn downwind
    (e) Increase scope

15. (a) Your boat is threatened by grave and imminent danger
    (b) 16
    (c) Name and call sign of your boat; position of your boat; description of your boat; number of people aboard and any injuries; nature of your problem and type of help you need; any other information which will facilitate rescue

SECTION D: *(page 174)*

1. Scale; projection; unit of measurement for depths, elevations and clearances
2. (a) Meridians of Longitude
   (b) One minute of arc on a Great Circle equals one nautical mile
   (c) On the scale provided
   (d) On the latitude scale at the side of the chart
   (e) One tenth of a nautical mile
3. (a) The plane of reference, or baseline, for soundings
   (b) 0.0 m or 0.0 ft.
   (c) They are the same
4. (a) Drying areas between the high and low water lines; foreshore that covers and uncovers
   (b) Elevations above chart datum
5. (a) 7   (g) 8
   (b) 10   (h) 6
   (c) 12   (i) 11
   (d) 4   (j) 13
   (e) 3   (k) 9
   (f) 1   (l) 2
                (m) 5
6. (a) From seaward, towards the headwaters of a river, into a harbour, or with the flood tide
   (b) Green; red
7. (a) Starboard hand have pointed tops; port hand have flat tops
   (b) Green square
   (c) Yellow
   (d) 2 black cones pointing away from each other
   (e) Black with one red horizontal band and 2 black spherical topmarks
   (f) To the named side of the buoy
8. (a) 1455 PDT; 5.8 ft. or 1.8m.
   (b) 23.8 ft.
9. 0510 PDT; 6.9 knots
10. 0130 PDT; 0145 PDT; 0200 PDT
    0750 PDT; 0820 PDT; 0850 PDT
    1350 PDT; 1420 PDT; 1450 PDT
    1915 PDT; 1930 PDT; 1945 PDT
11. (a) ⊕   (d) 26 R
    (b) +   (e) ● (1)
    (c) ✳ (2₄)   (f) S G
                             (g) 〜

GLOSSARY

Abaft – Behind.
Abeam – Off the boat, and at right angles to the fore and aft centreline of the boat.
Aft – On the boat, towards the stern.
Ahead – Off the boat, and in front of it.
Aids to navigation – Devices or systems external to a vessel which are provided to help a mariner determine position or course, to warn of dangers or obstructions, or to advise the location of the best or preferred route.
Amidships – In the middle of a boat, between bow and stern.
Apparent wind – The combination of true wind and boat wind. The wind by which the sails are set.
Astern – Off the boat, and behind it.
Backing – A wind shifting in a counter-clockwise direction (e.g. W to S to E). In the northern hemisphere a backing wind frequently heralds the approach of poor weather.
Backstay – Wire running from the top of the mast to the stern. Prevents the mast falling forward and controls fore and aft mast bend.
Battens – Wooden or plastic slats of varying lengths set in pockets with access at the leech of the sail.
Beam – The widest part of the hull.
Beam reaching – Sailing directly across the wind, with the apparent wind on the beam.
Bearing away (bearing off) – Altering course away from the wind.
Beating – Sailing to windward in a series of tacks, closehauled first on one tack, then the other.
Belayed – Secured, made fast to.
Bend on (a sail) – Attach a sail to mast, boom or stay.
Bifurcation – Junction
Bight – Loop of line.
Bilge – The lowest inner part of a vessel's hull.
Bitter end – The free end of a line (the other end is the **standing end)**.
Boat wind – The wind created by a boat's forward motion.
Boom – A horizontal spar or pole attached at one end to the mast, to support the lower edge of a sail.
Boomvang – Block and tackle leading diagonally from the boom to the base of the mast. It controls the tension of the after edge of the mainsail.
Bow – The forward part of a boat.
Breastlines – Mooring lines that run from bow and stern at right angles to the dock, to keep the boat from moving out from the dock.
Broad reaching – Sailing in any direction between a beam reach and a run.
By the lee – Sailing downwind with the wind on the leeward side, i.e. the same side of the boat as the mainsail is being carried.
Cabin – A below-deck compartment for living quarters.
Cable – Distance of 0.1 nautical mile.
Cardinal aids to navigation – Aids indicating the location of hazards and of the safest or deepest water by reference to the four cardinal points of the compass. These aids are positioned so that the safest or deepest water is to be found to the named side of the buoy (e.g. to the north of a north cardinal buoy).

Catboat – A one-masted sailing vessel flying no foresail.
Chainplates – Strong metal fittings attached to the hull externally or internally, to which the shroud turnbuckles are attached.
Chart datum – Plane of reference, or baseline, for **soundings** (depths).
Chock – A metal fitting used as a guide for a mooring line or anchor rode.
Cleats – Fittings for gripping or securing lines.
Clew – Lower aft corner of a sail.
Close reaching – Sailing in any direction between closehauled and a beam reach.
Closehauled (on a beat)– Sailing as close to the wind as possible, without the sails luffing.
Cockpit – An open well in the deck from which the boat is steered.
Companionway – Stairs or ladder aboard a boat, leading from one level to another.
Cringles (grommets) – Metal rings worked into a sail.
Cunningham – Line adjusting the tension of the forward edge of the mainsail.
Current – Horizontal flow of water.
Cutter – A sailing vessel having one mast and flying two foresails.
Deck – Horizontal top surface that secures to and encloses the hull.
Degree – A distance of 60 nautical miles; one 360th of a circle; one degree of latitude.
Deviation – Compass error caused by the magnetic properties aboard a boat or of items aboard a boat, and/or the boat itself.
Downhaul – A line connected to the tack of the sail or gooseneck which is used to adjust the luff tension of a sail.
Ease – Let out; let off (e.g. a sheet).
Fairleads – Fittings through which lines are led to guide them or to change their directions.
Fathom – A measure equal to 6 feet.
Fenders – Bumpers made of soft material which hang over the sides of the hull to protect it when tying alongside a dock or another vessel.
Fetch – The distance over open water that the wind has blown.
Flaked – (1) Line piled neatly back and forth so it can run freely. (2) Sail folded back and forth, accordion style.
Float – A floating dock.
Foot – The lower edge of a sail.
Forestay – Wire running from the top of the mast, or near the top of the mast, to the bow. Prevents the mast falling backward and supports the foresail.
Forward – On the boat, towards the bow.
Genoa – A large foresail which overlaps the foretriangle formed by mast, deck and forestay.
Give-way vessel – Vessel required to keep clear of a **stand-on** vessel.
Gooseneck – A hinged fitting attaching the boom to the mast
Gust – A temporary increase in wind speed lasting a few seconds.
Gybing – Changing tack while sailing downwind by changing the sails from one side of the boat to the other.
Halyards – Lines of rope or wire and rope for raising and lowering the sails.
Hanks – Clips on the luff of a foresail by which the foresail is attached to the forestay.
Hard over – All the way over (refers to the tiller, wheel, or rudder).
Harden – Tighten; put tension on (e.g. a sheet).

Head – (1) Top corner of a sail. (2) A marine toilet.
Head to wind – The bow of the boat is pointed directly towards the direction from which the wind is blowing.
Heading up (luffing, luff up) – Altering course towards the wind.
Heaving to – A means of minimizing way and motion of the boat at sea by adjusting sails and lashing the tiller to leeward (wheel to windward).
Heeling – Leaning over (of the boat).
Helm – (1) Steering mechanism of a vessel. (2) Person steering the boat (also **helmsman**).
Hull – The shell or body of a boat.
Hypothermia (exposure) – A condition resulting from a lowering of the body's core temperature due to heat loss from the body.
In irons – The boat is head to wind, with no steerage.
Jib – A foresail that is approximately the size of the foretriangle, or less.
Jiffy (slab) reefing – A means of reducing the size of a sail by partially lowering it and securing the lowered part with lines and ties.
Kedging – Pulling a boat by its anchor.
Keel – A weighted underwater extension below the hull. The keel has two functions: (1) It acts as a counterweight to keep the boat upright when the wind is pushing against the sail (it balances the force of the wind on the sails). (2) It reduces leeway (side slip) when the boat is sailing.
Ketch – A two-masted sailing vessel with a mainmast and shorter mizzen (aft) mast. The mizzen mast is stepped forward of the rudder post.
Knot – Rate of speed equal to one nautical mile per hour (e.g. 6 knots is a rate of speed of 6 nautical miles per hour).
Lateral aids to navigation – Aids indicating the location of hazards and of the safest or deepest water by indicating the side on which they are to be passed.
Lazarette – A storage compartment at the stern.
Lee helm – The tendency of a boat to turn to leeward.
Lee shore – The shore to leeward (downwind) of the vessel.
Leech – The after edge of a sail.
Leeward (downwind or lee) – Away from the direction from which the wind is blowing.
Leeway – The leeward motion of a boat, a side-slipping caused by the wind against the hull and rigging.
Lifelines – Wires running on each side of the boat from pulpit to pushpit above deck level.
Luff – (1) Forward edge of a sail. (2) A fluttering in the forward edge of a sail. (3) To alter course towards the direction from which the wind is coming.
Luffing – (1) Fluttering in the forward edge (**luff**) of a sail. (2) Heading up.
Luff up – To head up, causing the sails to luff.
Lying ahull – Drifting with wheel locked to windward or tiller locked to leeward.
Made fast – Secured.
Making off – Securing the free end of a line (e.g. a halyard).
Mast – An upright pole to support the sails.
Masthead fly – A wind indicator (windvane) at the top of the mast.
Meridians of Longitude – Imaginary lines circling the earth in a north-south direction from pole to pole and converging at the poles.
Mooring lines – Docklines.

Nautical mile – The international nautical mile is equal to 1852m. or 6076 ft. is equal to 1 minute of latitude.

Outhaul – Line adjusting the tension of the lower edge of the mainsail along the boom.

Override – Wraps that have jammed on a winch.

P-effect (propwalk or transverse thrust) – The tendency of the stern of a boat under power to "walk" to port or starboard.

PFD – Personal Flotation Device.

Painter – The bow line of a dinghy.

Parallels of Latitude – Imaginary lines on the earth that are parallel to the equator.

Pintle and gudgeon – Two fittings working together to form a hinge. The pintle is the fitting with the pin. The pin is inserted into the socket of the gudgeon.

Points of sail – Directions in which a boat may sail in reference to the apparent wind. See closereaching, closehauled, beam reaching, broad reaching, running.

Port – When you face forward, the left side of the boat.

Port tack – Sailing with the wind on the port side (the boom is carried on the starboard side).

Portlights – Windows; portholes.

Power-driven vessel – Any vessel propelled by machinery.

Pulpit – (Bow pulpit) – Metal railing around the bow; the area enclosed by the pulpit.

Pushpit (Stern pulpit) – Metal railing enclosing the stern; the area enclosed by the pushpit.

Range (of the tide) – Difference in height between high and low water in a tidal cycle.

Reaching – Sailing across the apparent wind in any direction between closehauled and running.

Reef points – Small cringles set into reinforced patches on a sail to accommodate reef ties.

Reference current stations – Main current stations

Reference ports – Main tidal ports.

Rode – The chain, cable or rope attached to an anchor.

Roller furling foresail (roller reefing foresail) – A foresail that rolls and unrolls on a rotating foil with a drum and controlling furling line at the bottom.

Rudder – A flat blade mounted near or on the stern, for steering.

Running (on a run) – Sailing directly to leeward (downwind, away from the direction of the wind).

Running rigging – The lines that control the sails, halyards, sheets, outhaul, cunningham, boomvang, topping lift. Running rigging may be adjusted while the boat is sailing.

Sailing free – A boat is sailing free on any point of sail other than closehauled.

Schooner – A sailing vessel having two or more masts of equal height, or with the taller mast aft.

Scope – Ratio of length of anchor rode deployed to the vertical distance from the deck to the sea bed.

Sea room – (1) Sufficient space on the water to perform an intended manoeuver without running into obstructions such as reefs, shallows, and anchored boats. (2) The water between your boat and the nearest obstruction e.g. your lee shore.

Seamanship – The skills of handling, maintaining and navigating a vessel.

Seaworthy – A boat that is safe to take to sea.
Self-bailing cockpit – A cockpit with drainage to the outside of the hull.
Shackles – Metal fittings (usually U-shaped) that close with moveable pins. Shackles attach lines to fittings.
Sheave – Roller or wheel to guide wire or rope.
Sheets – Lines which pull in or let out the sails.
Shrouds – Wires running from the mast to the deck to give lateral support to the mast and to control lateral bend. A boat may have several pairs of shrouds.
Slack water – The time of the turn of the current when there is little or no horizontal flow of water.
Slides – Fittings attached to a sail by which the sail is attached to the mast or boom.
Sloop – A sailing vessel having one mast and flying one foresail.
Sole – Cabin or cockpit floor, e.g. cabinsole.
Soundings – Depths
Spar – A mast, boom, pole or stick. May refer to mast or boom of a vessel.
Spinnaker – A large balloon-like sail, often brightly coloured, used when reaching or running.
Spreaders – Horizontal bars extending from each side of the mast to hold out the shrouds.
Springlines – Mooring lines running diagonally from the dock to amidships to prevent the boat from moving ahead and astern.
Squall – A temporary increase in wind speed lasting a few minutes.
Stanchions – Upright metal supports for the lifelines.
Stand (of the tide) – A short period during which there is no change in tidal height. This occurs when the tide has risen to either its high level or fallen to its low level.
Standing rigging – Wires supporting the mast not usually adjusted when the boat is sailing e.g. forestay, backstay, shrouds.
Stand-on vessel – Vessel required to maintain her course and speed at the approach of a **give-way** vessel.
Starboard – When you face forward, the right side of the boat.
Starboard tack – Sailing with the wind on the starboard side. The boom is carried on the port side.
Steerage – Ability of a boat to be steered. A boat can be steered only when water is flowing over the rudder.
Stern – The after part of a boat.
Storm jib – A small foresail made of heavy cloth which is used in very strong winds.
Tack – (1) Lower forward corner of a sail. (2) Port or starboard tack. (3) To change from one tack to the other.
Tacking (coming about) – Changing direction by turning the boat so the bow passes through head to wind.
Tail – (1) The bitter end of a sheet leading from a winch. (2) To pull on a sheet.
Tang – A metal fitting, used to attach the upper end of a shroud or stay to the mast.
Telltales – Short lengths of wool, ribbon or audiotape attached to sails or rigging to indicate (tell tales of) the wind direction. Telltales on the sails may be called **ticklers**.
Through-hulls – Entrances and exits for water in the hull.

Ticklers – Short lengths of wood or ribbon attached to sails to indicate air flow across a sail.
Tide – Periodic rise and fall of the waters of the oceans.
Tide-rips – Areas of rough water caused when the wind blows in opposition to a strong tidal current.
Tiller – A handle attached to the top of the rudder to control it.
Toe rail – Low rail around the edge of the deck.
Topping lift – A line leading from the top of the mast to the after end of the boom to support the weight of the boom when the sail is lowered.
Topsides – Hull above the waterline.
Traffic separation schemes – Shipping lanes.
Transom – Flat area across the stern of a boat.
Trim (set) – Adjustment of a sail so it can work efficiently.
True wind – The wind felt when the boat is not moving.
Turnbuckles – Long, threaded, adjustable fittings used to tension wires such as shrouds, stays and lifelines.
Upstream – The direction taken by a vessel when proceeding from seaward towards the headwaters of a river, into a harbour, or with the flood tide.
Veering – A wind shifting in a clockwise direction (e.g. E to S to W). In the northern hemisphere a veering wind usually indicates improving weather.
Wake – The disturbance or waves caused by a boat moving through the water.
Waterspout – A funnel-shaped vertical column of water similar to a tornado but generally less violent.
Way – The motion of a boat e.g. leeway, headway, sternway, etc.
Weather helm – The tendency of a boat to turn to weather.
Wheel – A steering wheel to control the rudder.
Winch – A drum-like mechanical device which is rotated with a handle. A winch assists in hauling in sheets, halyards and other lines.
Wind chill factor – A measure of the combined cooling effect of wind and temperature. The larger the wind chill factor, the faster the rate of cooling.
Windward (upwind or to weather) – Towards the direction from which the wind is blowing. May be referred to as "eye of the wind".
Wing and wing – Running with the mainsail and foresail set on opposite sides of the boat.
Yawl – A two-masted sailing vessel with a mainmast and shorter mizzen (aft) mast. The mizzen mast is stepped aft of the rudder post.

Index

Abeam, 14
Accidental gybe, 139-140
Aft, 14
Ahead, 14
Aids to navigation, 153, 160-161
Anchoring, 24, 111, 169, 184-185, 187-189
Apparent wind, 16, 100-101, 127-128, 133, 139
Astern, 14
Backstay, 7, 110
Balanced helm, 99
Battens, 8, 41-42
Batteries (recharging), 57
Beam reach, 18-19
Bearing away, 20, 131
Beating, 20
Belaying, 37
Bending on sails, 41
Bilge pumps, 24
Bitter end, 35
Boarding ladder, 31, 181
Boat wind, 100-101
Boom, 6, 10, 40-42
Boomvang, 7, 127
Bow, 6, 14, 20
Bowline, 35, 85
Bouys, 163-166
Breast lines, 88
Broad reach, 18-19, 100, 133
By the lee, 139-140
Cabin, 6, 117
Cardinal buoys, 163, 165
Casting off, 68, 76-80, 125
Chainplates, 11
Charts, 29, 153-157, 159
Cleats, 12, 87
Clew, 8, 41, 43-44
Close reach, 18-19, 128, 130, 132-133
Closehauled, 18-20, 100
Clove hitch, 36, 42
Coastal navigation, 153, 191
Cockpit, 6, 10
Coiling a line, 37
Collision regulations, 25, 29, 49, 53-54, 56, 103
Compass, 30
Crew, 1, 5, 22-23
Crew overboard, 28, 153, 177-179, 183

Cringles, 8
Cunningham, 7, 118-120, 145-147, 150
Current, 29-30, 76-77, 79, 82, 84-86, 97, 153, 157, 167-172
Current tables, 29, 47, 97, 153, 167-168, 170
Deck, 6-8
Depthsounder, 30-31
Deviation, 30
Distress calls, 113
Distress flares, 26
Divers, 60
Docking, 68, 81, 84-87
Docklines, 78, 86, 88
Double sheet bend, 36
Downhaul, 42, 118, 120
Drifting, 24, 80-81
Emergencies, 22, 105, 111
Emergency steering, 29
Equipment – CYA, 26
Equipment – DOT, 23
Fairleads, 12, 43-44
Fenders, 79, 85-88
Figure eight knot, 35, 70
Fire extinguishers, 25
First aid kit, 26-27
Fisherman's reef, 144
Fittings, 9-13, 27-28, 31
Flaking, 42, 46, 122-123, 151, 190
Fog, 28-29, 54, 97, 103-104
Foot, 1, 8, 39-41, 44
Fore, 87
Foresail, 8-9, 12, 40, 43-46, 89, 106, 119-122, 127-130, 142-144, 148-149, 151, 187
Forestay, 8-9, 12, 43, 68, 89, 110, 151
Foretriangle, 8
Forward, 6-8, 14, 17, 73-74, 84-88, 99-100
Fouled propeller, 110-111
Genoa, 8, 89, 99-100
Gooseneck, 10, 41, 118-119, 145, 147, 150
Gybing, 19, 21, 137-140
Halyards, 7, 13, 123
Hanks, 12, 43, 46, 148
Head, 8, 22, 27, 41-45, 80, 90, 111, 117-119, 121, 135-136, 148, 152, 183

203

Heading up, 19-20, 131-132
Heaving a line, 39
Heaving to, 101, 142
Heeling, 82, 108, 144
Helm, 23, 76-81, 83, 86-87, 118-119, 121-122, 135-140, 142-143, 145-150, 152, 188-190
HELP position, 64
Hull, 6, 86-88, 105-107, 109
Hypothermia, 49, 61-64, 180
In irons, 17, 136
Inboard engine, 71, 81, 83, 89
Jib, 8, 89, 99-100, 142
Jiffy (slab) reefing, 32, 144
Kedging, 108-109
Keel, 6, 15, 107-109, 126-127
Knots, 35, 93-94, 170-172
Lateral aids, 161
Leadline, 30-31
Leaks, 71, 109
Lee helm, 99, 106
Lee shore, 102-103, 111, 116, 186-187
Leech, 8, 40, 42, 129-130, 144-147
Leeward, 15, 49-50, 80, 142-143, 149-150, 179
Leeway, 15, 49, 132
Lifebuoys, 25
Lifejackets, 24
Lifelines, 6, 10, 47, 68, 85
Lift, 126-128
Lightening ship, 108
Lights, 25, 54-56, 103, 160-161
Lines, 7, 9, 35-37, 39, 78-79, 85-88
Lowering the foresail, 148-149, 151
Lowering the mainsail, 150
Luff, 8, 12, 17, 41-42, 44, 127-132
Luffing, 17, 127-131, 133
Mainsail, 7-9, 40-43, 89, 99, 117-120, 128-130, 144-146, 150-152, 182, 187, 189
Making fast, 68, 87
Making off a halyard, 38
Mast, 6-8, 10, 13, 28, 37, 40-41, 43, 54, 56, 59-60, 66, 68, 89, 109-110, 117-122, 126-127, 144
Masthead light, 55-56
Mercator projection, 155
Meridians of Longitude, 155
Mooring lines, 79, 85, 88
Navigation equipment, 29-30
Navigation lights, 25
Navigation publications, 191

No sailing zone, 17-18
Outboard engine, 68-69, 81-82, 88
Outhaul, 7, 41, 119-120, 127
Overhead power lines, 59
P-effect, 81, 83, 85-86
Parallels of Latitude, 154-156
PFDs, 24
Pintle & gudgeon, 9
Points of sail, 18, 20, 106, 130, 133, 139
Polyconic projection, 155
Port, 14, 18-21, 50-51, 162-164
Port tack, 18-21, 50
Pulpit, 6, 68, 117
Pushpit, 6, 68
Radar reflector, 28, 104
Raising the foresail, 121-122
Raising the mainsail, 117-119
Reaching, 19, 100, 130, 133
Reduced visibility, 28, 103-104
Reef knot, 36
Reef points, 8, 147
Reefing the mainsail, 144-146
Refuelling, 57-59
Reversing, 83
Roller furling, 9, 44-45, 149
Roller reefing, 9
Round turn and two half hitches, 35
Rudder, 6, 9, 29, 76-77, 80, 83
Run, 18-19, 21, 87, 126, 130-131, 133-134, 136-141
Running aground, 107, 111
Running rigging, 7
Safety harness, 28, 61
Sail care, 35, 40
Sail selection, 91, 99, 101
Sail trim, 127-128, 130, 133
Sailing by the lee, 139-140
Sailing circle, 17-18, 139
Scope, 111, 185-186, 188-189
Self-bailing cockpit, 10
Shackles, 11, 27
Shaking out a reef, 147
Sheets, 7, 13, 121, 123, 127, 132-133, 136, 139, 149-150
Shrouds, 7, 10
Sidelights, 54-56
Slides, 13
Sloop, 8
Slowing, 131
Snugging down, 68, 87-88
Softwood plugs, 27
Sound devices, 25

Sound signals – 28-29, 31, 54, 97, 103-104
Sources of fire & explosion, 25, 57, 111
Spare parts, 27, 31
Special buoys, 163-166
Spinnaker, 8, 191
Spreaders, 7
Spring lines, 78-79, 86, 88
Stanchions, 6, 47
Standing end, 38-39
Standing rigging, 7, 110
Starboard, 14, 18-21, 50-51, 162-164
Starboard tack, 18-21, 50
Steerage, 17, 76-77, 79, 84
Steering, 6, 29, 68, 76, 80-81, 106, 135-137, 139
Steering failure, 29, 106
Stern, 6-7, 9, 14
Sternlight, 54-56
Stopping, 54, 82-84, 131-132
Storm jib, 8
Stowage, 31, 102
Tack, 8, 18-21, 41, 43-44, 50, 135-137, 139-140
Tacking, 19-20, 135-137, 139
Tang, 10
Telltales, 8, 16, 127-130, 136
Through-hulls, 27
Tide, 29, 107, 109, 166-169
Tide tables, 167-168
Tide-rips, 95, 173
Tiller, 6, 29, 76, 106
Tools, 27, 30-31
Topping lift, 7, 40, 119, 145-147, 150, 152
True wind, 99-101, 127-128
Triangle method, 181
Turnbuckles, 11
Unseaworthy, 23
VHF radio, 30, 91-92, 112
Weather, 3, 91-99, 142-143
Weather forecasts, 97, 115
Weather hazards, 95
Weather helm, 99
Wheel, 6, 29, 76, 80, 106
Winch, 13, 123-125
Winch techniques, 123
Wind, 15-20, 92-95, 97-103, 126-130
Windward, 15, 17, 19-20, 135-137, 141-144
Wing and wing, 133, 138

NOTES

NOTES

NOTES

NOTES

NOTES

NOTES

NOTES